PETER BERRESFORD ELLIS

celtic
dawn

the
dream
of
Celtic
unity

yLolfa

First published in Great Britain 1993 by
Constable and Company Limited

This revised and expanded edition: 2002

Cover design: Robat Gruffudd

ISBN: 0 86243 643 5

Published and printed in Wales by
Y Lolfa Cyf., Talybont, Ceredigion SY24 5AP
e-mail ylolfa@ylolfa.com
website www.ylolfa.com
tel (01970) 832 304
fax 832 782
isdn 832 813

Reviews of *Celtic Dawn*

A major contribution to the history of European ideas. Peter Berresford Ellis is a prophet of the Celtic Revival. His latest book prepares the way for a brighter future as well as documents the past. His name will certainly be honoured for centuries to come in all the Celtic countries.
    −*Irish Democrat*

Such books of reference are all too few. −*Irish Times*

Anyone interested in Celtic Studies may, by definition, be well acquainted with the name and works of Peter Berresford Ellis. The trademark of this truly extraordinary scholar is his painstaking care for smallest details. As a result, his books often contain information not found anywhere else. *Celtic Dawn* takes off from where *The Celtic Revolution* ended. Ellis' books are distinguished by a very clear personal involvement in the subject and an equally clear ideological declaration of sides by the author.
    −Dr Piotr Klafkowski, *Lingua Posnaniensis: Revue Linguistique Comparee et Generale*

This is a clear, concise analysis of the struggle to maintain and support the languages and cultures of the Celtic nations. −*Aberdeen Evening Express*

Clearly written, logically organised and observes due proportion. I recommend it. −*Academic Library Books Review* (USA)

Researched with enormous care. And written with not a little passion and vigour, this is a thoroughly readable, important book about the position of the modern Celts. −*Bangor and Anglesey Mail*

A mine of information about the modern Celts. −*History Today*

'So time in its passing draws each thing forth, with benefit to men, and Reason bears each thing into the realms of light.'

TITUS LUCRETIUS CARUS (98–C.55 BC)

Contents

Acknowledgments

Many people supplied me with information and advice. I would especially like to thank the following: Elisabeth Coin of Caen, for her pioneering work on Charles de Gaulle; Alan Heusaff; Gwynfor Evans, Séamas Filbin, Archibald C. MacPherson, Yann Fouéré, Clifford Ifan Bere, Tim Saunders, J. Bernard Moffatt, Hywel Francis (Coleg y Brifysgol, Abertawe), Davyth Fear, Séamus Ó Coileáin, Dr George Broderick, Dr Brian Stowell, Liz Curtis, Cathal Ó Luain and Gwyneth Williams. I would also like to express my gratitude to Dave O'Reilly of the University of East London for his senatorial eye. Finally, I would like to make a special acknowledgment to Dr Kenneth MacKinnon and Dr Mary Harris for having faith in this work.

Preface

WHEN this book was first published in 1993 it was impossible to imagine the rapid and tremendous political changes that would be made in the Celtic world during the following decade.

No one in the early 1990's, in those days of the stubborn dogmatic approach of the United Kingdom Tory centralist administration, really expected such dramatic progress as a peace agreement in Northern Ireland. No one dreamed that elected Sinn Féin representatives would be included in a Northern Ireland Government let alone that there would be a Sinn Féin Minister of Education and a Sinn Féin Minister of Health in Belfast. Nor could anyone imagine that the Irish language would have recognition in Northern Ireland or that Irish language medium schools would be in demand there.

No one expected to see, by the end of the century, the establishment of a Scottish Parliament, *Pàrlamaid na h-Alba*, nor witness the first debate in the Scottish Gaelic language (*a' Ghàidhlig*) in its chamber. The emergence of *Cynulliad Cenedlaethol Cymru*, a Welsh Assembly in Cardiff, was still a dream. As for the idea that the Cornish language would be spoken in the House of Commons as Members of Parliament called for that language to be given recognition, was considered a fantasy. Nor would the idea have occurred that four of Cornwall's five Members of Parliament would lead a campaign for the establishment of

Seneth Kernow, a Cornish Assembly, and that a petition for the assembly be presented by them at Downing Street.

For the Celtic peoples, this last decade has been one of breath-taking progress towards their goals of political and cultural autonomy, not just with the practical achievements, but in convincing people of the legitimacy of their case. Conversely, no one ever dreamt that the concept of Pan Celticism would be seen by certain of England's academics as such a threat to the 'British' *status quo* that attempts would be made to persuade people that the ancient Celts never existed, that the term 'Celtic' was a modern political invention which was both 'false and dangerous'. Never mind that Julius Caesar wrote '*Qui ipsorum lingua Celtae...*' In their own language they are called Celts... The term 'Iron Age people' started to be used *ad naseum* in the press and media at every possible opportunity. It was clear that advocates of the 'Celts do not exist' theory were arguing from a political perspective.

It was reminiscent of the introduction of the term 'British mainland' which crept into media and press 'newspeak' as a political idea after 1980. This had arisen from the desire to reassure Northern Ireland unionists of the link with the United Kingdom, overlooking the fact that Northern Ireland had never been part of 'Britain' and could not been regarded as 'offshore Britain', which was the logical interpretation of the term. The state was the United Kingdom of Great Britain *and* Northern Ireland. So concerned were broadcasters to strike home the political message that one newscaster actually referred to the Scottish Isle of Lewis as the British *mainland*.

However, the Celtic world now seems to have the bit between its teeth in spite of those who would attempt to turn back the clock on the events that began in 1997. In this respect the Internet has been a great boon to the centuries of controlled communication and throughout the world Celtic websites concerning language, culture, music, politics, history and other matters, are flourishing. The major Pan Celtic gatherings have continued to grow in support and frequency. As the Celtic Congress enters into its second century of existence and the Celtic League enters its fortieth year, Pan Celticism is an established fact. The Celtic League continues to argue for those political and cultural ideals for which it was founded on August 9, 1961.

As a *caveat*, in the last year or so, a new Celtic League has come into being. Far form being the old established political movement, this is a Rugby Union League with teams from only three of the Celtic countries - Ireland, Wales and Scotland. Some have felt that the confusion this has caused had almost been designed to deflect from interest in the political Celtic League.

We are still at the glimmerings of the new dawn for the Celtic peoples. So far, only four of the six Celtic nationalities have achieved various forms of political and cultural self-government. The Cornish claims to have their ethnicity recognised has yet to be accepted by Westminster and the Bretons are still being aggressively discouraged from asserting their nationality within the French State.

There is an ancient Irish proverb. *Tar éis a chítear gach beart*. It is afterwards that events are understood. There is truth in this but for all the unexpected developments that have happened in the Celtic world during the last decade, with all modesty, I believe it is true to say that in 1993 *The Celtic Dawn* was a herald of the new Celtic world.

Peter Berresford Ellis

Introduction

DURING the closing decades of the nineteenth century a phenomenon occurred which was called the 'Celtic Renaissance', in which the poets, writers, artists and musicians of Ireland, Scotland, the Isle of Man, Wales, Cornwall and Brittany turned to their cultural Celtic roots to seek inspiration for new forms of self-expression. This cultural renaissance, of which the Nobel prize-winning Irish poet, William Butler Yeats, became the best internationally-known representative, was inspired by a significant movement of the Celtic peoples to restore their declining languages, and reassert their cultural identity and political independence. This movement was looked at disparagingly by most of its English and French neighbours, into whose empires the Celts had become incorporated. They promptly dubbed it 'Celtic Twilightism'. To be interested in the 'Celtic Twilight' became the popularly dismissive term for anyone interested in Celtic matters, while the six Celtic countries were slightingly referred to as the 'Celtic Fringe'. The term was explicit: to be Celtic meant to be parochial, on the periphery of the 'real' world.

The renaissance was not a success. While an Irish state (albeit in a partitioned Ireland) emerged on 6 December 1922 and Manx 'home rule' had been recognized by Westminster in 1866, no other Celtic peoples secured independence and their languages continued to decline.

However, during the recent decades of the last century there has been an astonishing upsurge of interest in practically every aspect of Celtic life – in Celtic languages, culture, music and history. Celtic interest groups proliferate and not just in the Celtic countries but throughout the world. The Celtic Society of India is an active organization with its own publication and the Celtic Society of Japan has just held its twelfth annual congress. It, too, produces its own journal.

The Celtic Film and Television Festival is now in its second decade and there are two main Celtic International Music Festivals well into their fourth decade of existence. Throughout the 1980s, a quarter of a million people attended the Lorient Inter-Celtic Festival in Brittany each year, and a similar number participated in the annual Pan Celtic Festival at Killarney in Ireland. Major television series on Celtic matters have been produced by the BBC, ITV and French television, and shown in many countries throughout the world. Individual radio and television programmes on specific aspects of the Celtic world have also been broadcast.

There are now Celtic languages book fairs, Pan Celtic magazines, educational conferences and environmental groups and political organizations. There is even a Celtic equivalent of Disneyland – 'Celtworld', in Waterford, Ireland. 'Celtica', a Resource Centre and multi-media attraction draws many tourists to Machynlleth. A huge volume of books are produced about all aspects of Celtic life and culture. Esoteric centres (and books) teaching what purports to be pre-Christian Celtic philosophy and religion are to be found in the most unlikely places. Ancient druidic philosophy has been conjured to the 'New Age' movement.

Major exhibitions of Celtic art (ancient and modern) and historical artifacts have been held in many countries of Europe, from Venice to London to New York. Universities from the United States and Canada to Nagoya in Japan and Moscow and Petersburg in Russia have departments of Celtic Studies. And in the early 1980s, UNESCO launched its own permanent 'Project for the Study and Promotion of Celtic Cultures'.

Have we come through the 'Celtic Twilight' to witness a new 'Celtic Dawn'?

Interest in the Celts and their culture is certainly assuming dramatic proportions, although the paradox is that the Celtic languages are still teetering on the verge of death. Politically, four Celtic nations achieved various forms of self-government. A parliament has been established in Scotland a national assembly in Wales, and a peace process begun in Northern Ireland.

What has caused this new, late twentieth-century 'Celtic Renaissance'?

Of all the many books devoted to Celtic Studies there has, curiously, never been a study of the one dynamic force which, in my opinion, is responsible for the upsurge of interest in Celtic matters. In the 1860s, a vague and confused idea of Celtic cultural commonality was given a new philosophical directive by a Breton-language poet, Charles de Gaulle. De Gaulle was the uncle of the famous general – named after him – who became President of France. It was only from 1960 onwards that this movement began to exert a significant influence on attitudes and perceptions within the Celtic areas. But it is those changes of attitudes and perceptions that are so marked today in the modern 'Celtic Renaissance', the influence of which far exceeds the boundaries of the Celtic countries to reach almost everywhere a Celt has migrated throughout the world. The movement inspired by de Gaulle is Pan Celticism. Examples of the influence of Pan Celticism in the cultural renaissance include: being able to arrive in downtown Saratoga, New York, and find a shop called 'The Celtic Experience' devoted to selling products from the six Celtic countries; being able to find another Pan Celtic shop called 'The Celtic Corner' in the famous holiday resort of Lake Placid. Although it is, it seems to me, responsible for the entire modern Celtic renaissance, in terms of size, Pan Celticism is relatively small; it is not a mass movement. Politically, it has to be admitted that, in spite of the quarter of a million people attending the annual Pan Celtic Festivals at Lorient and at Killarney, the movement has never been anything more than peripheral to the mainstream of Celtic nationalism – that is, to the independence movements within the Celtic countries.

Some might argue that because it is confined to a minority of activists, albeit a vociferous minority which has grown in influence in recent decades, and has not been, prior to the current examination, a subject for either general or academic study, it can't be considered as being at all significant or relevant to the history of the Celtic peoples. This argument, I believe, can be answered by reference to Professor Edward H. Carr, and his outline of the process by which 'a mere fact about the past is transformed into a fact of history'. Professor Carr asks: what will decide whether facts become history? It will depend, I think, on whether the thesis or interpretation... is accepted by other historians as valid and significant. Its status as a historical fact will turn on a question of interpretation. This element of interpretation enters into every fact of history.[1]

This book is an entire series of proposals of facts about the past, presented in cohesive form, to demonstrate the origins, growth and ideas of a particular movement. The facts exist, but whether they are relevant depends on two separate judgments. Firstly, the judgment of whether Pan Celticism is a more influential movement than its size might suggest; and (or) secondly, the judgment of other future commentators on the Celtic countries.

Through examining the chronology of events, it is possible to explain the paradox of how Pan Celticism has had an effect disproportionate to the size of the movement. Commencing with the formation in the nineteenth century of Pan Celtic groups with specific aims, based originally on the ideas of a group of intellectuals, the appeal of Pan Celticism has certainly remained generally confined to academics, artists and individual politicians; in other words, members of an intelligentsia. But while it has never attracted a mass following, it has attracted the talents of many energetic individuals who have worked in particular areas of the cultural and political life of the Celtic communities, propagating the Pan Celtic idea, with the result that Pan Celticism has had a vast and disproportionate influence on people's attitudes both within the Celtic communities and the communities of their close neighbours.

Because the influence of Pan Celticism is not 'politically dramatic', as in the case of Pan Arabism or the Scandinavian example, it has not been previously perceived by commentators.

This book is the first attempt to chart the history of the Pan Celtic movement and the first effort to analyse and discuss the various philosophical concepts which are to be found within it. It attempts to examine the successes of the movement and in so doing reveals some little acknowledged influences on Celtic life. It shows in depth how the current 'Celtic Renaissance' is due to the efforts of individuals who have worked within the Pan Celtic movement rather than any pressures from a mass movement.

The principal sources for this work, as the first study of Pan Celticism, tend to be the corpus of printed material emanating from the Pan Celtic movement itself, in terms of journals and books. Some interviews have been done and I have had access to some personal papers. The perceptions and attitudes expressed in the sources are self-explanatory.

The need to rely on this particular corpus of material for the study becomes obvious when it is observed that there has been little in the way of detailed critical evaluation from outside the Celtic movement, not even in studies devoted to the world's various 'Pan Movements'. The works of such specialists as Professor Alter and Dr Hechter do not even refer *en passant* to Pan Celticism.

Outside of the work of authors propagating the ideas of Pan Celticism, the movement is mentioned only in passing in a few works on related subjects – for example, in Dr Ruth Dudley Edwards' biography of Pádraic Pearse, and Dr Hanham's study of Scottish nationalism.

As a result of this, in dealing with sources, the source notes have had to be lengthier than is usually found in a study of this nature, in order to accommodate discussion on source and background information.

This study is also an attempt to examine where Pan Celticism is heading. What future does the movement envisage for the fifteen-and-a-half million Celts who dwell on the islands and peninsulas of north-western Europe?

Of those fifteen-and-a-half millions living in the Celtic areas, only two-and-a-half million can now speak a Celtic language, the result of centuries of systematic persecution and suppression of those languages. It has been estimated that there might be a further two-and-a-half million Celtic-speakers living beyond the Celtic areas due to the tremendous amount of immigration suffered by the Celts. But the decline of the Celtic languages remains a serious issue. Some optimists can argue that the 1991 census figures show that, for the first time since the census was taken, the number of speakers of nearly all the Celtic languages has risen. In previous years, the figures have showed a dismal, steady decline. Moreover, the Irish language appears to have regained speakers in large quantities. There are two exceptions: Scottish Gaelic, the number of speakers of which has declined by 14,000 since 1981, and Breton, about which we have no reliable figures due to the French Government's unwillingness to enumerate speakers. Cynical observers may argue that all the figures need to be taken with 'a pinch of salt', and are not reflective of the real situation. However, when one views them, it is beyond doubt that the Celtic languages are still in great danger.

Perhaps, indeed, the Celts have come to the end of their long march through European history; for, by their own definition, and indeed, by any meaningful definition, when the Celtic languages have passed beyond any means of resuscitation, then the Celtic culture and its civilization, the very Celtic people themselves, will have become extinct.

Are we then truly witnessing a new 'Celtic Dawn', with the upsurge of interest in Celtic matters, or taking into account the precarious state of the Celtic languages, are we merely witnessing the last glow of the 'Celtic Twilight'; to mix metaphors without apology, are we simply seeing a flurry of sparks from the last dying embers of the fire before it is finally extinguished?

Will the upcoming twenty-first century see the end of one of Europe's oldest civilizations, indeed, the first known civilization to appear north of the Alps, which has contributed so much to the emergence of Europe? By the start of the twenty-second century, will our descendants talk of the Celts as we now speak of the Etruscans? *The Times*, back in August 1970, anticipated such an obituary by solemnly informing its readers both that the Celts no longer existed and that 'little definite is known about the Celtic peoples because they left no written records'.

More learned opinion observed, as M. Szabo in *The Celtic Heritage in Hungary* (Budapest, 1971):

> The ancient Celts bequeathed more than language, literature and works of art to European civilization; they gave it the heritage of a sensitivity and an intellectual disposition which, down the centuries, remains the protagonist in a continuing dialogue with the various manifestations of the classical tradition. These two intellectual concepts only appear to oppose each other; two systems of thought and expression of differing nature, they are to some extent complementary...

Not to recognize the validity of the specific characteristics of the historic Celts is to deny the existence of a deep-rooted dialectic system which has, with remarkable energy over the ages, given form to a European culture which is an integral part of our inheritance.

This book is concerned, however, not with the ancient Celts but with the modern Celts, and it is presented as an attempt to understand the Celtic phenomenon of recent decades.

Note

1   E.H. Carr, *What is History?* (Macmillan, 1961); quotation from second revised edition (Penguin Books, London, 1987), p.12.

1: The Galician crisis: definition of Celtic

P AN Celticism, according to its advocates, is a recognition by the Irish, Scots, Manx, Welsh, Bretons and Cornish of a special relationship they have with one another due to their common Celtic origins.[1] This definition raises more questions than it answers and we should seek to clarify it before we proceed further. So even before we can address 'What is *Pan* Celticism?' we have to ask 'What is a Celt?' We may have an easier acceptance of what constitutes the individual Irish, Scots, Manx, Welsh, Breton or Cornish people than what creates their Celtic commonality. What special relationship does a person from Cornwall have with someone from Ireland, or someone from Brittany have with a person from Scotland?

To ask 'What is a Celt?' can be equally as confusing, or simple – depending on one's perception – as asking, 'What is a Slav?' A Slav is generally identified as being a member of Europe's largest linguistic group; a speaker of a language belonging to the Slavonic subfamily of the Indo-European family of languages. They are divided into West Slavs (Poles, Czechs, Slovaks), South Slavs (Serbs, Croats, Slovenes, Macedonians, Bulgars) and East Slavs (Russians, Ukrainians, Belorussians). Over the centuries they have intermixed with Turko-Tartars, Germans, Mongols, Finns, Greeks and Illyrians. Because of this intermixing, the only meaningful definition of a Slav is a linguistic one. So, too, with the definition of a Celt.

All the leading Celtic scholars have agreed on this issue since Edward Lhuyd's pioneering linguistic work on the Celtic languages – *Archaeologia Britannica* (Oxford, 1707). The influential

Celtic scholar, Henri Hubert (1873–1927) stated it clearly: 'The Celts are the group of the peoples which spoke or still speak dialects of a certain family, which are called the Celtic languages.'[2] On the question of language and race, Professor Max Müller (1823–1900), the noted German philologist teaching at Oxford, in his lectures 'Science of Language' (1861–63) pointed out that an ethnologist who spoke of 'race' was 'as great a sinner as a linguist who speaks of a dolichocephalic dictionary or a brachiocephalic grammar'. He argued that the peoples of Europe were mixtures of the same races.[3] Professor Eoin MacNeill (1867–1945) endorsed Mílller's argument and took it further, adding: 'In the case of populations which are recognized to be Celtic, it is particularly true that no distinction of race is found among them.'[4] Professor MacNeill referred back to the descriptions of a 'typical Celt' supplied by classical writers such as Tacitus, Florus and Livy. In these descriptions there is a remarkable range of 'racial' characteristics. Therefore, in Greek and Roman perceptions the only distinguishing factor which marked the Celts off from other peoples was their language and culture. The definition popularly used by all Celtic national organizations, which includes those who constitute the Pan Celtic movement, comes from the definition used by Pan Celtic scholars,[5] and it can be said that it is from the inception of Celtic studies, specifically from their foundation at university level in the mid-nineteenth century, that the Celts have been identified by their languages and attendant cultures.

In 1986 the Celtic League, the principal organization of the Pan Celtic movement, underwent a crisis on this matter. At the League's annual general meeting in Edinburgh on 11–12 October 1986, on the single casting vote of the chairman of the session, the League accepted the principle that the Galicians and Asturians of North-West Spain constituted Celtic communities. No Celtic language had been recorded as being spoken in this area since the ninth century AD. This decision caused an immediate controversy for it implied that the linguistic criterion was no longer valid. How then was a Celtic community to be defined? By race, religion or some other outwardly identifiable form? The ensuing debate, known in the Pan Celtic movement as the 'Galician crisis', caused the definition of a Celt to be thoroughly analysed and assessed. The outcome of this was that the linguistic definition became firmly reinforced with the League's 1987 annual general meeting.

Even so, the answer to this core question is still not necessarily commonly accepted even among Pan Celticists. For example, *Carn*, the quarterly journal of the Celtic League, through 1992 and 1993 continued to run contentious correspondence on the question, 'What Is A Celt?'[6] But the linguistic criterion prevails as the League's policy and certainly no Celtic scholar would identify a Celtic people in any other way.

What does this linguistic criterion entail? *Kernow* reported in 1989:

A Celtic people are a people who speak, or were known to have spoken within modern historical times, a Celtic language. The term 'Celtic' is indicative of a linguistic group. Therefore, there are only six modern Celtic nationalities – the Irish, Scots and Manx (speaking the Goidelic or 'Q' Celtic), and the Welsh, Bretons and Cornish (speaking a Brythonic or 'P' Celtic)[7]

The important part of this criterion was, of course, that the community was recognized not only if the people spoke a Celtic language, but also if they had spoken such a language within 'modern historical times'. This allowed recognition of those communities where the Celtic languages were in recession or had passed out of general use within the community (as in Cornwall and the Isle of Man).

Important when considering this definition must be a questioning of whether it is accepted generally among those populations recognized as 'Celtic' under this guideline. In spite of the occasional philosophical disputes among the intelligentsia about the definition of 'Celtic', there is to be found a general awareness, among most Celtic communities, of cultural links with other Celtic communities. The awareness certainly varies from those with specific knowledge to those with only a hazy idea of the commonality. For example, a few decades ago Welsh villagers accepted the travelling Breton onion-seller into their midst as a 'cousin'. They shared an awareness that their languages were similar; an understanding that together they constituted members of the same 'ethnic group' which was different to their respective state 'nationalities' – English or French. Incidents of this nature proliferate in Celtic oral folklore and I have witnessed several myself.

While staying in the Welsh-speaking village of Trefor, on the Llŷn Peninsula, in 1983, I witnessed the arrival of a Breton onion-seller, an aged man with fairly limited English. As a Breton-speaker he was given a special welcome and many locals, with some pride, volunteered to inform me how the Bretons were first cousins to the Welsh. Another incident occurred in St Ives, Cornwall, where I lived in the late 1960s. Often, Breton crab-boats would put into the harbour. The local Catholic priest had learnt Cornish, and he would go to the harbour and act as an interpreter for the Breton-speaking fishermen. Cornish fishermen and farm workers explained to me the closeness of the 'old tongue' to Breton, and the fact that the two peoples were thus cousins. They had not learnt this from books; it was through folk-knowledge of the commonality of language that they identified themselves as 'fellow Celts'.

So even where language has been lost, there remains a distinct folk memory of relationships based on the similarity of a language historically spoken. This is true in all the Celtic communities. It becomes obvious that the Celtic communities see themselves as members of a political state who are distinct from the dominant cultural group, English or French; they see themselves as cut off and marginalized from the mainstream culture, but as members of a wider cultural group which embraces communities from other states.

As cited previously, only around two and a half million of those who live in the areas deemed to be Celtic countries (2,559,925 precisely) speak a Celtic language. Of the other two and a half million speakers of a Celtic language, it has been estimated that as many as one million may live in England alone. In London, for example, in 1984, it was privately estimated that there was a community of 100,000 speakers of a Celtic language, Welsh being predominant in this group, there being, at that time, eighteen Welsh-speaking chapels and a Welsh language medium school. 250,000 speakers of Breton are thought to live in France, outside of Brittany.[8] Migration to Patagonia in the 1860s, in an attempt to form an independent Welsh-speaking state called *Y Wladfa*, has resulted in a Welsh-speaking community surviving along the Chubut Valley in this area of what is now Argentina. A Scottish Gaelic-speaking area of Cape Breton (Nova Scotia) has survived in Canada following the eighteenth-century 'ethnic cleansing' of the terrible 'Highland Clearances'. It is the existence of immigrant pockets in other areas, where a Celtic language has survived to some degree, that explain estimates giving a further 1,250,000 speakers of a Celtic language.[9]

Does the linguistic criterion make membership of the Pan Celtic movement, with its various branches, exclusive, with admittance governed only by virtue of being born within the community where a Celtic language is spoken or was known to have been spoken within modern historical times? The answer is 'No'. Membership of organizations such as the Celtic League has been open to anyone, regardless of nationality, racial origin, religion or any other distinguishing features:

> The League believes that every person born or living in any of the Celtic countries, regardless of racial origin, religion or any other distinguishing features, is heir to the local Celtic language and culture and has the right to participate in the efforts to secure the conditions under which that culture can survive and thrive again.[10]

But if the linguistic criterion is so clear and well-established, how did the Galician crisis of 1986 come about?

The Galicians of North-West Spain constitute a population of two million people. The Galician language (Galego), now spoken by less than half of the population, is a sister language of Portuguese, deriving from an Hispanic dialect current in North-West Spain in the Middle Ages. The first extant record of Galician dates from AD 1192. The language became the medium of a rich lyric poetry during the thirteenth and fourteenth centuries during which time it was little different, as a standard, to Portuguese. From the fourteenth century it grew away from Portuguese, evolving its own standard, but during the eighteenth century it drifted into the Castilian orbit due to various political, economic and cultural factors. Galician, therefore, with its attendant culture, is one of the Romance family of Indo-European languages. This is an entirely distinctive family from the Celtic.[11]

Why, then, was there such confusion within the Celtic League? Celtic links with the Iberian peninsula commenced during the first great Celtic expansion in about the ninth century BC, when the Celts were establishing themselves throughout Europe. The Celts spread themselves throughout the Iberian peninsula from the north to as far south as Cadiz (Gades). The Iberian Celts were subjected to the *Pax Romana* and by the early Christian epoch had been subdued and assimilated.[12]

When the ancestors of the English began to settle in Celtic Britain in the fifth century AD, Celtic tribes – fleeing from the 'ethnic cleansing' of the Angles and Saxons – began to migrate to Armorica (Brittany) and other areas in Europe. During this migration, in the fifth and sixth centuries, several tribes settled on the northern seaboard of the Iberian peninsula, mainly in what is now Galicia and Asturias, between Lugo and Oviedo. The Celtic migrants settled among what was then a Latinized population and soon began to merge their culture into that of the people they found there.

At the same time as the Celts were arriving in this area, a Germanic group, the Suevi, were also settling in Galicia and they, too, merged their culture into the Latinized culture of the area.

Because of the distinctive Celtic style of Christianity brought to the region, it took a while for religious practices to merge completely. The Council of Lugo in AD 567 recognized the Celtic elements, for ecclesiastical purposes, as constituting the See of Bretoŷa (See of the Britons), whose bishop Mahiloc signed the *Acta* of the Second Council of Braga in AD 572. Celtic Church practices ceased when Roman orthodoxy was accepted at the Council of Toledo in AD 633. After this, the evidence is that the Celtic settlements were quickly absorbed. There is no evidence to suggest that a Celtic language survived in the region later than the seventh and eighth centuries.[13]

It is true that a number of Celtic loan words are now found in Galician, along with a few identifiable folk customs – and local traditional music has a distinct echo of Celtic roots.

Galicia was united with Asturias under Alfonso II of Asturias in the eighth/ninth century. The monarchy of Alfonso moved its borders eastward and by the following century, under Ordoño, Galicia had taken up its rôle as a province rather than the centre of a kingdom. The next century saw the rise of a state centred on Castile and the start of Castilian cultural dominance.

The Galicians have always been aware that their distinction as a national grouping lay in their own Romance language and its culture. At no time was there any widespread support for the idea that their national cultural heritage was Celtic. In 1980 Galicia received a measure of home rule from Madrid, along with the Basques and Catalans. But their national movements had never based their claims to a separate identity on any Celtic element either in their history or culture. Their identity was clearly defined by Galego, the language they had been known to speak for 1,200 years. In their submission to the United Nations in June 1965, the Galician National Council had argued their right to self-determination and autonomy on the fact of their Latin nationality being 'as different to Castilian as French to Italian'.

However, during the late 1960s and 1970s, as the interest in things Celtic became widespread in Europe, and the struggles of the Celtic countries to obtain varying degrees of self-government became better known, there was a realization by some Galicians of their tenuous Celtic connections. They saw the Celtic element in their history as a means to reinforce their 'differences' from Castilian culture, according to the Celtic League subcommittee report to the 1987 AGM. Certain members of the Galician and Asturian independence movements sought to ally themselves with the Pan Celtic movement and especially the Celtic League.

Many Galicians joined the International Branch of the League, the League's membership being open to anyone who supported its aims, and these members pressed the general secretary to be separated into their own 'national' branch which would, of course, mean recognition of Galicia as a Celtic nation. By the 1970s Galician musicians were showing a high profile at Celtic musical gatherings in Lorient and Killarney and were being thought of by many people as an integral part of the Celtic world. Indeed, UK television's Channel 4 series 'How to be Celtic' accepted the Galicians as Celtic but completely excluded the Manx.

In *Carn* (Autumn 1980), Paul Mosson made a plea for the League to recognize the Galicians and Asturians as Celtic. He was supported by J.L. Pacios of the Astur-Galician Open Council. A *Lliga Celta d'Asturias* (Celtic League of Asturias) had also been formed. Mosson claimed that the Celtic loan word survivals were grounds for recognition, believing that 'the cultures of Galicia and Asturias are very much Celtic in nature'. It was this growing pressure that made the Celtic League give serious consideration to the Galician question at the 1986 AGM and which led to the 'Galician Crisis'.[14]

But in no way could the Galician claim meet the linguistic criterion. There were far more Celtic loan words in English and French than to be found in Galego. In spite of Galicia being granted a limited self-government within the new democratic Spain, in 1980, some Galicians continued moves to achieve official recognition within the Celtic Congress and Celtic League. In 1986 the League appeared to accept the principle of recognizing Galicia as a Celtic country and the idea of establishing a 'national branch' there.[15]

The proposer of the motion, a former general secretary of the League, Alan Heusaff, actually asserted in his preamble 'the Celtic League position, that the possession of a Celtic language is the essential characteristic for a nation to be recognized as indisputably Celtic'.[16] But the resolution itself embodied a policy which ignored the linguistic criterion.

While the resolution was adopted by the casting vote of the chairman of the session, it provoked such strong dissent that it was agreed that a subcommittee be set up to investigate before the resolution was fully implemented. The subcommittee's findings for the 1987 annual general meeting were two-fold. Firstly, that the acceptance of the resolution by the casting vote of the chairman of the session was invalid under the League's constitution. Secondly, they also reiterated the linguistic criterion and pointed out that the concept of recognizing the Galician claim was a departure from this definition of Celtic, which had been the cornerstone of the Pan Celtic movement.

The 1987 AGM reaffirmed that linguistic criterion as the only definition of a Celt. The League reiterated its position in line with the accepted teachings of Celtic scholars and the Pan Celtic movement since 1904. The official position was later stated in *Kernow*:

> The use of the linguistic criterion does not mean that the Celtic League, any more than the Celtic Congress, or Celtic scholars, says that no individual can be regarded as Celtic unless they speak a Celtic language. I have heard some people saying indignantly, 'I

don't speak Cornish, but I *am* Cornish!' Surely; but will their great-grandchildren be Cornish? The linguist, Professor Timoti Karetu, says: 'Language is central to the cultural identity of both the individual and the community... if a language is lost, the cultural identity of the group is considerably weakened.'

The League regards the national languages as the well-spring of Celtic culture. Its members seek to ensure the return of the languages to a viable rôle in the life of the community, if not for themselves, then for the unborn generations who will be so far removed from it, in the specific case of the Cornish, that they may lose all memory of it. It is those future generations who will become truly English.

Not being able to speak the language does not exclude your right to be considered Celtic – look at the wording of the linguistic criterion carefully – at this stage of historical development. We are still close to the well-spring of language. But unless the language is restored, unless one recognizes what it is one is tossing aside, it will be the future generations who will cease to be Celtic.

I say again, once the language disappears beyond all hope of resuscitation, then the Celtic community disappears.[17]

It is this definition of what constitutes a Celtic community, the acceptance of the Irish, Scots and Manx, Welsh, Bretons and Cornish as Celtic by virtue of their related languages and attendant cultures, which this study will subscribe to in tracing the history and philosophy of Pan Celticism.

Notes

1   Celtic League Policy Statement and Recruitment Pamphlet, 4pp, n.d. (c. 1987)
2   *The Rise of the Celts*, Henri Hubert, translated by Marcel Mauss, Raymond Lantier and Jean Marx (Kegan Paul, Trench Trubner & Co., 1934), p. 33.
3   *Phrases of Irish History* Eoin MacNeill (M.H. Gill, Dublin, 1919).
4   Ibid.
5   'The Linguistic Criteria' in *Kernow* (Liskeard, August-September, 1989). The anthropologist Dr Jean Finot (1858–1922) in *Le Préjugé des Races* (Felix Alcan, Paris, 1908) was very specific in identifying the Celtic peoples as a linguistic group and the Pan Celtic movement as a linguistic/cultural movement.
6   *Carn*, Nos 77–81 (1992/93).

7   'The Linguistic Criteria' in *Kernow* (Liskeard, August–September, 1989).

8   *Le Peuple Breton*, No. 225 (March, 1985).

9   'London and the Future of the Celtic Languages', Proceedings of Celtic
     League/Conradh na Gaeilge Conference (County Hall, London, 21 January
     1984). Estimates given in 'Scríf-Celtic Programme Booklet' (London,
     April, 1985).

10   Celtic League Policy Statement and Recruitment Pamphlet, 4pp, n.d.
     (c. 1987/8) quoted in *Peninsula Voice*, No. 75 (June/July, 1989).

11   *History of Spain & Portugal*, William C. Atkinson (Penguin Books,
     London, 1960), p. 19.

12   *The Celts*, Nora Chadwick (Penguin Books, London, 1970), pp. 184–
     185.

13   *Celtic Civilization*, Jean Markle (Gordon Cremonesi, London, 1976), p.
     149. See also *Celtic – a Comparative Study*, D.B. Gregor (Oleander Press,
     Cambridge, 1980), pp. 78–79.

14   *Carn*, No. 56 (Winter, 1986).

15   Ibid.

16   *Carn*, No. 59 (Autumn, 1987). See also the Celtic League 'Galician
     Subcommittee' report to League AGM, 1987.

17   *Kernow* (Liskeard, August-September, 1986).

2: The Celtic nations

As early as the Pan Celtic Congress of 1904, delegates recognized, by the linguistic criterion, that there were only six Celtic communities which had survived into modern times. Although this book is not concerned with charting or analysing the individual national movements of these six Celtic peoples with their varying political philosophies, and is not concerned with the complexities of the history of conditions and national political attitudes of these countries, it is necessary to provide a thumbnail sketch of each country in order to show its cultural and political position.

The six Celtic countries comprise the following (in alphabetical order):

Brittany

Brittany (Breizh). Population: est. 3,500,000. Breton-speaking: no figures are given by the French authorities, but it has been estimated by *Le Monde de l'Education* that there are about 700,000–800,000 people who speak Breton as a first language.[1]

Brittany was an independent, prosperous trading state in medieval Europe but it was always the object of territorial ambition by France and, at one period, England. In 1488 its armies, under the ruler Francis II, were defeated by the French at Aubin St Cromier. Francis II accepted French suzerainty. Then came a Union of Crowns in which France still recognized the autonomy of Brittany within the French state, allowing the continuance of its parliament. But during the next two centuries, the French monarchy made repeated efforts to centralize the state and suppress Breton autonomy. The 'Rights of Man' and republican fervour found enthusiastic adherents in Brittany, and it was from Nantes and Rennes that the fires of the French Revolution were started. Many Bretons had fought in the American War of Independence. Over 300 Bretons distinguished themselves as officers in the American Revolutionary Army, including the Marquis Lafayette and the Marquis Armand Tuffin de la Rouerie, known to the Americans as 'Colonel Armand', who was appointed a brigadier general by Washington at Yorktown.

In 1790 the new French National Assembly declared France to be a centralized state, abolishing the Breton Parliament. The Marquis Lafayette had previously made an impassioned plea for Breton autonomy but accepted the annexation. 'Colonel Armand', however, built up a Breton army, and a Breton War of Independence, sometimes called the war of the *chouannerie*, took place between 1793–1804. The actions of the French republic pushed many Bretons into the royalist camp with the Bourbons promising them a return to the old situation of autonomy. The war became confused with Breton republicans fighting French republicans and Breton royalists, and Breton royalists fighting both. The Bretons, both republicans and royalists, were defeated and since then Brittany has been an integral part of metropolitan France. At the Bourbon restoration the French monarchs were delighted to inherit the centralized state bequeathed them by the republic and Napoleon's empire. Nevertheless, a Breton movement for cultural and political independence has always been active, and often resorts to violent protest against French intransigence to their demands. Even cultural demands are severely repressed.

The Breton language is allowed no official status in Brittany and there is hardly any state backing for educational facilities.[2] Indeed, on 14 March 1981, before his election, François

Mitterand told a Breton audience in Lorient:

> It is now time that a status for the languages and cultures of France
> be established, so that France should no longer be the only
> European country to refuse its minority cultures fundamental rights
> which are recognized in international conventions signed by her.

By 1993, after over a decade of Mitterand's presidency, no such status for Breton had been granted nor would France agree to sign the European Convention for Regional or Minority Languages.

Cornwall

Cornwall (Kernow). Population est. 439,000. Cornish-speaking: Cornish died as an everyday means of communication in the late eighteenth century. Enthusiasts started a language revival at the turn of the twentieth century.[3] There has been no state recognition nor encouragement and the language revival has been a purely private enterprise. In 1989, however, the Cornish Language Board received financial grants from the European Commission for Lesser Used Languages and from Cornwall County Council's Educational Department. It is privately estimated that there are only 500 speakers with any degree of fluency.[4] Some teachers have tried to introduce it into schools as an optional environmental study, mainly concerning the interpretation of place-names.

Cornwall was conquered by Athelstan in AD 931 but native princes continued to rule under English suzerainty. Cadoc was the last native ruler. His daughter married a son of Henry I (1100–1135), who then inherited the 'earldom of Cornwall'. Until the Tudor period, laws had to be passed *in Anglia et Cornubia*.

The idea of Cornwall having a special position within the state was reinforced by recognition of the ancient Stannary Parliament whose rights have been confirmed in various English

Royal Charters since AD 1198. In 1508, the Stannary Parliament of Cornwall was granted a power of veto over laws made at Westminster relating to Cornwall by Henry VII. In 1337, Cornwall was created a Duchy, reinforcing its special position, with the eldest son of the ruling monarch being appointed as Duke, authorized to give assent to Stannary legislation. But, at the same time, Tudor centralist policies continued on other levels. Cornish uprisings in 1497 and 1546 were the last 'kick' of the Celtic community before it was absorbed into the English cultural ethos and state. The 1546 uprising, for example, was a protest against the introduction of English into the ecclesiastical life of Cornwall instead of there being a switch from Latin to Cornish.[5] Curiously, the Tudors did not suppress the Stannary Parliament in the wake of Sir Anthony Kingston's infamous 'pacification' of Cornwall after the defeat of the Cornish army by the Earl of Bedford.

The Stannary Parliament continued to meet until 1753 when its right of veto over Westminster was, surprisingly, reaffirmed by the monarch. However, in 1888, the County Councils Act determined that elected councils would take over the duties of the justices of the peace and for the first time Cornwall was designated an 'English' county. This was not confirmed until a year after the other county councils came into being because of the unique constitutional position of Cornwall, and lawyers have argued that the institution of Cornwall as a county was not in accordance with constitutional law.

While Cornwall has its independence parties, such as Mebyon Kernow and the Cornish National Party, many believe that Cornwall retains its own parliament in the Stannaries. In 1974, Cornish lawyers, having examined the corpus of Stannary Law, believed that they had the authority to recall the Cornish Stannary Parliament, and this was done on 20 May 1974. But it was not until 1990 that the Cornish Stannary Parliament came into direct conflict with Westminster. In 1989, the UK

Parliament imposed a community charge, popularly known as the Poll Tax. A large number of Cornish people refused to pay the tax on the grounds that the Stannary Law showed they were exempt from such taxes if Westminster did not have authority and approval from the Stannary Parliament. In May 1991, a test case against a Cornishman, the writer Tim Saunders, came before Cardiff Magistrates. The magistrates accepted Saunders' case put forward under Stannary Law and adjourned the case against him *sine die*. Westminster is still pursuing a case against the officers of the Stannary Parliament in the English High Court.[6]

However, in one case involving the British Atomic Energy Authority, being heard before the Cornwall County Court (Stannary jurisdiction), the English lawyer for the Authority began to submit that the Stannary Parliament and Stannary Law no longer existed in Cornwall. District Judge Adams interrupted and told the lawyer to go away and prepare his case properly. Judge Adams pointed out to the startled lawyer that the case was being heard in the *Stannary Jurisdiction* of the County Court of Cornwall and that he, as judge, held his position by virtue of Stannary Law.

Ireland

Ireland (Eire). Partitioned into the twenty-six county Republic of Ireland, and the UK province of 'Northern Ireland', which contains six of Ulster's nine counties. Irish-speaking: the 1991 census figures were, unfortunately, not available at the time of publication of this book. However, the 1986 mid-term census figures showed that, in the Irish Republic, out of a total population of 3,540,643, some 1,042,701 citizens returned themselves as Irish-speaking, just over a third of the population. This was a slight increase compared to the 1981 census, held five years earlier, when out of a population of 3,537,195, Irish-speakers were returned at 1,018,312 (31.6 p.c.).[7]

In the Partitioned Six Counties, the 1991 population was

1,502,385. Some 142,003 people were returned as having various degrees of competence in Irish but only 79,012 claimed total literacy.[8] This represented 10.6 p.c. of the population. No census had been taken there after 1911 due to the Partition in 1921, for obvious political reasons. The UK Government kept a promise for an enumeration in the 1991 census.[9] The promise was made after a campaign by the Celtic League and Irish language bodies. As it turned out, the Celtic League argument, derided at the time, was that some 60,000 people in the Six Counties could speak Irish. The results showed that the League was making a conservative estimate.

The Anglo-Normans invaded Ireland in 1169. Henry II defeated the Irish High King, Ruaidhri Ó Conchobhair (d. 1198). In October 1175, by the Treaty of Windsor, Ruaidhri recognized Henry as his suzerain, establishing the Angevin emperor's claim over Ireland. Irish resilience in absorbing the conquerors into their cultural ethos, in terms of language, acceptance of Irish law and social customs, continued until the seventeenth century, at which point the native Celtic order was devastated by further conquests and a systematic colonization designed to eliminate the Irish nation.[10] The native ruling class and intelligentsia were generally dispersed to Europe and the native Irish legal system, the oldest complete codified law system in Europe based on Indo-European custom and not Roman Law, was suppressed. Carefully organized attempts were made to suppress the Irish language, which is Europe's oldest literary language after Greek and Latin.

In 1801 the 'Colonial Parliament' in Dublin, having tried to wrest greater independence from England, as the American colonists had done, accepted a Treaty of Union against the background of an Irish republican uprising. This parliament was as representative of the native Irish as George Washington's Congress was representative of the aspirations of the American Indians. The state of the United Kingdom of Great Britain and Ireland was created with this union.

In spite of the gradual easing of the Penal Laws, prohibiting Irish Catholics and Dissenting Protestants from civil rights, passed in the late seventeenth and early eighteenth centuries, the Irish continued to rise in arms to establish their independence. A deliberate policy of 'divide and rule' was then used by the UK Government following the suppression of the 1798 uprising. The Dissenting Protestants, who had been the foremost supporters of republicanism in Ireland, were 'weaned' away from their Catholic compatriots by financial incentives and better rights and privileges. The process was not complete until 1834 when Presbyterians, the majority Protestant sect, were allowed to join the élite Anglican Orange Order.

Uprisings against English rule continued through the nineteenth century. With the failure of the Fenian uprising of 1867, the Irish people turned to the new 'constitutional path' opened for them by the Catholic Emancipation Act and Parliamentary Reform Act. An Irish Party was established to achieve self-government and over the next forty years this party held four-fifths of all the Irish seats available to them within the UK Parliament. In the first few years of its existence, the Irish Party presented no less than twenty-eight self-government bills. The democratically-expressed wish of the vast majority of Irish people was dismissed out-of-hand by successive London governments.

In the general election of 1910, the Irish Party, having won yet another majority with eighty-four seats out of the 105 Irish seats, found that they held the balance of power between the major English parties. It seemed inevitable that the Irish would achieve a measure of self-government. But the proposals for 'home rule' were delayed and finally shelved when Britain entered the Great War in August 1914. The republican movement, and those who favoured physical force, could justifiably claim that 'democracy' and the UK 'constitutional path' did not apply in Ireland. On Easter Monday, 24 April 1916, the Irish rose in arms again. After a week the insurrection was crushed and the leaders were executed by firing squad over a protracted period, to instil maximum fear and obedience into the population. This policy had the reverse effect.

In 1918, a General Election was called. At the dissolution of parliament the Irish Party held sixty-eight seats, Independent Nationalists held ten, and Sinn Féin, which had turned from independence under a dual-monarchy system to declaring itself a republican party, held seven seats. Unionists held only eighteen seats. Sinn Féin now swept to power with seventy-three seats out of the 105, the Irish Party held only six seats while the Unionists increased to twenty-six seats – winning several on the split votes between Sinn Féin and the Irish Party. In accordance with its manifesto, Sinn Féin refused to take the seats won in Westminster but reaffirmed the Irish Republic declared in 1916, and established its own parliament – the Dáil- in Dublin.

The UK response was to declare the Dáil an illegal assembly and send in troops, ordering the arrest of all republican members of the parliament. Conducting a war on one hand and a propaganda campaign on the other, the Westminster Parliament could not shake the allegiance of the Irish electorate for the republic. In January 1920, in the municipal elections, Sinn Féin won seventy-two town and city councils with coalitions of Sinn Féin and the Irish Party controlling a further twenty-six town and city councils, which made ninety-eight out of 117 town and city councils controlled by the republicans. In June 1920, elections for the county and rural district councils and boards of guardians took place. Sinn Féin won twenty-eight out of the thirty-two county councils, 186 out of the 206 rural district councils and 138 out of the 154 boards of guardians.

A Government of Ireland Act, creating a Partition of Ireland, was passed by Westminster without the sanction of the Irish electorate, nor consultation with the majority of elected representatives, and was then enforced by British troops in an attempt to divide and rule once more. A General Election was subsequently called by the UK Government for 'northern' and 'southern' parliaments, as a last ditch attempt to decrease the support given to Sinn Féin. Taking the all-Ireland figure for the new elections, out of 180 seats, Sinn Féin won 130, the Irish Party won six, while the Unionists only held forty-four. But the military enforcement of Partition against the democratically-expressed will of the Irish people has left a legacy of bitterness and bloodshed which continues today.

The War of Independence 1916–21 was therefore only partially successful.

The state of the United Kingdom of Great Britain *and* Northern Ireland finally came into existence on 7 December 1922. On 5 December 1922, by Royal Proclamation, a thirty-two-county Irish Free State had been recognized. But on 7 December, as had been foreseen, the Unionists meeting in Stormont sent a petition to the King, asking that the Six Counties be allowed to use their option clause in the Articles of Agreement between *Ireland* and *Great Britain* to withdraw from the Free State. A Boundary Commission were supposed to meet to draw up a border, as two of these Six Counties had clear nationalist majorities, and in the other four counties, the Unionists only had significant majorities in two of them. But the Boundary Commission never met because the Unionists, having seized their territory, refused to cooperate with any discussion on boundaries. Partition became a *fait accompli*, carried out by military force by the UK against the clearly expressed democratic wish of the majority of the Irish nation. As the Unionist leader, Lord Carson of Duncairn, commented without any guile: violence had created 'Northern Ireland' and only violence would destroy it.

The sectarian Unionist Government, established in the Six Counties, reinforced their position by disenfranchising Catholics, bringing segregation to education and setting up an apartheid system with discrimination stretching to jobs and housing. Sir Basil Brooke (later Viscount Brookeborough), prime minister of the Six Counties 1943–63, once told the Derry Unionist

Association: 'I recommend those people who are Loyalists not to employ Roman Catholics...' In spite of the fact that over a third of the population were Catholics, in April 1934, Lord Craigavon, the first prime minister of the Six Counties, was able to boast: 'We have a Protestant Parliament and a Protestant state'.

But the Unionist failure to coerce their fellow countrymen or drive them out of the Six Counties altogether, by sporadic pogroms, had become obvious in the 1960s, even to the UK Parliament which had tried to ignore the situation and simply bolster the Unionists when requested with troops and weapons, every time the nationalist population resorted to an armed protest. The last republican campaign prior to the current warfare was from 1954 to 1962.

During the late 1960s, the unrest, which had been endemic in the Six Counties, led to the creation of a Civil Rights Movement. The right of every citizen to the electoral franchise was particularly sought. Catholics, who constituted the majority of the nationalist population, had been denied such rights under the Unionist Government, which was drawn from the majority Protestant population. With the Unionist backlash against the Civil Rights Movement and the sending in of British troops yet again, the then moribund Irish Republican Army returned to an active rôle and began 'the long war' of republicans against Westminster, in an attempt to reunite the country. Stormont was abolished in 1972 and the Six Counties became ruled directly from London.[11] It was obvious that British troops in Ireland were not part of a solution to the problem but an integral part of the problem itself.

While Article 2 of the 1937 Constitution of the 26 County Irish state makes a territorial claim over the Six Counties, a 1949 United Kingdom Government Act guarantees to the Unionists that those counties will remain part of the UK so long as Unionists remain a majority there. As Partition was undemocratically drawn-up to ensure a permanent Unionist majority, the idea of any possible democratic 'choice' can be dismissed. The result is violence and impasse until the UK Government decides to disengage from Ireland.

To divert people from this tragedy, there has been an amusing attempt to change 'labels' to help confuse people about the Irish situation. In 1980, with the then prime minister Thatcher's more aggressive attitude to Ireland, a new term began to permeate all Press and media reports on Northern Ireland – observers began to speak of '*mainland* Britain'. The clear implication was that Northern Ireland was an integral part of Britain – and, indeed, that the entire island of Ireland was simply an offshore part of Britain. The phrase was never used prior to 1980 and it was obviously politically conjured. A bemused president or prime minister of the sovereign Irish Republic could be informed that when they went to visit their opposite numbers in London, they were simply journeying to the 'mainland' – the insult seems to have been lost on the Press and media of the UK.

In 1949 the Free State became the Republic of Ireland and was deemed by Westminster to have left the Commonwealth.

While the Irish language is 'the first official language' of the twenty-six county Republic,[12] it has no official status in the Six Counties, although it has been taught in many schools – some Protestant, as well as the majority of Catholic ones.[13]

Between 1963 and 1983 the average number of pupils passing GCE 'O'-level in Irish in Northern Ireland was 1,800 per year while the number passing 'A'-level was 300. However, typical of the lack of status given to the language in Northern Ireland is the case of Breandán Ó Fiaich, a 27-year-old Irish language teacher from Andersonstown, Belfast, who was fined for failing to give information in English to the police and army when stopped by a military patrol in the city.[14] Ó Fiaich did, in fact, give the relevant information in Irish and had adequate identification on him, but he was taken to Queen Street police station, suffered verbal and physical abuse, and was told he must speak English and give information under Section 18 of the

Emergency Provisions Act. On being brought before a magistrate's court the following morning, the magistrate allowed Ó Fiaich an interpreter and satisfied himself that he had complied with Section 18, which did not stipulate that the information had to be given in English only. The charge was dismissed. Ó Fiaich, however, was immediately rearrested by the RUC who tried to pressurize him into answering their questions in English. He was then held in police cells over a weekend and appeared in another magistrate's court on 14 May. This time he was charged with obstructing police officers in the course of their duty. Resident Magistrate Basil McIvor was able to convict him of the charges and fine him £50. According to McIvor, English was the language in which the business of the courts was conducted and he 'could not accept that a man living in Belfast did not speak or understand it'.

Such confrontations over language regularly occur in Northern Ireland. In March 1980, Seán Ó Canainn was fined £25 or one month's jail for trying to conduct his defence in Irish before the Derry Magistrate on a summons of failing to tax his car. In spite of attempts to bring his case before the Court of Appeal, Ó Canainn was arrested and jailed. Continuing similar cases highlight the hostile attitude of the authorities in Northern Ireland towards the Irish language.

However, it cannot be assumed that because Irish is the 'first official language' of the Republic, it actually prospers there. Although Irish was made an optional subject in secondary schools in 1878, and a bilingual education policy, using Irish as a medium of instruction, was approved in 1906, which made it a subject for matriculation in 1909, the creation of a state in 1922 pledged to supporting the restoration of the language has not led to anything more than Irish being used in schools almost as a 'dead language'. Irish-speaking areas (*Gaeltachtaí*) have continued to decline, particularly due to inmigration for they are generally socially deprived areas.

Outside of the school system there has been little attempt to use the language or create an Irish environment, apart from the declining *Gaeltachtaí*. The state broadcasting company (RTÉ) until recently only broadcast 1.6 p.c. of its programmes in Irish. Under the constitution, an Irish citizen can, theoretically, live life through the medium of Irish. Yet in February 1984, Mr Justice Ryan could dismiss the request of an Irish-speaking defendant for his trial to be held in Irish as an 'impertinence',[15] and this was followed by an Irish Supreme Court ruling that judges did not have to hear cases in Irish even within Irish-speaking areas of the country.[16] There is an appalling lack of local and central government bilingual forms or forms in Irish which should be available according to the constitution. The lack of facilities and the Irish Government's lack of commitment to the state-founding principles of halting the decline of the national language evidence a curious paradox. While citizens with a knowledge of the language have, according to the census, been steadily increasing, the position of the language in Irish life is rapidly diminishing.[17]

Isle of Man

Isle of Man (Ellan Vannin). Population 65,000. Manx-speaking: the last census was in 1991 and enumerated 643 able to speak, read and write it, and 497 able to read it and 343 able to write it.[18]

The government of the newly created Great Britain bought the 'lordship of Man' from the 3rd Duke of Atholl in 1764. The title was then bestowed on the reigning monarch who became 'Lord of Man'. In 1866, however, the island's parliament – Tynwald, one of the oldest in the world, dating back to the early tenth century – was reconstituted by the Governor, appointed by the London Parliament, and the Island was recognized as having 'home rule'.[19] Tynwald drew more and more political and fiscal control away from London over the years. The last Royal Commission on the island's status in 1959 declared it to be a Crown Dependency outside of the territory of the UK with full fiscal autonomy.[20] Tynwald has always maintained the theory that the Manx language is as valid as English on the island.[21] However, this has not been so in practice and in spite of a commitment to 'the preservation and promotion of Manx Gaelic' by the Manx Government, on 10 July 1985, no immediate legislation in support of the language has been made.[22] However, in January 1992, Dr Brian y Stoyll was appointed Manx Language Officer by the Manx Department of Education to devise a programme for the language to be taught in Manx schools as an optional subject. Two peripatetic language teaching posts were created and it was announced that a programme would be available to pupils by September 1992.[23] The 1992 Secondary Curriculum Policy Statement carried a foreword by the Minister of Education, announcing that the Manx language would henceforth be available 'to all pupils wishing to study it'.[24] A Broadcasting Bill went before the Manx Parliament in 1993 with a clause to make Manx language programmes an integral part of broadcasting on Manx Radio.[25]

Many Manx wish even greater independence from the UK, which has authority over the Island's foreign relations and defence policy, and Mec Vannin is a republican party which, at varying times, has won seats in the Manx Parliament.

Scotland

Scotland (Alba). Population: 5,136,50. Scottish Gaelic-speaking: the 1991 census showed a significant drop from 79,309 (1.6 p.c.) to 65,978 (1–4 p.c.).[26]

The process of the erosion of the Scottish Gaelic language within Scotland began when Scotland was still independent, following the death of MacBeth (1040–57), with the gradual Anglicization of the native ruling and merchant classes. This Anglicization did not mean an acceptance of an Anglophile attitude, as was discovered during the War of Independence following Edward I of England's claim to suzerainty over

Scotland in 1291. The language, however, suffered particular suppression during the Reformation, and in 1616 the Privy Council decided in favour of the universal 'planting' of the English language and the abolition and removal of Scottish Gaelic. This was confirmed by the Scottish Parliament in 1631.[27] The Stuart monarchy was offered the Crown of England on the death of Elizabeth I. James VI became James I of England in 1603. He was a strong advocate of Anglicization and complete union. However, his plan to unite both parliaments of Scotland and England was rejected by the English in 1607. In 1707, because of the commercial rivalries whereby Scottish commercial concerns, such as the Darien Company, were seen as threats to English trading companies, the English Parliament decided to press for a union to control such enterprises. They managed to obtain a majority for union in the Scottish Parliament, which also had hitherto rejected the proposal, by the liberal use of bribes. In 1708, realizing that the English-dominated London Parliament was breaking the terms of the Treaty of Union, the Scots rebelled. Even many who had advocated the Union in the Scottish Parliament now led the movement for insurrection. In 1714, an attempt to introduce a Self-Government for Scotland Bill in the House of Commons was defeated. The Speaker informed the Scottish Members that England 'had catch't Scotland and would keep her fast'.[28] From 1715 through to 1820 a number of major uprisings against the Union took place, some in the form of support for the Jacobite cause, because the Stuarts promised a restoration of the Scottish Parliament – while in 1797 and 1820, risings took on a radical republican outlook. The modern Scottish self-government movement began in 1886 and from 1889 through to 1927, some twenty-one Self-Government for Scotland Bills were introduced in the House of Commons. Of those allowed to come to a vote, on every occasion the Bills were defeated by the inbuilt English majority, in spite of an average 80 p.c. support vote by Scottish members. There have been only half-a-dozen attempts to present Self-

Government Bills since 1927, none of which have come to a vote.[29] In the General Election of 9 April 1992, 75–5 p.c. of those who voted did so for parties pledged to re-establishing a Scottish Parliament (of these, 21.5 p.c. voted for complete separation from England). The issue of a Scottish Parliament had been made into a prominent factor in the election. Nevertheless, the victorious Conservatives, returned to power in England, resolved to maintain the *status quo* within the United Kingdom. Scottish Democracy was set up as a cross-party movement to confront the Tories, uniting all those who believe in self-government for Scotland from devolution to full independence within the European Economic Community. On 12 December 1992, 30,000 Scots marched to St Andrews House to hear a Declaration of Scottish Democracy read.

The position of Scottish Gaelic has been considerably eased since its suppression by law was confirmed by the UK Parliament in the late eighteenth century. At one point, even wearing the kilt and playing bagpipes was suppressed by English law. A Gaelic clause was finally allowed in the 1918 Education Act but it was common, even until the 1960s, for Gaelic-speaking children attending State schools to be taught in English throughout the entire course of their schooling, and for them to be the subject of corporal punishment if overheard speaking their own language. A more liberal attitude has prevailed since the late 1960s, although the language is given no official status by the UK state within Scotland.[30] This attitude is actually in contravention of the Universal Declaration of Human Rights as well as the European Convention and the European Charter for Minority or Regional Languages, which the UK has now signed. Speakers are still placed at a disadvantage within the state.

Bilingual education policies have, however, been adopted at local government level, particularly in the Western Isles, and adult classes are mushrooming throughout Scotland. The announcement in 1990 of the establishment of a Scottish Gaelic medium television station has been a major breakthrough for those who have pointed out that the language was poorly served by broadcasting, with just a few minutes a week on regular television schedules and not much more on radio. However, a new Scottish Gaelic soap opera called *Machair*, shown at peak-time on Independent Television, with English subtitles, attracts a viewing figure of eight times the official number of Scottish Gaelic speakers. Producers of the Gaelic learners series 'Learning Our Language' say that there has been a whole new resurgence of interest in the language since *Machair*.

But such concessions as there are to the language have so far been too little and perhaps too late. Of all the Celtic languages, with the possible exception of Breton, whose position, as discussed earlier, we do not know with any degree of accuracy, Scottish Gaelic has declined the most rapidly in the last ten years with its apparent drop of 14,000 speakers.

Wales

Wales (Cymru). Population: 2,807,200. Welsh-speaking 508,100 at the 1991 census, representing 18.7 p.c., and showing a fairly stable situation since the 1981 census which returned 503,549 speakers (18.9 P.C.).[31]

When Llywellyn ap Gruffydd ap Llywellyn (1246–82) was slain near Cilmeri, his brother Dafydd became the last native Welsh ruler for a period of six months before he was captured and executed by the English, having been 'tried' before the English Parliament. Wales then came under English control. There was a period of restlessness and uprisings and, from 1400, Owain Glyn Dŵr became ruler of an independent Wales. By 1409, however, the Welsh struggle for independence was being won by England and by 1415 Wales was once more firmly under English control. In 1535 and 1542, by Acts of the English Parliament, Wales was incorporated into England and divided into shires. The Welsh language was to be 'utterly extirp'd'. Wales, as a separate entity to England, did not re-emerge until

1951 when a Minister for Welsh Affairs was appointed. This post developed into that of Secretary of State for Wales in the 1960s due to nationalist pressure. During the 1960s a campaign of civil disobedience by Cymdeithas yr Iaith Gymraeg (Welsh Language Society) caused a Royal Commission on the Welsh Language to recommend that the Welsh language have equal validity throughout Wales. Legislation in 1968 fell short of this. However, in terms of government recognition and support, Welsh now fares better than the other Celtic languages within the UK. Nevertheless, other pressures continue to be exerted on the language. The main one is that created by the immigration of English families into Wales. They establish English language areas, and this is a problem over which the Welsh people have no control because Wales is not a separate political entity to England and cannot enact protective legislation for the indigenous communities.[32]

It is, however, theoretically possible to live one's life through the medium of Welsh. One can receive an education from playschool through to higher education – that is, primary degree level. S4C, the Welsh television channel, the use of Welsh on the radio, in newspapers, and in the production of Welsh films that have won international awards, are of great assistance to· the way Welsh people perceive the language and, in this respect, with bilingualism as a visible aspect of moving through Wales, the availability of bilingual local and central government forms, arising out of the campaign of civil disobedience by Cymdeithas yr Iaith Gymraeg, places Welsh in a stronger position than its sister Celtic languages.

* * *

These six peoples comprise the modern Celtic homelands or countries. The recognition by these six peoples of their common cultural ancestry is the basis for Pan Celticism.

Because only two of the Celtic countries are self-governing, the Pan Celtic movement subscribes to the aim of self-government for all the Celtic peoples. Mainstream Pan Celticism today is therefore a 'nationalist' movement. At the same time, mainstream Pan Celticism believes in formal political links between such self-governing Celtic countries, with many pointing to Scandinavia as a 'rôle model'. The mainstream movement is therefore also 'supranationalist'.

I will comply with the terminology which has been used by Celtic nationalists since the nineteenth century. The six separate Celtic communities, as defined by the linguistic criterion, are 'nations' because they constitute distinct peoples, characterized by a common descent, language and history with the additional factor of having once been organized into political states at some recent epoch in their history. There is, therefore, in Celtic perception, a difference between the terms *state* and *nation*.

The acceptance of this interpretation of these terms makes it easier to follow the logic of the Pan Celtic argument. I am, however, aware that such definitions can be argued. From the seventeenth century, the terms *state* and *nation* have been used synonymously. E.A. Freeman argued that the Swiss constituted a *nation* which consisted of four *ethnic* groups.[33] Yet this would seem a slight tautology, for 'ethnicity' comes from the Greek meaning 'pertaining to *nation*'. It was then argued that an ethnic group became a nation only when it demonstrated a political self-awareness as a cohesive unit. While the latter criterion would certainly apply in the Celtic case, it is easier, for the purposes of this study, to accept the Pan Celtic definition.

A state, therefore, is a territory confined within political borders which more often than not comprises several nations. There is usually a dominant nation and several peripheral nations. In our consideration of definitions, we have to point out that there is no British *state* let alone a British *nation*. The United Kingdom of Great Britain *and* Northern Ireland is thus a *state*, containing a dominant English nation but incorporating the Welsh, Cornish, and Scottish *nations*, and a section of the Irish *nation*. The Manx, as has been pointed out, are not part of this state but deemed to be a Crown Dependency.

It follows that nations often exist without the protection of a state. A nation comprises a homogeneous community, which possesses a common language, culture and history. Such a community can overlap the borders of several states as in the case of the Kurds. Kurdistan, whose 7.6 million population is marked by a language, common culture and history, is divided between the states of Turkey, Iraq, Iran, Syria and Armenia. The Basques, as another example, are a nation also identified by a common language, culture and history, but they are members of two states – being citizens of France and Spain. Yet in both French and Spanish perceptions there is such an entity as a Basque *country* (*Le pays Basque* and *El pais de los Vascos*), implying recognition of a territory just as Kurdistan is similarly identified. To the Basques, there is no doubt about the identification of their territory; they live in *Euzkadi* and have a clear perception of its historical borders. Similarly, Celts refer to their *countries*, recognizing the historic political borders which existed at the time of their former independence.

'Nationality' is, therefore, not the same as 'state citizenship'. Therefore I make reference here to Celtic *nations*, *communities*, and *peoples*, all of which mean the cultural nation sharing an historically recognized territory – that is, a country. True, there is some double-edge recognition of the Celtic countries by the state apparatus. For example, while Wales is constitutionally still annexed to England, with no political recognition of territorial separation, for the purposes of sport (specifically football) in the UK, Europe and world leagues, it is recognized as a *nation*. The same view holds for Scotland. In June 1993, a television advertisement for a forthcoming game between the British Lions rugby team and the New Zealand All-Blacks showed the words 'Ireland, Wales, Scotland, England = the British Lions'. Correctly-speaking, Ireland cannot be included in the *British* equation.

But to what degree are Pan Celts nationalists?

Pan Celticism is interpreted varyingly from simple recognition and a wish to maintain and improve cultural links between the six cultural groupings within current political structures, to a more radical political undertaking with the aim of achieving organized relations not only on the cultural level but at the political and economic levels, with the long-term aim of a formal association between self-governing Celtic nations. This last concept was first argued in the nineteenth century but it has not been until recent decades, with the rise of the Celtic League and other political groups, that it has emerged as a serious political consideration. For the purposes of this book, all these varied opinions are referred to as the Pan Celtic movement.

While arguably little known or discussed outside the Celtic communities, Pan Celticism has, since 1865, been an increasingly influential movement in changing attitudes and perceptions within those communities and has resulted in the establishment of some organized relations already between the peoples of the Celtic nations which now have the potential to affect future social and political developments. Pan Celticism can, therefore, be described as a social movement.

As with most social movements, it is often difficult to demonstrate the extent of the following and support that Pan Celticism actually receives for one does not need to have a membership card unless one belongs to a particular group or organization, such as the Celtic League. Indeed, supporters of the political aims of Pan Celticism can be found in many unrelated political groupings, from the UK Labour Party and the UK Liberal Democrats to the Irish Fianna Fáil, the French Socialist Party or the individual Celtic nationalist parties such as Plaid Cymru, the Scottish National Party, Mebyon Kernow, Social Democratic Labour Party (Northern Ireland), Sinn Féin, Mec Vannin, Union Démocratique Bretonne and so forth. Therefore, as with social movements such as the women's movement, one cannot point to a card-carrying membership nor enumerate all who are or would be supportive to Pan Celticism.

But whatever the varying political objectives, almost from its inception, mainstream Pan Celticism accepted the idea that the survival of the Celtic communities, which, because of the very definition of 'Celtic' implies the survival of the Celtic languages and the cultures they enshrine, means the re-emergence of politically independent Celtic units. The creation of protective borders and legislation was seen as essential to the defence and recovery of the Celtic languages. But, once again, the definition of 'independence' can vary from mere 'devolution' within the current state framework, to 'home rule', or complete sovereignty as independent republics.

Now, 'nationalist' is regarded as the term for describing anyone who argues for some form of self-government for the Celtic peoples, and the restoration of their languages and cultures. But nationalism, like the word 'love', is frequently misused and often misunderstood. To simplify, there are two types of nationalism. There is the nationalist who believes in the superiority of his nationality and who tries to impose his language and culture on another people, stamping out the other nation's nationality. Such nationalism is, of course, imperialism. England's Victorian Empire was built on such concepts. This national superiority is the same 'nationalism' that built all the world's empires, that created Nazi Germany, and inspires modern Serbian aggression over their neighbours in the Balkans. It is xenophobic and regressive.

The second form of nationalism is a reaction to imperialism; it is a striving to prevent the nation's language and culture from being destroyed and the people from being economically exploited by the dominant nation. This nationalism strives to return the national community to a position of political independence, but has no desire to extend the native language and culture beyond the national community, or seek political domination beyond the borders of the country for which independence is sought.

The Celtic nationalists see their nationalism as being the second of the two types. They argue that their nationalism, by which they mean the advocacy of the freedom of national communities from the cultural, political and economic exploitation of other nations, is integral to the policy of a truly liberated society. They further argue that national and social freedom are not two separate and unrelated issues but are two sides of one great democratic principle, each being incomplete without the other.

On the basis of such 'nationalism', they would argue that they are true internationalists because the way to a sound internationalism is through recognition, not repudiation, of the fact of nationality. The solidarity of the peoples of the world must, accordingly, rest upon a pact between national units, associated in a common purpose and destiny.

'Pan Celtic movement' is used in the following pages as a means to indicate Pan Celticism in all its various aspects and diversity of aims and attitudes; it does not imply the existence of a monolithic group.

In defining precisely our terms, we come face to face with the fact that sociologists are disputing with each other what a social movement is. In recent years, they have conjured a bewildering variety of groups to their arguments. The Pan Celtic movement does, however, fulfil all the major criteria offered. It is a 'collective attempt to restore, protect or create values (or norms) in the name of a generalized belief'; it is a form of 'collective action aimed at social reorganization'; and it is also an attempt 'to bring about or resist large scale change in the social order by non-institutionalized means'.[34]

The Pan Celtic movement, which includes varying interpretations of its central concept, the special relationship of the six communities recognized as Celtic, covers the spectrum of the whole society within those communities and, because it fulfils the differing criteria, one can in fact come to the conclusion that it is almost all things to all people. As A. Melucci has cynically suggested, there are such a variety of interpretations as to what a social movement is, that 'if it moves' it can be called a social movement.[35] But in the meantime, the Pan Celtic movement conforms with most of those proposed.

One thing Pan Celticism does not do, however; as discussed earlier, is to constitute a *mass* social movement, for it has not gathered a large number of active supporters even though most members of the Celtic community can express a sympathy with one or other of its aims. The fact that Pan Celticism has not emerged as a mass movement does not mean that it does not possess the potential to do so at any future date. M. Weber stated that western societies, increasingly organized and bureaucratized, make the charismatic mobilization of people behind a small social group necessary to change it to a big one, an unlikely event.[36] But such a breach of Weber's 'rule' has happened, and in a Celtic country too; in Ireland, when the period 1916–1918 saw the remarkable swing in popular support from the Irish Party's 'home rule' within the UK to Sinn Féin's republican separatism and the prospect of an entirely new social order. The point is that no rule on mass social behaviour can be writ in stone.

Notes

1   *Le Monde de l'Education*, Paris, September, 1976.
2   *Separatism in Brittany*, M.J.C. O'Callaghan (Dyllansow Truran, Redruth, 1983). See also *The Bretons*, Patrick Galliou and Michael Jones (Basil Blackwell, Oxford, 1991).
3   *The Story of the Cornish Language* (Tor Mark Press, Penryn, 1990). See also *Kernewek Hedhya: 1984 Report on the State of the (Cornish) Language* (Cowethas an Yeth Kernewek, Truro, 1984).
4   *Covath*, Falmouth, Autumn, 1990.
5   *A History of Cornwall*, F.E. Halliday (Duckworth, London, 1959), p. 116. See also *Tudor Cornwall*, A.L. Rowse (Jonathan Cape, 1941), pp. 253–290,
6   'The Cornish Stannary Parliament', Paul Laity, *Carn*, No. 66 (Summer, 1989). See also 'The (Dis)United Kingdom', *Gulliver*, No. 31 (1992, Argument-Verlag, Berlin).
7   *Statistical Abstract of Ireland for 1981*, see Table 37, Irish Language. The 1986 census figures supplied by the Central Statistics Office, Dublin.

8   The 1991 Northern Ireland census summary report (Table 2–3),
     Population aged 3 years and over by knowledge of Irish language. See: *Irish Dialects and Irish-speaking Districts*, Dr Brían Ó Cuív (Dublin Institute for Advanced Studies, Dublin, 1967). Tables for Ulster, pp. 81–85.

9   *Irish Democrat*, April, 1988.

10   *The Fortunes of the Irish Language*, Daniel Corkery (Cultural Relations Committee of Ireland, Dublin, 1954), p. 95.

11   *The Course of Irish History*, ed. T.W. Moody and F.X. Martin (Mercier Press, Cork, 1967), and *Northern Ireland: The Orange State*, Michael Farrell (Pluto Press, 1976), give an excellent historical overview.

12   *Bunreacht na hÉireann* (Constitution of Ireland), Article 8, Paragraph 1.

13   'The Case for Ulster Irish on Ulster Radio and Television'; report by study group under chairmanship of Patrick Clarke (Belfast Gaelic League, September, 1978), 18pp.

14   *Belfast Telegraph* and *Irish Times*, 14 May 1984.

15   *Inniu*, 10 February 1984.

16   *Carn*, No. 44 (Winter, 1984). The case cited is that of Tomás Ó Monacháin versus the State.

17   An outline of the position of Irish within Ireland is given in 'Irish; An EEC Language', *The Incorporated Linguist*, Vol. 2–3, No. 4 (Autumn, 1984). One of the best studies on the attitudes contributing to the failure of the Irish language revival is *The Great Silence*, Seán de Fréine (Mercier, 1978 – originally published in Irish by FNT, Dublin, in 1965, and revised for the English language edition). More recently *The Cultural Conquest of Ireland*, Kevin Collins (Mercier, 1990), examines the cultural transformation which has continued under native Irish governments.

18   Isle of Man census, 1991. Also *Carn*, No. 78 (Summer, 1992).

19   *A Brief History of the Isle of Man*, G.V.C. Young (Mansk-Svenska Publishing Co Ltd, Peel, 1983).

20   *Report of the Commission on the Isle of Man Constitution*, 2 Vols (London, 17 March 1959).

21   Yn Cheshaght Ghailckagh (Manx Language Society) statement, 20 March 1968: 'With regard to the legal position of the Manx language, Manx has every bit as much status as English in theory but unfortunately not so much in practice.'

22   *Report of the Select Committee on the Greater use of Manx Gaelic* (Tynwald, July, 1985).

23   *Carn*, No. 75 (Autumn, 1991) and *Carn*, No. 77 (Spring, 1992).

24   *Carn*, No. 81 (Spring, 1993)

25   *Carn*, No. 80 (Winter, 1992/93).

26   Census of Scotland, 1981 (Gaelic summary report), 1982.

27   *Gaelic in Scottish Education and Life, Past, Present and Future*, John Lorne Campbell (Saltire Society, Edinburgh, 1950), p. 48.

28   *The Anglo-Scottish Union of 1707*, Oliver Brown (Scots Independent Publication, Perth, n.d.), p. 17.

29 *The Treaty of Union Between Scotland and England, 1707: The Legal Basis of the United Kingdom of Great Britain* (The Scottish Secretariat Ltd., Glasgow, 3rd revised edition, 1955), pp. 27/29. For an overview of developments see *Scottish Nationalism*, H.J. Hanham (Faber & Faber, London, 1969).

30 *The Lion's Tongue*, Kenneth MacKinnon (Club Leabhar, Inverness, 1974) p. 65.

31 1991 Census County Report Series CEN 91 Nos 47 to 54 and Census of Wales, 1981 (Welsh Summary Report), 1982.

32 For an overview see: *The Historical Basis of Welsh Nationalism*: a series of lectures by A.W. Wade-Evans, T. Jones Pierce, Ceinwen Thomas, A.O.H. Jarman, D. Gwenallt Jones and Gwynfor Evans, Plaid Cymru, 1950. For specifics on inmigration see Cymdeithas yr Iaith Gymraeg's various reports and factsheets (ie *Cynllunio a'r Iaith − Planning and Language*, n.d.1982, and *Tai yn yr Ardaioedd Gwledig − Housing in Rural Areas*, n.d.).

33 Edward Augustus Freeman (1823–92), *History of the Norman Conquest*, 6 Vols (Oxford, 1867–1879).

34 For a discussion on the varying interpretations of what constitutes a 'social movement' see *Social Movements: the Politics of Moral Protest*, Jan Pakulski (Longman Cheshire, Australia, 1991), particularly his 'Introduction', pp. xiii − xvi. Also chapter three on social movement theory. See also *Ideology of the New Social Movements*, A. Scott (Unwin Hyman, London, 1990).

35 'Social Movements and the Democratization of Everyday Life', A. Melucci, in *Civil Society and the State: New European Perspectives*, ed. J. Keane (Verso, London, 1988), pp. 245–260.

36 *The Theory of Social and Economic Organization*, M. Weber (The Free Press, New York, 1947).

3: Origins of Pan Celticism

ANY study of Pan Celticism must ask is it a modern concept, an idea which emerged in the nineteenth century from romantic literary movements within the Celtic countries, the so-called 'Celtic Renaissance'? Most people do immediately associate Pan Celticism with W.B. Yeats and 'Celtic Twilightism'. But did Pan Celticism have a reality at some historical point? Was there such a reality as a Celtic consciousness before the nineteenth century?

In seeking to answer these questions, especially in a survey limited by space, there is a tendency to seize on particular anecdotal evidence to demonstrate links. But such evidence, expressive of a greater field of material, is valid.

In early times we find accounts of military and political alliances and, from the late eighteenth century, these turn into the formation of cultural links and societies. Although the evidence is anecdotal by the nature of its brevity, the links do demonstrate a long and continuing tradition of awareness of common ties between the disparate Celtic communities.

The Celtic scholar, Henri Hubert, has spoken of 'the solidarity of Celtic societies' in the ancient world, in the years before the start of the Christian epoch. Hubert demonstrated that the ancient Celts 'were in communication, they were inter-connected'.[1] He cites evidence to 'show that the Greeks of Marseilles and of Lampsacos' (in Asia Minor) 'knew that they would find among Celtic peoples living very far apart a *sense of oneness*' (my italics) 'of which the Romans had been aware some years earlier when they had sent ambassadors to ask the Volcae to be neutral when Hannibal passed through the country.'[2]

Celtic scholars, along with Hubert, have been unanimous in pointing to the tremendous sense of kinship, of common origin, of philosophy, mythology, ritual practices and legal institutions shared by the Celts. This sense of kinship was frequently remarked upon by Greeks and Romans. Hubert argues:

> This solidarity of the Celtic peoples, even when distant from one another, is sufficiently explained by the sense of kinship, of common origin acting in a fairly restricted world, all the parts of which were in communication.

Celtic scholars generally agree that the sense of unity was cemented by language and cultural attitudes. It was manifested in a common religion and social ideas which bound them in a shared legal system. There are similarities between the Brehon Laws of Ireland and the Laws of Hywel Dda which, it can be argued, support the idea of a commonality of an earlier Celtic legal system, which also has many parallels to Hindu Law and which would support the hypothesized common Indo-European link.[3] As the Celtic world diminished, because of conquests, assimilation and extermination, firstly under the onslaught of the Roman Empire and later because of the western expansion of the Germanic peoples, the Celts were eventually pressed back into the islands and peninsulas of north-west Europe where the early medieval Celtic nations emerged, retaining their sense of kinship through a phenomenon which we recognize today as the Celtic Church, which was not finally absorbed by Rome until the fourteenth century. Indeed, the religious functions of the druids were replaced by those of the 'saints' or missionaries of this Church. The term 'Celtic Church' is not strictly an accurate one because the early Christian churches among the Celtic peoples, in most essentials, were part of the Roman Church. Neither was the Celtic Church an identifiable organization with a central leadership. Nevertheless, the insular Celts of the British Isles developed their own particular

Christianity, clinging to the original computations of the dating of ceremonies and freely mixing many pre-Christian traditions and social concepts into their Christian philosophy and ceremonials. Moreover they thus developed as a distinct cultural entity within the wider Christian movement. It was a Church delineated by individual cultural philosophies, social concepts and art forms with a distinct asceticism and monastic extremism.[4]

Professor Cecile O'Rahilly, in a pioneering study,[5] has charted the historical and literary relationships between the Irish and Welsh during the Dark Ages, which was for the Celts, incidentally, a 'Golden Age' of learning, literacy and development.[6] Citing events and examples in both Irish and Welsh annals, O'Rahilly has described the links between these two Celtic countries during the early medieval period and until the Tudor times. Naturally, we have to be careful to avoid ascribing Pan Celticism to these links when geographical proximity and identification against a common enemy might be considered a more reasonable cause. However, the cultural, political and social linkage between the two Celtic communities, as recorded in the *Annals of Tigernach*, *Annals of Ulster*, and others, do indicate an awareness of their Celtic commonality.[7] Professor O'Rahilly's study is crucial to any work on Pan Celticism, demonstrating, as it does, the cultural interaction between all the Celtic countries in the early and late medieval period. The Scottish historians John de Fordun (*Chronica Gentis Scotorum*, c. 1380) and Hector Boece (*Historia de Scotia*, 1527), using now lost references, told of an alliance between the Britons, Scots and Picts in the period ascribed to 'King Arthur', and speak of a combined army marching to Kent in the early sixth century to face the aggression of the Anglo-Saxons (referred to specifically as the Jutes). They claim that this early 'Celtic alliance' was able to thwart a Jutish invasion of the Isle of Wight at this time.

We find two major poems demonstrating how this Celtic commonality found expression in the unification of different

Celtic communities against a common foreign enemy. From the sixth century we have *Y Gododdin*, written by Aneirin, about a Celtic raid on Catraeth (Catterick) which had been recently captured by the Anglo-Saxons. The Gododdin (the Votadini of the Roman period) were a tribe whose capital was situated on the site of modern Edinburgh, and the poem mentions Celtic leaders from Dumnonia (Devon and Cornwall) as well as Wales, joining together in a military alliance with the Celts of southern Scotland in the attempt to recapture Catraeth.[8] The poem contains, incidentally, our first recorded reference to Arthur – but as a hero already dead at the time of its composition. This poem, known as *Y Gododdin*, would seem to support the lost authorities used by de Fordun and Boece.

However, nowhere is the concept of Celtic unity better illustrated than in the tenth-century poem, now ascribed to Welsh literature, *Armes Prydein Vawr* ('The prophecy of Great Britain'), which survives in the 'Book of Taliesin'.[9] The poem consists of 199 lines and calls upon the Welsh to unite with the Irish, the Manx, the Scots, the Cornish and the British Celts of Cumbria and Strathclyde, as well as the Danes of Dublin, in an alliance to drive the Anglo-Saxons from Britain.[10] The inclusion of Danes, both from Dublin, the Isle of Man and the Western Isles of Scotland, absorbed into the Gaelic world, tends to underscore the fact that the Celts did not believe in 'racial' exclusiveness. Their badge was a cultural one.

O'Rahilly comments, 'It was, unfortunately, but a poet's dream, and no such powerful confederation ever opposed the Saxons in Wales'.[11] O'Rahilly was too particular in her vision, for in AD 937 such a confederation did emerge. Constantine II (AD 900-942) of Scotland, Owain, King of Cymbria, Olaf Godfreyson of Dublin, Aralt, King of Man and the Isles, Hywel Dda of Wales, Donnchadh, High King of Ireland and Cynan of Cornwall formed an alliance with the Dane Anlaf against the Anglo-Saxon king Athelstan. The confederation, whose fleet numbered 600 ships, was defeated after a two-day battle at

Brunanburgh (a site not identified but thought to be on the Northumbrian coast), which is recorded in the *Anglo-Saxon chronicle* and in Icelandic saga. It is my contention that *Armes Prydein Vawr*, whose title must seem to translate ironically to the modern Celt, was written in support of this Celtic confederation, which sought a return of a Celtic Britain.

The concept of cooperation between the Celtic peoples continued after this defeat. It re-emerges in 1176 when Rhys, Justiciar of Deheubarth, organized the first Eisteddfod in Wales that we have any record of. This was held at Christmas at Aberteifi (Cardigan) Castle, but had been proclaimed the year beforehand 'not only in Wales but in Ireland and Scotland too, showing that there was still some consciousness of the old Celtic relationship'.[12]

There are several examples of cooperation through an awareness of common origins in the late medieval period. In the summer of 1171 we find Ruadhri Ó Conchobhair, the High King of Ireland (1117–1199) using Archbishop Ó Tuathail of Dublin to ask assistance from the Scots and Manx, to aid him against the 'common enemy', the Anglo-Normans.

When Robert Bruce regained independence for Scotland, defeating the English at Bannockburn in 1314, he also liberated the Isle of Man from English overlordship. According to Ronald McNair Scott, Edward II of England's 'defeat at Bannockburn by a mainly Celtic army roused the expectation of his subject Celts'.[13] Indeed, Bruce's victory was greeted with joy in both Ireland and Wales and envoys were sent to him. Bruce's reply to the Irish makes clear his sense of common Celtic kinship:

Whereas we and you and our people and your people, free since ancient times, share the same national ancestry and are urged to come together more eagerly and joyfully in friendship by a common language and by common custom, we have sent over to you our beloved kinsmen, the bearers of this letter, to negotiate with you in our name about permanently strengthening and maintaining inviolate that special friendship between us and you, so that with God's will your nation may be able to recover her ancient liberty.[14]

Edward Bruce, Robert's brother, was crowned King of Ireland on May Day 1316. According to Dr Edmund Curtis, who based his assessment on an analysis of the letters of the Bruce family now held in the Harris Collection of the National Library of Ireland, 'The Bruces in fact planned a general revolt of the Celtic race everywhere against the English.'[15]

Colm McNamee, a research officer for the Northern Ireland Parliamentary Boundary Commission, writing in *History Ireland* (Spring, 1993) states: 'In the thirteenth century there is evidence of a growing "Celtic" consciousness...' He asks the question: 'Did the Bruces aim to build a grand "Celtic" alliance against England?' He argues that 'Edward I discovered that he could not suppress the revolts of the Welsh without causing unrest in Ireland. In the recent past, Welsh and Scottish leaders had made formal complaints against the English to the Pope, which may have served as models for Donal O'Neill's Remonstrance.' In 1317, O'Neill, king of Ulster and claimant to the High Kingship, together with the Irish princes and chieftains, wrote a Remonstrance to Pope John XXII denouncing the English conquest and rule of Ireland. This document clearly shows that the concept of a single nation state had long been established in Ireland.

Colm McNamee, in pointing out Robert Bruce's appeal to the Irish on grounds of common ancestry, language and customs, says 'a similar letter was also circulated in Wales'.

Certainly the initial victories of the Bruce family caused the Welsh, led by Gruffydd Llwyd, to invite them to aid Wales in securing her independence. Edward Bruce promised the Welsh military aid on the provision that he rule Wales 'as your prince (Llywelyn) formerly most fully used to exercise'.[16] Gruffydd Llwyd's uprising was defeated in the wake of Edward Bruce's own defeat and death in Ireland. Llwyd was imprisoned in Rhuddlan Castle. According to McNamee, however, 'in 1327

Robert (Bruce) was thought to be contemplating an invasion of Wales by way of Ireland'. But only Scotland and, for a while, the Isle of Man, remained free from English dominance.

It can be argued that the Bruce family were not 'Celtic idealists' but were merely out for territorial aggrandizement. However, the significant point is that they could use the 'Celtic idea' as part of their political strategy, thus demonstrating that the concept of Celtic commonality did exist in the minds of the Celtic populations.

Owain Glyn Dŵr's first priority, after re-establishing Welsh independence in 1400, was to make treaties with his Celtic neighbours. He entered an agreement with Robert III and later James I of Scotland, and began negotiations with Yann V of Brittany.

There was considerable intermingling between the Bretons and Cornish until the sixteenth century, when the Cornish language went into a period of decline. Bretons were found to be living in Cornwall in large numbers until the Reformation, which gave the final blow to the Cornish language.

The Tudor family, thoroughly Anglicized by the time Henry Tudor seized the English throne in 1485, were not above using a Pan Celtic 'rallying card' to get support from the Welsh, Bretons and Cornish. Henry Tudor used the name of the Celtic hero 'Arthur' to rally the Celts, naming his eldest son Arthur and proclaiming him Prince of Wales in 1489. Henry Tudor had spent considerable time in exile in Brittany. The battle of Bosworth, which overthrew Richard III, was fought for Henry mainly by Welsh and Cornish troops with support from Brittany. Yet the Tudors, once in power, were the most virulent anti-Celts, ruling from London, making centralist policies and laws designed to destroy the Celtic languages and cultures. Even Cornwall was provoked into three uprisings against Tudor centralization.

That the cultural relationship of the Welsh, Bretons and Cornish was generally recognized in this period may be seen from the episode in which Henry VIII met François I of France at 'the field of the Cloth of Gold' near Boulogne (1520). It is recorded that Welsh and Bretons met in a friendly wrestling contest before the battle. A similar wrestling contest was held in 1551 between Bretons and Cornish. The similarity in the style of 'Celtic wrestling' has been retained until modern times and since 1927 an annual Celtic wrestling tournament has been held.

It is not within the scope of this study to examine all the examples of Celtic cooperation, based on the recognition of a common cultural bond, which can be enumerated over the centuries. Collectively, however, they provide a powerful argument for the existence of a consciousness of a common identity among the Celts.

The Scottish scholar, George Buchanan (1506–1582), seems to have been the first person to state clearly, in a form which modern linguists can appreciate, the common identity of the Celts, by pointing to the relationship of their languages in his study published in Edinburgh in 1582.[17] However, as noted earlier, the Welsh scholar Edward Lhuyd is generally acknowledged as the founder of modern Celtic scholarship. Lhuyd is particularly recognized as the founder of comparative Celtic philology, having travelled in most of the Celtic countries and collected material, which was published as the Glossography volume of *Archaeologia Britannica* (Oxford, 1707). It is unfortunate that the planned subsequent volumes were not published. Lhuyd was arguably the main link between some of the last traditional custodians of medieval Celtic learning and lore and those who followed him. It was Lhuyd who reintroduced the term 'Celtic' into vernacular use.

Some have argued that the Breton Abbé Pezron, rather than Lhuyd, laid in 1703 the foundations for the eighteenth-century Celtic 'vogue', as it was he who was the 'creator' of the use of the modern term 'Celt'. But Pezron was considerably less scientific in his scholarship than Lhuyd, although his work prompted Johann Kaspar Zeuss to turn to Celtic philological studies. Zeuss' *Grammatica Celtica* (1853) became the later cornerstone of all modern Celtic scholarship.

James MacPherson was the person who set the cultural 'bomb' which created a Romantic Pan Celtic movement and influenced the Romantic movement in Europe. A Scotsman, James MacPherson of Kingussie (1736–96) published *Fragments of ancient poetry collected in the Highlands* (1760), *Fingal* (1762) and *Temora* (1763), all of which, he maintained, were translations from ancient Scottish Gaelic manuscripts. They became known collectively as *Ossian* (Oisín being the son of Fionn MacCumhail in Gaelic mythology).

Dr Samuel Johnson denounced MacPherson's work as a forgery, causing a bitter controversy. However, whether the work was a forgery or merely a highly subjective rendering from Gaelic oral tradition, or even translations of lost manuscripts, the work brought things Gaelic and Celtic to wide public attention outside the Celtic world as well as within the Celtic communities themselves. There began a resurgence of interest in things Celtic not only in the Celtic countries but throughout Europe. *Ossian* was to have a profound effect on other European literatures and influenced writers as diverse as William Blake (himself of Irish parentage), J.W. Goethe and Lord Byron, and it even had influence on political figures such as Napoleon Bonaparte and Bernadotte. Bernadotte, who married the daughter of Dublin émigrés living in Marseilles, became King of Sweden and thereafter Sweden has had several Kings called Oscar (named after the son of Ossian).

Through the wave of interest in his literary achievement, attention was drawn to the commonality of the Celtic peoples, and *Ossian* became the literary parent to works on similar traditions in the other Celtic countries, in which authors pointed out the Celtic cultural connection. These were: in Ireland, Joseph Walker's Historical memoirs of the Irish bards (1786), *Reliques of Irish poetry* by Charlotte Brooke (1789) and *Irish minstrelsy* by James Hardiman (1831); in Wales, *Specimens of the poetry of the ancient Welsh bards* by Evan Evans (1764) and *Musical and poetical relics of the Welsh bards* (1784); in Brittany, Hersart de la Villemarqué's *Barzaz Breiz: chants populaires de la Bretagne* (1836). All these works awoke a new sense of a common Celtic identity among Celtic antiquarian and literary circles.

One of the most remarkable effects on the Romantic movement in Wales was the re-establishment of a regular Eisteddfod in 1789 by the political Radical, Thomas Jones of Corwen. At the same time another member of the radical Gwyneddigion group – Edward Williams – more popularly known as Iolo Morganwg – recreated a Gorsedd ceremony based on his perception of ancient Celtic druidic rituals. The Gorsedd, first held on 21 June 1792, was accepted as an integral part of the Eisteddfod in 1819. Iolo Morganwg's idea, a resurgence of an annual gathering of Celtic bards, with ritual and regalia, was a little comical to many who did not like its semi-fantastical outlook. It was not until 1901 that the Bretons instituted their own Gorsedd ceremony, or until 1918 that the Cornish held their inaugural Gorsedd. The three Gorseddau of Wales, Brittany and Cornwall joined together on 3 September 1971, deciding that while each of the Gorseddau should retain complete autonomy in domestic affairs, all three would acknowledge a Gorsedd of Bards of the Isle of Britain with the Archdruid of Wales as its leader. Thus the three Brythonic Celtic communities were united in these annual cultural events.

In Scotland in 1820, the year of the last major uprising against the union with England by a republican radical movement, a Celtic Society was formed. It was, however, an association of middle class intellectuals led by Walter Scott. Dr Durkacz observes: 'Having discovered a landscape which filled their imagination, they set out to fill it with trusty sons of Ossian.'[18] This Celtic Society was peopled by 'drawing room' Celts. According to Dr Durkacz: 'The Celtic Society's ambivalent attitude towards Gaelic, and the ambivalent attitude of the romantic movement towards Celtic culture generally, led it into a curious pseudo-support for the Gaelic language. The members of the Celtic Society would have been the last to encourage a vigorous Gaelic periodical literature, or any encouragement of vernacular Gaelic teaching in the Schools. The Highland myth they constructed had no place for Gaelic as a vehicle of political expression or of day-to-day communication.'[19]

Nevertheless, in spite of the attitudes of Walter Scott's Celtic Society, the 'Celtic idea' which it propagated spread rapidly through the nineteenth century. The *Celtic Magazine*, which ran from 1875–1888, did much to stimulate Pan Celtic concepts while mainly dealing with Scotland's own Celtic culture.[20] It was replaced by *The Celtic Monthly* which, in 1893, was able to comment with misplaced satisfaction that the 'Celtic Renaissance', in all parts of the Celtic world, had given new impetus to the attempts to revive the languages. 'The Celtic Renaissance has given new life to the language, and active steps are being taken in all directions to foster and encourage it.'[21]

A sense of solidarity emerges not only in cultural terms but in political terms, inspiring, in the late eighteenth century, a great stirring in the spread of Celtic independence movements and the creed of republicanism. In the 1790s, when the Scottish Friends of the People tried to establish a Scottish Republic, they sent delegations to the United Irishmen conventions. Reciprocal delegations were received from Ireland. Thomas Muir, named in a secret document as President of the Scottish Republic during the rising of 1797, was made an honorary member of the United Irishmen. Thomas Paine's *Rights of man* became a bestseller in its Scottish Gaelic translation. We find records of meetings between the Irish, Scots, Welsh and Breton movements and their representatives through this period.[22] And it is particularly interesting to note that the case for French aid to help the Irish and Scots achieve independence was put in the French National Assembly by Breton deputies, such as Armand Kersaint and the Marquis Lafayette, a descendant of the counts of Cornouaille in Brittany. Lafayette signed a declaration of the

Breton Parliament which denounced French centralism and he made an impassioned speech in the États Bretagne in support of Breton autonomy.[23]

There has been little work on Wales' revolutionary links with such movements as the United Irishmen, United Scotsmen and with the Breton movements. Judging from the background and close ties between the other Celtic countries, it seems inconceivable that such links did not exist. However, there has also been little work so far into the Welsh republican movement of the late eighteenth century, although we know such a movement to have existed. The Cymdeithas Gwyneddigion, founded in 1771, was greatly influenced by the French Revolution, becoming radical and republican. A subject for a further study would be the influence on French Revolutionary leaders of Welshmen like Robert Price, whose work *Civil liberty* (1776), was written in support of the American Revolutionaries. When Price died in 1791, the French National Assembly went into mourning for him. Another Welshman, David Williams, an ardent republican, was asked to assist in drawing up the constitution of the French Republic. He became an honorary French citizen. Both Rousseau and Voltaire declared themselves 'his ardent disciples'. Much of the material for such a study exists in Welsh sources, such as Thomas Roberts' *Cwyn yn erbyn gorthrmderr* ('A Complaint Against Oppression'), 1790, and other works. Tomos Glyn Cothi (the Unitarian Minister, Thomas Evans) is reported to have translated the 'Marseillaise' into Welsh only to find himself in Carmarthen Jail.[24]

One of the most fascinating anecdotal accounts of Pan Celticism in action actually concerns the famous literary family Brontë. Patrick Prunty (who later changed the name to Brontë) came from Co. Down, while his wife, Maria Branwell, was Cornish. Patrick's father was Aodh (Hugh) Prunty of Emdale, Ballynaskeagh, near Loughbrickland, Co. Down. Aodh Prunty came from a Protestant family but had rejected organized religion. He married a Catholic, Alice McClorey, in the

Protestant Church at Magherally, in 1776. Patrick was their first son, born on 17 March (St Patrick's Day), 1777. Aodh Prunty was a well known local *seanachie*, or storyteller, whose first language was Irish. He was very much a freethinker of his age. He is recorded as stating:

> Ireland was governed by a gang of rapacious brigands... he was unable to obey the laws of the country, as those laws were made by an assembly of landlords purely and solely to serve their own rapacious desires, and not in accordance with any dictates of right or wrong. As soon might the lambs respect the laws of the wolves as the people of Ireland respect the laws of landlords.

While Patrick Prunty apparently kept out of politics, his younger brother Liam (William) joined the United Irishmen, the revolutionary force seeking to establish an independent Irish Republic. In the 1798 uprising, Liam Prunty was in the ranks of a unit commanded by Henry Monroe, a Protestant Republican from Lisburn. He was part of the force that occupied Ballynahinch on 12 June 1798, when Major General George Nugent's forces attacked the insurgent positions with Howitzers, leaving 400 dead and killing many as they fled the battlefield.

Liam Prunty was one of those who escaped back to his father's house at Emdale. Near Rathfriland a company of Welsh Dragoons (22nd Light Dragoons) spotted him. Liam reached the house and hid in the loft. The Dragoons arrived, under the charge of an English officer. Alice Prunty, with the younger children clutching her apron, tried to plead with the English officer. But the grandmother of the famous Brontë sisters only spoke Irish. The officer ordered his men to set fire to the house and then rode on. Aodh Prunty then arrived and also 'appealed to the Welsh soldiers in Irish, whereupon they at once joined him in extinguishing the flames'. The Welsh soldiers found they had more in common with their fellow Celts than with their English officer.[25]

Patrick Prunty was 21 years old at this time and probably away teaching at Drumballerony. He was to go to England in

1802 and, so far as is known, never returned to his family home again. Nor does it appear that he ever kept in touch with his family. He certainly rejected their politics and cultural concerns, changing his name first to Branty and then, when Horatio Nelson became Duke of Brontë in Sicily, he adopted that spelling which approximated with the sound of his name. It is interesting to note that the first language of the father of the great English novelists must have been Irish, but there is no hint that he ever passed on that knowledge to his famous children. As for his wife, Maria Branwell, she was born in Penzance in 1783, scarcely a mile from where the last group of native speakers of the Cornish language were then living. Many critics, such as Phyllis Bentley, have argued that the Celtic parentage of the Brontë sisters produced a 'Celtic strain' in their writings not found in other Yorkshire writers of the day.

There are many anecdotal accounts of interaction between the Celtic peoples during this period which imply their awareness of common identity. For example, in 1867, many Scots supported the Irish Fenian movement on the grounds of a common Gaelic identity. The 73rd Foot stationed near Cahirciveen in Co. Kerry were a mainly Scottish Gaelic-speaking regiment. It is on record that when they moved into action against Colonel O'Connor's Fenian troops in Kerry, they formed picket lines, having surrounded the Irish, and began conversations with the Irish through the medium of Gaelic. Discovering they had more in common with the Irish than with their English officers, they let the Irish slip through their lines and escape.[26] This was not an isolated incident.

As with the later period with which this study is concerned, the history of Pan Celticism from earliest times until the nineteenth century remains a generally unexplored area. However, it can be seen that this examination of the initial origins of Pan Celticism has demonstrated that it was not simply a nineteenth-century romantic concept. There existed an awareness and a tradition which originated in the pre-Christian period and continued until the Romantic Period and the national movements of the nineteenth century. It can be seen that this brief summary has also demonstrated that it was not the Romantics who 'invented' Pan Celticism; they merely picked it up and gave it a new dimension and impetus.

One man, however, is responsible for turning a generally accepted, but often vague, recognition and emotional sympathy into a series of practical ideas and aims.

Notes

1   *The Greatness and Decline of the Celts*, Henry Hubert, trs. M.R. Dobie (Keann Paul, Trench, Trubner & Co., London, 1934), p. 187.
2   Ibid., p. 188.
3   Ibid.
4   *The Religion of the Ancient Celts*, J.A. MacCulloch (T. & T. Clarke, Edinburgh, 1911).
5   *Ireland and Wales: their Historical and Literary Relations*, Cecile O'Rahilly (Longmans, Green and Co., London, 1924).
6   See 'Ireland's Golden Age' in *Phrases of Irish History*, Eoin MacNeill (M.H. Gill, Dublin, 1919).
7   O'Rahilly (as above), pp. 63–67. See also Dr Kuno Meyer, 'Early Relations between Gael and Brython' (Honourable Society of Cymmrodorion, London, 1895).
8   *Cymmrodor*, Morris Jones, xxviii (1918), p. 7
9   *Four Ancient Books of Wales*, ed. William Skene, 2 Vols (Edinburgh, 1868), pp. 123ff.
10 O'Rahilly (see above), pp. 72/73.
11 Ibid.
12 *Aros Mae*, Gwynfor Evans, Abertawe (Wales, 1971), p. 143.
13 *Robert the Bruce*, Robert McNair Scott (Hutchinson, London, 1982), p. 172.
14 See Scott (above), p. 172- quoting from Harris, *Collectanea*, Vol. 1, p. 395 (1310); 19 folio MS volumes in National Library, Dublin, compiled by Walter Harris (floruit, 1686–1761); now calendared by Charles MacNeill in *Analecta Hibernica* (1934), Vol. vi.
15 *A History of Medieval Ireland from 1086 to 1513*, Edmund Curtis (Methuen, London, 1938 – a completely revised edition to the Maunsel and Roberts first edition of 1923), p. 183.
16 Ibid. quoting Powell's *History of Wales*, pp. 311–312.
17 *Rerum Scotiarum Historia*, George Buchanan (Edinburgh, 1852).
18 *The Decline of the Celtic Languages*, Victor E. Durkacz (John Donald, Edinburgh, 1983), p. 195.

19 Ibid.
20 *The Celtic Monthly*, Vol. VIII, No. 1 (1893), p. 120.
21 Ibid.
22 Ibid.
23 *Moniteur*, Paris, 3 January 1793.
24 See 'Wales and the French Revolution' by Dr David Williams, in *Wales through the Ages*, ed. A.J. Roderick, Christopher Davies, Carmarthen, Vol. 11, pp. 117–124.
25 *As I Roved out*, Cathal O'Byrne (Irish News Ltd., Belfast, 1946), pp. 366/367 and 394/395 Also *The Gaelic Source of the Brontë Genius*, Cathal O'Byrne (1940). And *Irish Democrat* ('The Brontë's Celtic Strain' and 'The Patrick Brontë's Enigma'), November and December, 1991.
26 'Fenianism and the Celtic Nations' by Pádraig Ó Snodaigh, in *Celtic Advance in the Atomic Age*: Annual Volume of the Celtic League, 1967, pp. 80–84.

4: Charles de Gaulle and Pan Celticism

THE latter half of the nineteenth century witnessed the establishment of the first organizations specifically devoted to a set of written goals for Pan Celticism.

Charles de Gaulle (1837–1880) was the first person to commit to writing a number of aims for Pan Celticism. General Charles de Gaulle (1890-1970), the first President of the Fifth French Republic in 1958 was not above capitalizing on the reputation of his uncle. During an official visit to Brittany, 1–3 February 1969, he went so far as to quote one of his uncle's poems – *Da varzad Breiz* – to win favour with the Breton audience at Quimper:

> *E Paris va c'horf zo dalc'het*
> *Med daved hoc'h nij va spered*
> *Vel al labous, a denn askel,*
> *Nij da gaout he vreudeur a bell.*

> In Paris my body is held,
> But towards you my spirit flies,
> Swiftly, like a bird,
> To meet his far away brothers.

The General was not given a friendly reception as his visit came in the wake of a French crack-down on the Breton movement, at a point when over fifty Bretons, ranging from priests, a headmaster, a doctor, an architect, a town councillor, farmers and factory workers had been arrested. They were suspected of being members of the Front for the Liberation of Brittany. The FLB had become active in the early 1960s with a series of bomb attacks on Government installations. The last of the suspects was released nearly twelve months afterwards without charge.[1] The Breton audience felt that de Gaulle, fresh from his *'vive Quebec libre'* speech in Canada, was insulting the Breton people by quoting his uncle's poetry, and drowned him out with hissing and booing.

It is through pointing to achievable objectives that Charles de Gaulle, the poet, developed a philosophy of Pan Celticism which was of considerable importance on the Pan Celtic movement.

De Gaulle, although born in Valenciennes, in the north of France, became, as noted earlier, a Breton language poet, and also learnt Welsh and Irish, becoming deeply involved in Celtic cultural matters. Oddly enough, in seeking a Celtic family connection, it was with Ireland rather than Brittany that such a link could be made, through a maternal grandparent, Marie-Angélique McCartan, a descendant of Seán MacCartan of Co. Down, who had been a colonel in the French Irish Brigade.[2] De Gaulle never visited a Celtic country for he fell ill as a youth and become paralysed, as a result being confined for the rest of his life to his apartment at 286 rue Vaugirard, Paris. However, he became secretary of Breurez Breton, a society of Breton-speaking poets exiled in Paris, whose president was Théodore Hersart de la Villemarqué (1815–1895), author of *Barzaz Breiz: chants populaires de la Bretagne* (1836). Hersart had a profound effect on de Gaulle. It was reading *Barzaz Breiz* at the age of sixteen which inspired de Gaulle to learn Breton.[3]

In 1838, de la Villemarqué and the Breton scholar Jean-Francis Le Gonidec,[4] author of grammars and dictionaries and a founder of the Celtic Academy in Brittany in 1805, had been among the delegates to a meeting in Abergavenny, Wales, organized by Cymdeithas y Cymreigyddion y Fenni, which was regarded as a meeting of major importance to the Bretons. This visit inspired the resuscitation of the Association Bretonne.

The Association Bretonne had originally been formed by Armand de la Rouerie in 1791 to restore Breton autonomy under the Treaty of 1532, by force of arms if necessary. De la Rouerie had been a supporter of the French Revolution until the abolition of the Breton Parliament by the French National Assembly. Indeed, he had fought for the American colonists in their American War of Independence as a colonel. De la Rouerie had laid the groundwork for Breton resistance against the French should Breton autonomy be threatened. He had died in 1793, just as the war broke out. Although the Association Bretonne was initially successful, with the French signing a treaty at the Castle of La Mabilais in April 1795, with the *chouan* leader, Baron Cormartin, warfare broke out again – this time leading to the defeat of the Bretons.

The Association Bretonne was proscribed but reformed in 1843 to seek a return to the autonomous position occupied by Brittany from the Treaty of 1532 until 1790. This Association was suppressed in 1858 by the French authorities.[5] Also attending the Abergavenny meeting was the Breton writer Alexis-François Rio, whose work on the Breton War of Independence, *La petite chouannerie* (1842), was an influential work on de Gaulle and opened up a Breton perception of the history. De Gaulle was able to reject French centralist attitudes. Rio was married to a Welsh woman, Apollonia Jones.[6]

De Gaulle, unlike his contemporaries, was not content to write sorrowful laments about the loss of Breton independence, the glories of ancient Breton poets and the suppression of the language. Writing as Charlez Vro-C'hall (the Breton version of his name) he took a revolutionary line, demanding the return of Breton autonomy. He was both a devout Catholic and a monarchist; very much a rightist, and these attitudes coloured his writing. [7]He was, to some extent, influenced by the Tréguier writer Ernest Renan (1823–1892), who published his *Essai sur la poésie des races Celtiques* ('Essay on the poetry of the Celtic races') in 1854, revising it in 1859. Renan argued for the study of Celtic literature but as a 'medieval' subject and he gave undue emphasis on the 'race' elements in talking of the cultural composition of the Celts for which he was criticized by the anthropologist Jean Finot.[8]

When Renan spoke of a Celtic 'race', Finot immediately referred to the linguistic definition:

> In the present state of science… it is becoming impossible for us to distinguish the ethnic origin of peoples. On the contrary, the elements are so entwined that the partisans of inequality must admit the common parenthood of all races.
>
> Ethnic psychology has understood this so well that far from taking into consideration the present state of the Celtic issue, which forbids any generalization, which recognizes that the science of 'race' cannot be relied on. Do those that use this 'science' to depict the Celt, do so only according to the needs of his personality and his cause?

De Gaulle, accepting Renan's argument that Celtic literature should be made a study for universities, however, also held that language was the deciding cultural factor, not 'race'. The national community disappeared once its language disappeared and simply became assimilated into the culture of the dominant group. Once the Breton language vanished, so would the Breton people. Brittany would be merely a geographical expression for a province of France.

Politically, he sought the return of the Breton Parliament as it was constituted by the Treaty of 1532, prior to its destruction in 1790. The Kings and Emperors of France would be recognized once more as Dukes of Brittany. In this idea he seems to have been supported by the illegal Association Bretonne.[9]

In 1864, de Gaulle wrote a long article in the *Revue de Bretagne*, which was a royalist and Catholic magazine edited by the historian Arthur de la Borderie.[10] De Gaulle stated that it was the right of individual nations to decide their political and cultural future for themselves – that is, to have self-government.

Brittany and indeed the other Celtic countries should be autonomous. Far from resigning themselves to the destruction of their languages and cultures, their very survival depended on the preservation of their languages which were 'the external sign and fortified wall' of nationhood. He wrote that 'so long as a conquered people speaks another language than their conquerors, the best part of them is still free', which echoed the maxim of Tacitus that 'the language of the conqueror in the mouth of the conquered is ever the language of the slave'. In this polemical work, de Gaulle made clear that language was the basis of recognition of the Celts as distinct communities, thereby departing from Renan and thus subscribing to the linguistic criterion which has been officially held by the Pan Celtic movement from that time.

He urged that it would be better for the Irish 'to speak Gaelic under the English yoke than to submit to the English language with complete political freedom'. He urged Bretons to follow the example of the Welsh who were concentrating on protecting their language and culture rather than seeking political goals, and he also suggested that those Celts who felt forced to emigrate to the New World for economic reasons should settle in one area – Patagonia. This shows that de Gaulle was fully acquainted with Michael D. Jones' attempt to set up an independent Welsh-speaking colony in that country – Y *Wladfa*. But de Gaulle warned that the Celtic settlers in Patagonia must ensure that the aboriginal inhabitants, the Araucan Indians, retained their own cultural and political rights and would thereby be persuaded to support the colony.

The basis of de Gaulle's article was revised and published as a major work, *Les Celtes au dix-neuvième siècle – appel aux représentants actuels de la race Celtique* ('The Celts in the nineteenth century – an appeal to the present representatives of the Celtic race'), and published both in Paris and Nantes in 1864.

For the first time plans for a 'Celtic Union' were put forward[11] in which de Gaulle argued that regular and frequent contacts between the Celtic communities, at the level of cultural and political groups and societies, was the first goal. He wanted a *Celtic Review*, a journal common to all Celtic countries, discussing common problems and dispensing information. He gave great weight to the importance of such a Pan Celtic journal and was very specific as to its potential contents. It was in 1873 that such a journal, the *Revue Celtique*, was launched under the editorship of de Gaulle's friend Henri Gaidoz. This became the premier journal of Celtic studies during the late nineteenth century, more academic in content than de Gaulle had envisaged.

De Gaulle became the first person to propose a Celtic 'Esperanto' in order that the six Celtic nations would not have to rely on either English or French as a *lingua franca*. He felt that a language based on Celtic grammatical constructions, with words coined from roots common to the two forms of Celtic, would close the growing gap between the peoples. He felt all learned Celts should make themselves familiar with such a language.

He argued for an annual congress, rotating in each of the Celtic countries in turn, which would also give awards to those who had done estimable work in the service of the various Celtic languages and cultures.

He argued for a re-examination of history where there had been a tendency to attempt to separate the Celts and show them as antagonistic to one another. More studies were needed to bring to light Pan Celtic cooperation over the centuries, he argued. The negative tendencies, he felt, had been purposely exaggerated by the imperial powers.

Above all, cried de Gaulle, 'unity is strength!' There was a need for the Celtic nations to unite in their shared history, social and economic and cultural problems. He proposed *l'union celtique*.[12]

Putting his words into action, de Gaulle wrote to political and cultural leaders in Wales, Scotland and Ireland and proposed a Pan Celtic Congress to be held in Saint Brieuc in Brittany in 1867. To see this in context, the project of a Breton Eisteddfod in Quimper in 1866 had been prohibited on the direct intervention of the French Minister of the Interior as 'subversive'. But the prospective attendance of representatives from Ireland, Wales and Scotland forced the authorities to allow the Congress to go ahead. The Congress was organized through the Association Bretonne, proscribed in 1858, but working underground. De Gaulle could not attend because of his paralysis, but wrote an address which was read out in which he urged his Pan Celtic proposals.[13] The St Brieuc Pan Celtic Congress is regarded as the second Celtic Congress to be held.[14]

De Gaulle had, for the first time, committed to paper a series of aims and aspirations for Pan Celticism. Although only 43 years old when he died, he had achieved a tremendous amount. Although his political work was never translated out of French, leading individuals within the Celtic countries argued the principles he taught and some tried to influence organizations, such as the Irish Republican Brotherhood, Cymru Fydd, and the Irish and Scottish Land Leagues, to take them up. Indeed, some even set about the formation of Pan Celtic groups. A Glasgow Celtic Society was in being in October 1867, and presented its 'Breton brothers' with a volume of Scottish history. An attempt was made to set up a Celtic League in 1886. It was not until 1900 that de Gaulle's proposal for a regular and annual Celtic Congress came into being (through the organization of the Celtic Association formed in 1899). His ideas, however, albeit somewhat modified, would eventually form, as noted earlier, the basis of the modern Pan Celtic movement.

In the UK, which then incorporated five out of the six Celtic communities, de Gaulle's influence was immediate. Particularly in Ireland (then ruled from London) he had found supportive correspondents in such leading scholars as John MacHale, Archbishop of Tuam (1791–1881); the Belfast Protestant republican Samuel Ferguson (1810-1886), who was President of the Royal Irish Academy; Whitley Stokes (1830–1909), the philologist; and Ulick Bourke (1829–1887), one of the leading language revivalists.

There was now a fertile soil at an academic level and, indeed, there had been some tremendous strides forward in the scholastic field. By the 1880s, chairs of Celtic Studies had been established at Oxford, Edinburgh, Trinity College, Dublin and in Belfast and Cork. This was achieved as a response to the pleas of the English critic and poet Matthew Arnold (1822–1888), holder of the chair of poetry at Oxford, who gave a series of four lectures entitled 'On the Study of Celtic Literature', which were published in the *Cornhill Magazine* and later in book form in 1867.[15]

Matthew Arnold's position was simply that of an onlooker perceiving an interesting culture dying with no academic studies being made of it. The last thing he supported was cultural or political nationalism. Indeed, he urged the quick demise of the Celtic languages as everyday means of communication:

> The fusion of all the inhabitants of these islands into one homogeneous, English-speaking whole, the breaking down of barriers between us, the swallowing up of separate provincial nationalities, is a consummation to which the natural course of things irresistibly tends; it is a necessity of what is called modern civilization, and modern civilization is a real legitimate force; the change must come, and its accomplishment is a mere affair of time. The sooner the Welsh language disappears as an instrument of the practical, political, social life of Wales the better for England, the better for Wales itself.

He argued that: 'Cornwall is the better off for adopting English.' He urged the Celtic peoples to:

> ... consider that they are inextricably bound up with us, and that, if the suggestions in the following pages have any truth, we English, alien and uncongenial to our Celtic partners as we may have hitherto shown ourselves, have notwithstanding, beyond perhaps any other nation, a thousand latent springs of possible sympathy with them. Let them consider that new ideas and forces are stirring in England, that day by day these new ideas and forces gain in power, and that almost every one of them is the friend of the Celt and not his enemy. And, whether our Celtic partners will consider

this or no, at any rate let us ourselves, all of us who are proud of being the ministers of these new ideas, work incessantly to procure for them a wider and more fruitful application; and to remove the main ground of the Celt's alienation from the Englishman, by substituting in place of that type of Englishman with whom alone the Celt has too long been familiar, a new type, more intelligent, more gracious, and more humane.[16]

Celtic studies were made 'respectable' in English eyes for the first time, albeit by the intervention of someone with an 'outsider's' perception who supported the continuing erosion of the Celtic languages and cultures as a modern phenomenon but saw their value merely in terms of 'medieval studies'. In this respect, Arnold was similar in attitude to his French counterpart Renan, who had also argued for Celtic studies. However, the new academic status provided a focus and the universities became a meeting place for scholars and intellectuals to consider cultural and political aspects of Pan Celticism.

Three separate strands began to emerge in the growing Pan Celtic movement. Firstly, and momentarily in the ascendant during the period known as the 'Celtic Renaissance', there was a cultural group, as typified by the poet W.B. Yeats, who saw Celtic culture as merely an historical treasure trove to be plundered for his English literary purposes. Yeats and those who followed him, in dressing themselves in 'gold embroidered Celtic fringes', as James Joyce once disparagingly dismissed Yeats' work, seemed more in tune with Renan and Arnold than de Gaulle.

There was, secondly, another cultural group who accepted the Celtic languages as living vehicles of a culture in danger and made efforts to save them from extinction within the existing political framework.

But the third group saw that the preservation and restoration of the Celtic languages and cultures could, in their eyes, only be achieved by political means and safeguarded by the achievement of independent states. It was from the third group that de Gaulle's ideas really took shape, and eventually the concept emerged that like-minded movements in each Celtic country should bind themselves together in a union.

According to Dr Durkacz:

> By the 1870s cultural and national resurgence had manifested themselves throughout the Celtic fringe. There was land agitation in Scotland and Ireland hastened by the depression in agricultural prices. In Wales, disestablishment and anti-tithe feeling ran high. The revival of Celtic culture provided new arguments for the restoration of the Celtic languages in national life. Just as the land question drew the national question in its train, so the national question drew the language question behind. But it must be said that the nationalistic assertions in favour of the Celtic languages were made in a thick atmosphere of cultural imperialism emanating from Whitehall.[16]

In the 1880s the Land League movement, formed to obtain fair rents and a fixity of tenure in Ireland and overturn the remnants of the Penal Law code under which the Irish suffered a feudal landlord system, spread from Ireland to both Scotland and Wales, each country forming movements suited to their own national land problems. It was this movement which became the focus for the Pan Celtic idea.[17]

The awareness of the 'Celtic dimension' was being considered by many prominent Land Leaguers. William O'Brien (1852–1928), the Irish Party MP for Mallow (1883–1918), was one of the first Irish politicians to make serious arguments for Pan Celticism. He had become acquainted with de Gaulle's study. As editor of the campaigning *United Ireland*, he was an influential figure. In *The influence of the Irish language on Irish national literature and character*, published in 1892, and owing some influence to de Gaulle, he went so far as advocating 'a worldwide Celtic League' which echoed de Gaulle's Celtic Union.[18] Such ideas were not only being expounded within the 'constitutional' national movement but among revolutionary republicans in Ireland. The former Fenian leader John O'Leary wrote: 'I am strongly of the opinion that we should do all that is in our power to bring ourselves into touch with our Celtic brethren all the world over.'[19]

Prominent adherents to the idea of achieving organized cultural links and cooperation among Celtic movements seeking political independence included Michael Davitt (1846–1906), a former Fenian revolutionary who founded the Irish Land League and who served as an Irish Party MP from 1882–92 and from 1895–99. He influenced the Welsh politicians T.E. Ellis and Michael D. Jones, who were influential in forming the Cymru Fydd (Future Wales) group in Wales. The Irish Party MPs frequently addressed meetings in Wales. David Lloyd George, whose early career was with Cymru Fydd, supporting self-government for all the Celtic countries during his early years in parliament, had been persuaded to enter parliament by Davitt and Jones who had spotted his talent at a meeting in Wales.[20] Lloyd George won the Caernarfon seat on 10 April 1890, and in his maiden speech he expressed his support of Pan Celticism:

> The current of the time is sweeping to nationalism. Wales, in throwing in her lot with Ireland in the self-government struggle, has struck a blow not only for the national rights of another Celtic country but also for her own.

In March 1895, Lloyd George supported Sir Henry Dalziel's Bill for self-government for the Celtic nations of the UK. The Bill was defeated by only twenty-six votes. Lloyd George had observed:

> Welsh nationality has survived two thousand years in spite of every human effort to crush out its vitality.
>
> The strongest governing forces in the world have successively attempted to crush it, to coax it, and even to pray it out of existence: the Roman, the Saxon, the Dane, the Norman, and lastly the race which is a blend of all...
>
> Still, after all, here were are... claiming the same measure of self government as our forefathers fought and died for.

The Welsh had influenced the (Scottish) Highland Land League meeting in September 1886, at Bonar Bridge, to debate the idea of growing cooperation between the Celtic peoples, and a proposal was enthusiastically endorsed inviting the Welsh and Irish to join the Scots in a 'Celtic League' as a practical aid to their struggle.[21] There were already three Welsh delegates at the meeting supporting the idea: Michael D. Jones (founder of the Welsh Patagonian colony in 1866), Dr E. Pan Jones (who was to become his biographer) and Keinion Thomas, editor of *The Celt*, a leading Welsh newspaper. Dr Pan Jones, responding to the Celtic initiative, declared: 'Hitherto and no further – here shall we make our stand for Welsh were [sic] similar to Scottish, Irish and Cornish grievances.'[22] Michael Davitt, the former Fenian leader and Irish Member of Parliament, as a frequent visitor to Scotland and to Wales, also supported the idea.[23]

The Celtic League of 1886 did not get off the ground as a separate organization. However, the cooperation between the Land Leagues continued. In practical terms Welsh delegates were able to give evidence to the 1884 Crofters' Commission while Scottish delegates supported and gave evidence to the Commission on Land in Wales in 1896. On the 'Home Rule' front, the Irish Party found it could cooperate with Cymru Fydd (Future Wales) and the Scottish Home Rule Association.[24]

In Ireland the Pan Celtic idea led to the foundation of a Pan Celtic Society, formed in Dublin on 1 March 1888.[25] The society was to be purely cultural, with the accent on language and literature. The prime movers behind this Pan Celtic Society were Gerald C. Pelly, a medical student, Dr Augustine F. Downey and a lawyer named M.D. Wyer. But there is little evidence that it ever developed any really strong links with the other Celtic nations. Indeed, it was to vanish within three years but it can be said that it had a tremendous influence on the 'Celtic Renaissance' in Ireland by attracting to its membership many leading literary figures such as Douglas Hyde, A.P. Graves, Maud Gonne, Katharine Tynan, P.J. McCall and others. According to W.P. Ryan, writing ten years later: 'it may be said that the Pan Celtic Society is still living in that promising organization [the National Literary Society] in which so much Irish intellectual hope is centred.'[26] The Pan Celtic Society produced only one publication – *Lays and Lyrics of the Pan Celtic Society*, in 1889.[27]

But the more important development was the consolidation of the language movements in each of the Celtic countries in the last decades of the century. A number of societies formed: the Society for Utilising the Welsh Language in 1885; An Comunn Gàidhealach (Scottish Gaelic movement) in 1891; Conradh na Gaeilge (Gaelic League of Ireland) in 1893 and Kevredigez Vreizh (a new Association Bretonne) in 1895. These movements are regarded by historians of the 'Celtic Renaissance' as its foundation stone. The most successful of them at the time was Conradh na Gaeilge who successfully campaigned for the Imperial Government to give Irish status in Intermediate Irish Schools from 1901 and adopt a bilingual education policy in schools in Irish-speaking areas from 1906. A few years later the language renaissance had spread to the Isle of Man and even into Cornwall with the formation, in 1899, of Yn Cheshaght Ghailckagh (Manx Gaelic Society), and in 1901, of Kowethas Kelto-Kernuack (Cornish Celtic Society).

These language societies, formed to preserve, promote and restore their Celtic languages to positions of prominence within the Celtic communities, cooperated with one another, inevitably bringing their membership towards the concept of a Celtic commonality and to the idea of bringing the diverse energies of the individual movements together under a 'Celtic umbrella'.

It can be seen that by the end of the nineteenth century, de Gaulle's ideas were having a significant and widespread effect in most of the Celtic countries and Pan Celticism had moved from being a somewhat hazy and emotional concept, to having a set of aims and objectives which could be achieved through practical endeavour.

Notes

1   *Celtic News*, No. 21 (Spring, 1961).
2   'De Gaulle, Fils du Nord', Special Number of *Journal Nord-Eclair*, No. 1, pp. 22–23.
3   'Charles de Gaulle; Barde Breton' by Elisabeth Coin, *Chronique du Landévennec*, No. 58 (April, 1989), p. 63. See also 'Charles de Gaulle est né à Valenciennes!' by Elisabeth Coin, in *Valentiana*, No. 6 (December, 1990), pp. 39–50. Letters from de Gaulle in Breton on Celtic subjects also appear in 'Charles de Gaulle, Parisien Bretonnaut' by F. Gourvil, *Nouvelle Revue de Bretagne*, Nos 1 & 2 (1947)) pp. 5 and 90/93.
4   Le Gonidec seems to have had many Welsh links and in 1824 he was asked by a Welsh Bibliographical Society to make a Breton translation of the New Testament. This was published in 1827. He died in 1838 just after his visit to Wales.
5   'Charles de Gaulle; Barde Breton' (see above).
6   Ibid.
7   *Le Bretonisme, les Historiens Bretons au XIXé siècle* (Société d'Histoire et Archéologie Bretagne, Mayenne, 1984), pp. 68–69.
8   *Le Préjugé des Races*, Jean Finot (Paris, third edition, 1908).
9   *Les Celtes au Dix-neuvième Siècle*, Charles de Gaulle (Nantes & Paris, 1864), p. 351.
10 Ibid.
11 Ibid. pp. 351–358
12 'Charles de Gaulle; Barde Breton' (see above).
13 Ibid. See also *Revue de Bretagne*, October and November 1867 issue ('Le Congrès Celtique International'). A report of the second session of Le Congrès Celtique International is contained in *Revue de Bretagne*, July 1869 issue.
14 *Histoire Chronologique des Pays Celtiques*, Jakez Gaucher (Association Keltica International, Guerande, Bretagne, 1990), p. 231.
15 *The Study of Celtic Literature*, Matthew Arnold (Smith, Elder & Co. London, 1867), pp. xviii–xix.
16 *The decline of the Celtic Languages*, Victor E. Durkacz (John Donald, Edinburgh, 1983), p. 203,
17 *Crofter Power in Easter Ross: The Land League at Work 1884–8*, Rob Gibson (Highland Heritage Educational Trust, Easter Ross, 1986). See also *Scottish Nationalism*, H.J. Hanham (Faber & Faber, London, 1969) pp. 123/125.
18 *The Influence of the Irish Language on Irish National Literature and Character*, William O'Brien (Guy & Co, Cork, 1892), p. 135.
19 *Recollections of Fenians and Fenianism*, John O'Leary (Dublin, 1896), p. 285.
20 *Ireland and Wales*, Cecile O'Rahilly (Longmans, Green & Co, London, 1924), pp. 89/90.

21 *Ross-shire Journal*, 24 September 1886.
22 *Scottish Highlander*, 7 October 1886.
23 Ibid.
24 *Crofter Power in Easter Ross*, p. 20.
25 *The Irish Literary Revival: its History, Pioneers and Possibilities* (W.D.
    Ryan, London, 1894), p. 49.
26 Ibid.
27 This volume was edited by A.R. Stritch but W.P. Ryan observes (p. 49)
    that it 'was not a collection that can be fairly considered representative of
    Pan Celtic poetical effort'.

5: The Celtic Congress

THE Celtic Congress, first meeting in 1900, has become the longest surviving Pan Celtic organization. Initially attracting those with a political commitment to Celtic independence, during the First World War, in the wake of the 1916 Irish uprising in which many Pan Celts took part, the Congress became purely cultural in outlook and the political Pan Celts looked to other organizations to fulfil their needs.

In 1899, a Celtic Association was formed with the purpose of organizing joint festivals and gatherings of representatives in the fields of Celtic scholarship, literature, the arts and music. The inspiration for this new Pan Celtic movement came from a very unlikely personality – Bernard Edward Barnaby Fitzpatrick, 2nd Baron Castletown of Upper Ossory (1849–1937). Lord Castletown was one of the wealthiest landowners in Ireland, owning a 20,000 acre estate at Doneraille, Co. Cork, and a manor at Abbeyleix. He was London-born, educated at Eton and Brasenose, a former Colonel of the Prince of Wales' Leinster Regiment, and former Liberal MP for Portarlington Borough, fighting against an Irish Party candidate. He had resigned when he succeeded to the title, taking a seat in the House of Lords. He was a staunch Unionist and in 1885 he was a founder of the Irish Loyal and Patriotic Union with Lord Longford.

His interests were listed in *Who's Who* as simply 'shooting, fishing, hunting and travelling'.[1] Nevertheless he was fluent in Irish and a passionate supporter of the language, who once insisted on his right to address the House of Lords in it. With his anti-Land League and Unionist politics and being a representative of the Protestant Ascendancy and Anglo-Irish aristocracy, he was distrusted and disliked by many members of the national movement in Ireland.

Castletown's publications ranged from *The ABC of the Irish land question* (1881), to *Random record of sport, service and travel in many lands* (1923). Lord Castletown married the Hon. Ursula (Clare) St Ledger, daughter of the 4th Viscount Doneraille. He served in the 1st Battalion, Life Guards, in the Egyptian Campaign and in the First Boer War, becoming Colonel of the Prince of Wales' Leinster Regiment. As well as his military decorations he was awarded the Companion of the Order of St Michael and St George and Knight of St Patrick. He was, therefore, a curious convert to Pan Celticism and it is obvious why he was regarded with such suspicion by Irish nationalists. But for Castletown, as with his cousin, the writer Emily Lawless (1845–1913), the idea of Pan Celticism was not incompatible with preserving the Union. Castletown could address a Unionist meeting in a saffron kilt and commence his remarks in Irish.

Father Peadar Ó Laoghaire (1839–1920), a leading figure in the language movement and an influential Irish writer, went so far as to say: 'I have known that man for fifteen or sixteen years. I would not sit down at the same table with him to save my life.'[2] But Ó Laoghaire's caustic pen was frequently wielded in attacks on those he disagreed with and often with personal rancour and prejudice. However, Castletown's track record was certainly a curious one.

Castletown was to be president of the Celtic Association while the secretary was a leading physicist, Dr Edmund Edward Fournier D'Albe. Born in London in 1868, he usually affected the name Edouard Fournier and claimed Breton ancestry, although it seems likely that he was actually of French Huguenot descent and had no connection at all with any Celtic country before he went to live in Ireland. Dr Fournier D'Albe was a senior lecturer in physics at Trinity College, Dublin, and a member of the Royal College of Science for Ireland. Fournier

D'Albe transmitted the first wireless picture broadcast from London on 24 May 1923, and was also the inventor of the optophone, an instrument which enabled blind people to read ordinary print by a light cell. He was also an enthusiastic linguist and had, among other languages, mastered Irish and published several works in it and translations from it.

With Lord Castletown, Dr Fournier D'Albe began to organize the Celtic Association, with the idea of holding a Celtic Congress in Dublin in 1900. A quarterly journal entitled *Celtia* was launched in March of that year. While the Celtic Association found many supporters in the Celtic countries, in Ireland, among the Irish nationalist movement, there were also those who dismissed Pan Celticism with vociferous bitterness. The idea was called a 'highly impolitic and undesirable step'.[3]

In its narrowest form, the opposition to the new movement was on the basis that the Irish should not have anything in common with Anglo-Irish aristocrats nor 'British' Celts who were supporters of the Empire. At the time nationalist Ireland was vehemently anti-English, anti-monarchical and vocally pro-Boer. The second Boer War (1899–1902) fed the imaginations and political longings of the people. Nowhere were the suspicions about Lord Castletown and Pan Celticism stronger than among sections of Conradh na Gaeilge (The Gaelic League), the Irish language movement.

Conradh na Gaeilge's president, Dr Douglas Hyde (1860–1949) had expressed himself in favour of Pan Celticism and he was asked to serve on the committee of the Celtic Congress. He referred the matter to Conradh na Gaeilge's National Executive, who were not in favour of any links with the Congress. They placed no restriction on Dr Hyde attending in a private capacity but stated that they 'would be sorry that any of their members should give time or money to an enterprise that could not help the Irish language'. Dr Hyde then felt unable to support the Congress in case of any personal criticism being levelled at him.[4]

Dr Hyde was to become the first President of Ireland when the office was created under the Constitution of 1937. He became the first Professor of Modern Irish in University College, Dublin, in 1909 and held the chair until his retirement in 1932. An Irish Free State Senator in 1925/26, he always insisted that Conradh na Gaeilge, whose presidency he held from its foundation until 1915, should be non-sectarian and non-political. He remained a Pan Celticist from 1900 until his death.

Conradh na Gaeilge's weekly journal *An Claidheamh Soluis* dismissed the Congress. 'It is absurd to talk of the reunion of the Celtic nations,' it commented.[5]

Nevertheless, many radical members of Conradh na Gaeilge were interested in Pan Celticism. Among them was Dr Eoin MacNeill. MacNeill was Professor of Early Irish at University College, Dublin. He was chairman of the Irish Volunteers in 1913 (forerunner of the IRA) and later the Chief of Staff. In 1917 he was elected a Sinn Féin MP but supported the Treaty in 1921 and was a Minister for Education in the Free State Government. He left politics in 1927 to return to his academic work. He continued to have a scholastic interest in the Celtic cultures.

Two months after Hyde had been told that he could not officially support Pan Celticism, MacNeill and Dr Tadhg O'Donoghue of the National Executive of Conradh na Gaeilge proposed that Dr Hyde accept a place on the committee of the Congress. This proposal was defeated by the indignant opposition of P.J. Keawell, Mary O'Reilly and Norma Borthwick, who saw Pan Celticism as 'socially unacceptable with Irish nationalism'.[6] They said, 'Pan Celticism diverts attention from the real serious issue – the life and death of our own language, and this at a most critical time.'[7]

Pan Celticism was becoming a cause which was splitting Conradh na Gaeilge, the first mass movement in support of the Irish language. The split began to centre round two journals within the movement: *Fáinne an Lae*, a weekly (1898–1900) edited by Bernard Doyle, which supported Pan Celticism, and *An Claidheamh Soluis*, a weekly launched in 1899, edited nominally by Eoin MacNeill, the policies of which were dictated by Keawell, O'Reilly and Borthwick. *An Claidheamh Soluis* began to attack Pan Celticism in very contemptuous terms.[8]

In July 1899, Pádraic Pearse was delegated to attend the Welsh Eisteddfod by Conradh na Gaeilge. Pearse (1879–1916), poet, playwright and teacher, was to be executed for his part in the 1916 uprising, having been named 'President of the Provisional Government of the Irish Republic'. Pearse was the catalyst to resolve the Pan Celtic conflict. Pearse became a staunch supporter of Pan Celticism and believed it could be of benefit to the Irish movement.

Pearse firmly allied himself with the Pan Celtic idea and had two or three interviews with Castletown. This enraged Keawell and the anti-Pan Celtic group, and their attack in *An Claidheamh Soluis*, without the apparent approval of the editor, Dr Eoin MacNeill, caused Pearse to send a telegram of protest. Dr MacNeill then wrote a letter to the Irish nationalist daily *Freeman's Journal* disassociating himself from the attack. *Fáinne an Lae* issued a subsequent editorial in support of MacNeill on 19 August 1899. It was this incident which led to the defeat of the anti-Pan Celtic lobby on the executive. Norma Borthwick, however, continued to keep up a campaign against Pan Celts, even accusing Pearse of drinking the health of Queen Victoria while on a visit to Wales.[9] Pearse, writing to the Irish writer J.J. Doyle ('Beirt Fhear'), who became editor of *An Claidheamh Soluis*, felt that Conradh na Gaeilge had 'made a gigantic blunder' in initially deciding to have nothing to do with Pan Celticism.[10] Pearse himself went on to serve on the committee of the Celtic Congress.

In the ensuing conflict Pearse, Eoin MacNeill and Douglas Hyde forced the resignation of the anti-Pan Celts from the executive of Conradh na Gaeilge, and formed a new executive adopting a declaration which allowed members to become associated with the Pan Celtic Association.

The Celtic Congress began to gather strength. Among early enthusiasts was the Irish poet and writer Alfred Percival Graves (1846–1931), father of Robert Graves (1895–1985).[11] A.P. Graves became assistant editor of *Punch*, founder member of Conradh na Gaeilge (London branch), a member of the Irish Text Society and the Irish Literary Society. In later years, Graves' secretary, Mona Douglas, of the Isle of Man, became a leading Pan Celtic figure.

In the pages of *Celtia* letters and articles discussed the aims and concept of Pan Celticism. In an article called 'The Pan Celtic Idea', Fournier D'Albe argued that it was principally a cultural movement but, because most 'cultural nationalists' saw political action of one kind or another as the only means to wrest official status and recognition from the Imperial Governments (England and France), he seemed to draw a partial political conclusion. He suggested that the Celtic Congress could be the focal point of a federation of Celtic movements united for mutual assistance and encouragement. He wrote:

> It means the federation of the existing Celtic movements for mutual assistance and encouragement. It means the advent of the Celt as a powerful, and, possibly, a dominating factor in the development of the human race.[12]

Such a movement, he argued, could have more weight in dealing with the Imperial Governments than individual groups.

The magazine *Celtia* lasted only a few years although its contributors included most of the leading Celtic scholars of the day. It was published from Dublin from 1900–1903. However, a *Celtic Review* was launched to continue the sense of Celtic identity and in London, the *London Celt* had been launched in 1897 and continued until 1904.

The Celtic Congress was established in Dublin in 1900 with scholars from the Celtic countries giving keynote lectures, particularly on aspects of the languages and cultures. Although representatives from Cornwall attended the first meeting,

Lord Castletown, the Irish-speaking Anglo-Irish peer who was the unlikely leading spirit behind the Pan Celtic Association of 1899.

The enthusiastic Pan Celticist Douglas Hyde (1860-1949), first President of Ireland (1937-1945).

The committed Pan Celticist Pádraic Pearse (1879-1916), executed for leading the 1916 uprising.

Cornwall was thought to be too Anglicized to be considered one of the Celtic nations by the yardstick of the 'linguistic criterion'. From its inaugural meeting, the Congress had defined a Celtic people in accordance with the linguistic criterion. It was thought that Cornwall could not be recognized as Celtic because the language was dead. Indeed, Cornish had died out as a mother tongue at the end of the eighteenth century, although some scholars argue for individual survivals through the nineteenth century. At the second Congress, meeting on 15 August 1901, a formal application for membership was rejected by 31 votes to 22.[13] In spite of this, Kowethas Kelto-Kernuak (Celtic Cornish Society) was established by leading Cornish language enthusiasts and the Cornish Language Revival was started.[14] The Cornish were able to demonstrate to their fellow Celts that the language was far from dead and enough people spoke it, albeit as a revived language, to maintain Cornwall's claim to its Celtic origins.

> Today there is a growing movement among the lettered class in Cornwall to learn something of their own language; and in the programme of the new Celtic Cornish Society, which has for its object the study and preservation of everything of Celtic origin that remains in the country, place is found for the revival of Cornish.

So wrote L.C. Duncombe Jewell, the secretary of Kowethas Kelto-Kernuak, to the Celtic Congress.

On 31 August 1904, the Congress duly admitted Cornwall to membership[15] after Henry Jenner, 'Father of the Cornish Language Revival', had delivered an address called 'Cornwall: A Celtic Nation', which convinced the majority of delegates to support Cornwall's application to join. Jenner, while at the Congress, received a telegram of congratulations from Dr Hambly Rowe in Cornish, and he made a point of showing it to delegates to support his claim that Cornwall's Celtic language was not yet extinct. Among the Cornish language revivalists and Pan Celts of the Kowethas Kelto-Kernuak was the author 'Q' – Sir Arthur Quiller-Couch (1863–1944).

The Celtic Congress, which circulated in turn to each of the Celtic countries, was mainly academic in tone but most of the scholars supported, to varying degrees, the concept of political independence for each of the Celtic countries. At this time only the Isle of Man had self-government. More importantly, in view of the aims of Congress, members were pledged to the revival of each Celtic language and to some degree of 'official status'. Because of this, the early Celtic Congresses had a political hue. Indeed, the very act of speaking a Celtic language, let alone campaigning for its status, could be interpreted as an act of political expression when the Imperial government were actively discouraging the languages as a continuing part of their centuries-old policy of destroying them. The Celtic Congress was supported not only by leading scholars, writers, musicians and artists but by many leading political figures in the Celtic world.

It was, perhaps, inevitable that a comparison would be made between the Pan Celtic Movement and the Pan Slavic Movement. The comparison, again perhaps not surprisingly, came from a German Celtic scholar, Heinrich Zimmer (1851–1910).[16] Zimmer believed Pan Celticism was a parallel movement to Pan Slavism.[17] No one came forward to correct him on what was obviously a wrong analogy.

Pan Slavism is regarded as the earliest of what are termed the 'Pan Movements', all of which attempt to link together different nationalities sharing an historic ethnic commonality.[18] The concept arose in the mid-nineteenth century among the Slavic peoples living under Austrian rule. It was expressed through the subject Slav nationalities developing closer links with Russia, which was regarded as the only existing Slav state which could be turned to for protection. The first Slav Congress had been held in Prague in June 1848. But the Russian Tsars quickly moulded the movement into a tool of Russian imperialism in the Balkans. By the time of the second Slav Congress, held in Moscow in 1867, the idea of Pan Slavism had been defined as a confederation of Slavic peoples under the spiritual and political leadership of Russia.[19] It becomes obvious why any analogy between Pan Celticism and Pan Slavism is fallacious.[20]

The one question which does arise, however, from a consideration of the Pan Slavic Movement, and which needs a considered answer, is whether the rise of Pan Slavism and its philosophies gave any impetus to the growth of Pan Celticism. There is no indication that Charles de Gaulle, nor any of the others who formulated the basic ideas behind Pan Celticism, were acquainted with the work of Nikolai Danilevsky on Pan Slavism or its ideology, or that they attempted to modify such concepts for the Celts. Indeed, such are the basic differences in ideology (already commented on) that one can see that the two movements simply had separate parallel growth, the one not inspiring the other.

The outbreak of the Great War (1914–1918) stopped the Celtic Congress meeting between 1915–191. However, in 1917, the Congress met again, this time in Birkenhead, near Liverpool, for security reasons. The 1917 Celtic Congress (whose papers were published in volume form in 1918)[21] was subdued. This is understandable, for it was meeting in the middle of the 'Great War', a year after the Irish uprising, and many of its Irish supporters had been executed or imprisoned for their part in the insurrection. There was little emphasis on political nationalism, for obvious reasons.

From the Birkenhead Celtic Congress of 1917 to the present day, the Celtic Congress has held regular meetings. Since 1917, however, it has lost the political content of its first decade and a half. It has concentrated on the reading of academic papers on historical aspects of language, culture and history by leading scholars in the field, rather than applying historical lessons to contemporary situations or considering modern linguistic and cultural problems. In the years following 1917, many Pan Celticists, realizing that the Celtic Congress was no longer a meeting place to air political views, began to consider the formation of other organizations. These 'political Pan Celts' were simply individuals working within their own national independence movements who sought links with like-minded people in other Celtic countries. Many were the heirs of the militant groups of Welsh and Scots who joined the Irish republican forces during the War of Independence against England.

A month following the Easter Uprising in Dublin, Captain James Robert White DSO, the son of the late Field Marshal Sir George Stuart White VC of Antrim, was arrested in Wales. White had become both a convinced socialist and a friend of the Irish Marxist leader, James Connolly. He had helped to organize and train the revolutionary Irish Citizens' Army, which had been one of the two organizations forming the Army of the Irish Republic during the uprising. White was charged under the Defence of the Realm Act in Aberdare. It was revealed that he had made attempts to induce the miners of South Wales to support the Irish and organize a strike to prevent the government from executing James Connolly. Connolly was, in fact, executed by firing squad a few days after White's arrest, strapped to a chair because the wounds he had received would not allow him to stand. White's lawyer told the Stipendiary Magistrate on 24 May 1916 that 'the Welsh, being Celts, he' (White) 'thought he could rouse their sympathies more quickly'.

Explosives had been stolen from the South Wales collieries and sent to Ireland as events drew towards the start of the War of Independence (1919–1921). Some Welshmen went further than sending explosives to help the cause of their fellow Celts. Welsh miners from the Rhondda and Abertillery went to join the Irish Citizens' Army. Among them was Tom Gale from Abertillery who, after serving in Ireland, found it necessary to spend some time in America until it was safe to return to Wales.

But perhaps the most famous of the Welsh contingent was Arthur Horner, son of a Merthyr railwayman, born in 1894. A confirmed socialist and miners' leader, Horner was 25 years old when he went to Dublin. He worked as a druggist in central

Dublin, using the name 'Jack O'Brien'. In the evening he was out with the Citizens' Army. In his memoirs, *Incorrigible Rebel* (MacGibbon and Kee, 1960), Horner recalls taking part in several operations, including rescuing prisoners from jail:

> In the middle of Dublin, you rushed into a house and shouted 'Sinn Féin', every door shut behind you to keep out your pursuers; or in a crowd you could just vanish because no one would give you away. We were very much in the position of the men and women of the Liberation Movement during the Second World War.

Horner was arrested on a return visit to Wales carrying leaflets designed to raise support. Court-martialled and sentenced to imprisonment with hard labour, Horner was elected as 'checkweigher' for Mardy Colliery, an honorary position usually given to Members of Parliament. He went on to be elected chairman of the South Wales Socialist Society, secretary of the National Union of Mineworkers and member of the central committee of the Communist Party of Great Britain.

Pan Celtic support also came from Scotland, particularly from Scottish Republicans and socialists who followed Ruaraidh Erskine, John MacLean and Seumas MacGaraidh of Arbroath. Perhaps the most romantic and famous of these was Iain Mackenzie Kennedy, a Scottish Gaelic speaker from Inverness and a convinced Pan Celt. He went to Cork to learn Irish, earning a reputation as a folk singer and musician. He served in the West Cork Brigade of the IRA until 1921. At the outbreak of the Civil War he continued to fight for the republican side and was killed by Free State troops on 8 August 1922. His grave is in the republican plot of St Finbar's Cemetery, Cork. A Scottish Brigade was organized for the IRA by Jim Reeder of Glasgow during 1919–23.

The Irish struggle was supported among the Pan Celts throughout the other Celtic countries; one could either volunteer or spread propaganda. This participation brought forth the attention of the state apparatus of both the United Kingdom and France to the Pan Celts. It was this which caused, ultimately, the Celtic Congress to drop its political dimension, and concentrate solely on the scholastic.

The political Pan Celts, who were without a voice following the demise of the political side of the Celtic Congress, had many differing ideas of how a new political Pan Celtic movement should be established, which is reflected in the attempts they made during the two decades between World War I and World War II.

Political Pan Celticism was revived after the 'Great War' firstly in Brittany, where the Bretons were greatly encouraged by the outcome of the Irish War of Independence (1919–21) and the establishment of an Irish state, Partition not-withstanding. In 1923, Breiz Atao, the leading Breton independence party which had been formed in 1918, became the first political party in any of the Celtic countries to adopt an official policy of Pan Celticism.[22] The aim was to create formal links between the various Celtic political groups which desired to gain varying degrees of independence for the Celtic countries. Links were initially formed with Byddin Ymreolwyr Cymru (Home Rule Army of Wales) and Unvaniez Yaouankiz Vreiz, a pressure group of Breiz Atao formed in May 1920. Breiz Atao sent its first official delegation to Wales in 1923 to discuss its policy. Arising from this visit, the party's magazine, also entitled *Breiz Atao*, published a Pan Celtic supplement in Breton, Welsh, French and English. Then a new magazine entitled *Pan Celtia* was launched by *Breiz Atao* and the Breton literary magazine *Gwalarn* began to publish Breton translations of works from other Celtic languages.

In March 1925, just a few months before Plaid Cymru (Party of Wales) was formed, Morvan Marchal, a leading member of Breiz Atao, suggested to Welsh and Scots delegations that they form an International Committee for National Minorities. However, this committee was only briefly Pan Celtic for Marchal later invited representatives of the Basques, Corsicans and Flemings to join. Soon Breiz Atao's policy drifted away from Pan Celticism towards European federalism and by 1927 the party were propounding the idea of a European federation, in which each nationality was to be self-governing but would subscribe to a European parliament.[23] At this time, a half century before the development of the 'European idea', it was regarded as a wild and impractical dream.

The Pan Celtic idea now passed on to some individuals in Scotland where a *Celtic Magazine*, edited by Alexander Mackenzie, a Celtic scholar and vice-president of the Scottish Home Rule Association, encouraged the concept of Pan Celtic cooperation. In 1929 a Celtic League was formed by the Hon. Ruraidh Erskine of Marr (1870–1960) and an Irish-American, G.W. McCaffrey, who often used the Irish version of his name, Gearóid MacGafraidh. Louis LeRoux of Breiz Atao organized a branch of the League in Brittany.[24]

The Hon. Ruraidh Erskine of Marr, son of the 5th Baron, was president of the organization. Writer, translator, political activist and Marxist Socialist, Erskine was the founder of the radical An Comunn Albannach (Scots National League) in 1904, which dissolved in 1928 to become one of the movements forming the Scottish National Party. In the years before the Great War, Erskine had made the first tentative steps to Pan Celticism, seeking first a movement to unite the Gaelic Celtic nationalities (the Irish, Manx and Scots). He argued for a 'Gaelic confederation'.[25]

Believing in the idea of a Scottish socialist republic, Erksine worked with John MacLean (1879–1923), pioneer of Marxism in Scotland and a major architect of the 'Red Clyde' concept, who also formed the Scottish Workers' Republican Party. Among his 'disciples' were Lord 'Manny' Shinwell, James Maxton and Willie Gallagher, all of whom eventually rejected MacLean and his teachings on Scottish independence after being elected to Westminster. MacLean died aged forty-four as a result of the ill-treatment he received in prison for protesting against Scottish involvement in an 'imperialist war' during 1914–18. Ten thousand Glaswegians followed his funeral cortège. Both Erskine and MacLean were supporters of the 'Celtic Renaissance' and threw their support behind the Irish independence movement at the time of the 1916 uprising and during the War of Independence (1919–21).

Yet another Scottish supporter of the 1929 Celtic League was the writer Lewis Spence (1874–1955). Spence is regarded as one of the pioneers of the Scottish Literary Revival, and is an outstanding lyric poet with over fifty books to his credit. A supporter of Scottish independence from his youth, in 1924 he co-founded the Scots National League, which was one of the movements which merged to become the Scottish National Party four years later. Spence became vice-president of the new SNP and wrote its first manifesto, *The National Party of Scotland* (July 1928). He became the first SNP parliamentary candidate standing in North Midlothian but he was unsuccessful. Spence was an expert in world mythology as well as mysticism. His *Magic arts in Celtic Britain* (1945) and *The history and origins of Druidism* (1949) are still highly regarded.

In spite of significant intellectual support, the Celtic League of 1929 scarcely lasted into the 1930s and produced only one pamphlet. It also attempted to produce a Celtic anthem which was reprinted in *An Aimsir Cheilteach* in March 1948.

> Hark! The voice of Celtia calling!
> Rise or lie, forever crushed!
> Lift your birthright from the ruins,
> Where th' invader's footsteps rushed.
> Race and honour, life and triumph,
> Call us, wake e'er life is flown,
> Cymry, Gael, unite or perish!
> Celts, arise and claim your own!

Among its supporters were Spence's close friends, Compton MacKenzie (1883–1972), one of Scotland's best known novelists, and the poet Hugh MacDiarmid (Christopher Murray Grieve – 1892–1978) who, according to the critic Kenneth Buthlay, was 'the greatest literary force in Scotland'.[26] MacDiarmid was a leading figure in what became known as the 'Scottish Renaissance'. However, he believed in the restoration of Scottish Gaelic as the national language of Scotland. In his pamphlet *Scotland in 1980* (1935), he foresaw the reestablishment of a Gaelic Scotland with 'eighty per cent of all creative literature of any value' being written in that language. However, he did not, so far as is recorded, make any attempt to learn Gaelic nor write in it himself. Instead he revived the Scottish dialect of English, 'Lallans', which he saw as a halfway house to Gaelic, and he wrote poetry in that medium. But according to MacDiarmid, Scotland would become not only Gaelic-speaking again but self-governing and not merely self-governing but a radical socialist republic. He was an ardent Marxist, a co-founder of the Scottish National Party in 1928, but his independent temperament kept him from being in any party for long periods.

He saw his task as being to 'work for the establishment of Workers' Republics in Scotland, Ireland, Wales and Cornwall, and, indeed, make a sort of Celtic Union of Socialist Soviet Republics in the British Isles'.[27] MacDiarmid became one of the first to give political Pan Celticism a clear left wing ideology. It should not longer simply be a catch-all movement for cooperation between the Celtic cultural movements but a more significant movement linking the independence parties, and not just independence groups but those movements who were socialist in aim. Pan Celticism, he contended, should be concerned not only with national freedom but with social freedom. The aim, at this stage of political Pan Celtic development, was probably the cause of the early demise of the 1929 Celtic League. However, MacDiarmid continued to believe in Pan Celticism until his death, although his political attitudes did not suit many in

Scottish poet Hugh MacDiarmid (1892-1978) saw it as his personal task to 'work for the establishment of Workers' republics in Scotland, Ireland, Wales and Cornwall, and indeed, make a sort of Celtic union of Socialist Soviet Republics in the British Isles'.

The Caltic Congress of 1932 at Truro. Henry Jenner, bearded, stands almost centre while Douglas Hyde, soon to be Irish President, stands in the front row, third from Jenner's left hand side.

the independence movement in his native Scotland.

MacDiarmid was an individualist, a man of numerous social, political and even cultural contradictions, who did not find it easy to work within any one movement or group. His fellow Celts found it easier to revere him from a distance than attempt to work with him. Politically, he swung from Marxism to supporting Mussolini's Fascism, being thrown out of the Communist Party for 'national deviationism', but rejoining the Communist Party in 1956 at the time of the Soviet repression of Hungary. His arguing in favour of the restoration of Gaelic as Scotland's national language at the same time as making no attempt to learn it and writing in a Scots dialect of English (a language which he admitted to the current writer he had invented for literary purposes) is an example of a typical perversity of his.

Hugh MacDiarmid contributed a foreword to my book *The Scottish insurrection of 1820*, co-authored with Seumas Mac a' Ghobhainn, published by Victor Gollancz in 1970. While promoting the book in Edinburgh, March, 1970, I stayed with leading 'Lallans' poet, the late Sydney Goodsir Smith. At a dinner in his apartment, attended by Hugh MacDiarmid and Gaelic Poet Somhairle MacLean, both MacDiarmid and Goodsir Smith made no secret of the fact that the vocabulary they used owed more to their own inventions than genuine surviving forms used in the English spoken after the demise of Gaelic in southern Scotland and before the spread of standard English.

But if MacDiarmid was individualistic, it was a fault shared by many of his fellow Celts, and it was just this individuality of personality and attitude that led to the political Pan Celtic movements failing to survive between the World Wars.

Notes

1   *Who was Who*, 1937. Lord Castletown and his attitudes are sketched in Mark Bence-Jones' *Twilight of the Ascendancy* (Constable, 1987).

2   Quoted in *Patrick Pearse: The triumph of Failure*, Ruth Dudley Edwards (Faber and Faber, London, 1977), p. 35 (no source given).

3   *Patrick Pearse*, Edwards (see above), pp. 31–38.

4   *Patrick Pearse*, Hedley McCoy (Mercier, Cork, 1966), pp. 26/27.

5   *Patrick Pearse*, Edwards (see above), pp. 31–38. In fact, an editorial in *An Claidheamh Soluis* claimed that the Celtic Congress 'will do harm' to the Irish language movement.

6   Quoted in 'Aspects of the Cornish Revival', T.S. Saunders, Ph.D. (unpublished) thesis, 1982, University College of Aberystwyth, Wales. pp. 222–230.

7   Ibid.

8   *Patrick Pearse*, Edwards (see above), p. 35. Edwards gives a detailed account of the Pan Celtic rift in Conradh na Gaeilge and the role Pearse played.

9   MacNeill Papers (National Library of Ireland, 15 January 1900).

10 MacNeill Papers (31 August 1901).

11 Graves edited *The Celtic Song Book, being representative folk songs of the six Celtic nations*. While he had been given the task of preparing this at the 1901 Congress it was not published until 1928.

12 *Celtia*, March, 1901.

13 'Aspects of the Cornish Revival' (see above), p. 240.

14 Ibid.

15 *Celtic Review*, January, 1905.

16 Heinrich Zimmer was one of the pioneering Celtic scholars of the nineteenth century. *The Irish Element in Medieval Culture*, translated by Jane Long Edmonds (Knickerbocker Press, New York, USA), 1891; and *The Celtic Church in Britain and Ireland*, translated by A. Meyer (David Nutt, London, 1902), were two of his major works.

17 *Preussiche Jahrbücher*, Vol. 92/93, edited by Professor Heinrich Zimmer, Greifswald.

18 *Nationalism*, Peter Alter (Edward Arnold), translated by Stuart McKinnon-Evans (1989), pp. 89–90.

19 *Pan Slavism: its History and Ideology*, Hans Kohn, Notre Dame (Ind., USA), 1953. Nikolai Danilevsky wrote what is regarded as the 'Bible' of the movement in 1867. See also: *Nationalism*, Alter (above), p. 90; *Imperialism*, George Lichtheim (Allen Lane: The Penguin Press, 1971), pp. 91–92.

20 'Democratic Pan Slavism' by Frederick Engels, *The Pelican Marx Library*, gen. ed. Quintin Hoare, Vol. 1. *The Revolution* of 1848, ed. & intro. David Fernbach (Penguin Books, London, 1973), pp. 226–245; also quoted in *Imperialism*, Lichtheim (see above), p. 91.

21 *Papers of the Celtic Congress*, Birkenhead, 1917, preface by E.T. John, Perth, 1918.
22 *Separatism in Brittany*, M.J.C. O'Callaghan (Dyllansow Truran, Redruth, 1983), p. 50
23 Ibid.
24 *An Aimsir Cheilteach*, February, 1948.
25 *Guth na Bliadhna*, No. 11, Vol. II (1906).
26 *Hugh MacDiarmid*, Kenneth Buthlay (Oliver & Boyd, Edinburgh, 1964) p. 4.
27 *Lucky Poet*, Hugh MacDiarmid (Methuen, London, 1943), p. 26.

6: A Celtic Union?

THE late 1940s and early 1950s saw Pan Celtic sentiment used quite cynically by some leading members of the Fianna Fáil Party in Ireland. At the same time, Clann na Poblachta, one of the 1948–51 Coalition Government parties in Ireland, and their leader, Seán MacBride, began to give serious support to the concept of Celtic cooperation. The years 1948–1951 presented a missed opportunity for Pan Celts to create a broader-based movement.

During the 1930s and early 1940s, apart from the regular meetings of the Celtic Congress, and through it, a continuing Pan Celtic interest among individual members of cultural and political groups, there was no significant Pan Celtic development. After the demise of the Celtic League in the early 1930s, there were no further attempts to create a politically orientated Pan Celtic body until July 1947, when a Celtic Union was established. This body was, in fact, born at a 'fringe' meeting of the Celtic Congress. While it failed to last more than a couple of years it began the continuous phenomenon of the rise and fall of politically orientated Pan Celtic publications, the bodies and groups which published these eventually leading to the foundation of the modern Celtic League, formed in 1961.

In Dublin, during the July of 1947, the Celtic Congress was being hosted by the Irish Government. Eamon De Valéra's Fianna Fáil Party had given a tremendous boost to Pan Celticism that year by its official support, and financing, of the Congress which was opened on 24 July at University College, Dublin, by the Irish Minister for Education, Tomás Ó Deirg. The chairman

Seán MacBride (1904-1991) was converted to Pan Celticism when Ireland's Foreign Minister (1948/51), became Assistant Secretary-General of the United Nations and was holder of numerous honours such as the Nobel Prize for Peace (1974).

of the organizing committee was Ireland's Chief Justice Conor Maguire, and Congress not only received a visit from the Irish President, Seán T. Ó Ceallaigh, but delegates were invited to a special Garden Party at the Presidential residence in Phoenix Park.

De Valéra (1882–1975), who had been Prime Minister since 1932, had several times expressed his interest in the cultural problems facing Ireland's fellow Celtic nations.[1] On St David's Day, 1 March 1946, De Valéra had expressed his first Pan Celtic views by sending a message in Irish and Welsh to *Y Ddraig Goch*, the journal of Plaid Cymru.

> By their faithfulness to their traditions and their language, even under circumstances which might be judged overwhelming, the Welsh have proved that a nation can retain its individuality so long as the language, which gives the most perfect expression of its personality, remains in daily use. A strong link binds the people of Wales and Ireland together, not only because they derive from the same Celtic stock, but also because of their devotion to things of the spirit; as is proved beyond doubt by the passionate desire of the two nations to preserve their cultures. Both of our nations know by so doing they are safe-guarding something which can enrich all humanity, and in particular, strengthen those bonds which link the Celtic nations together.

The day before the 1947 Congress, De Valéra had chosen, with great political acumen, the Isle of Man as the place to make his first official state visit since the end of the war. He made a point of visiting the surviving native speakers of Manx. When he discovered nothing was being done towards making a recording of these last speakers, he personally asked the Irish Folklore Commission to make audio recordings of them.[2] Returning to Dublin, De Valéra held an official reception for Congress delegates, basking in their approval for his Pan Celtic enthusiasm.

The 1947 Congress was attended by many leading Celtic scholars, poets and political figures from all six countries. According to the Scottish Gaelic scholar, Revd John McKechnie:

'The Celtic Congress [is] the visible outward sign of the federation of the Celtic peoples.'[3] He pointed out: 'Let us be clear that there is a federation already in existence between the Celtic peoples.'

But the Dublin Government only supported the idea of cultural links. For the more politically-minded delegates, the federation as constituted by Congress was not enough. It was not the political federation that many wished for. Congress, however, did deal with some political problems in 1947. It supported Welsh and Scottish demands for their languages to be granted state recognition by the London Government and asked the French Government to allow the teaching of Breton in the primary and secondary schools of Brittany.[4] But a resolution asking Congress to support moves to alleviate the plight of Breton political refugees in Ireland was opposed by Scottish delegates, who believed the Bretons to be 'Nazi sympathizers'.[5]

Following the Allied landings in France in 1944, the French authorities started to repress anyone they claimed was pro-Nazi and collaborationist. Indeed, a small group of no more than seventy Bretons had been recruited into a military unit called Bezen Perrot, but mainly because they had been pushed into it by some extreme actions of the local Maquis. The unit was named after Father Yann Perrot, a priest in his late seventies, who had been gunned down by the local Maquis on the steps of his own church in Scrignac, and for no other reason than the fact that he was a Breton language enthusiast who had been a founder of Bluen-Brug, an organization for teaching Breton, in 1905. The unit was formed in 1943, under the leadership of Marcel Guieysse and Neven Henaff, and was incorporated into the ranks of the German SS. Bezen Perrot had little support among most Breton nationalists, many of whom, understanding the nature of Fascism, were fighting in the Free French forces. But the French authorities used Bezen Perrot as an excuse to smash the Breton movement once and for all. Assassinations of members of the Breton movement occurred, even of Bretons who had fought against Nazi Germany. Poets, such as Barz ar Yeodet, the historian Madame du Gerny, writers such as Louis Stephen and Yves de Cambourg, were all shot out of hand because of their adherence to the Breton language. Bretons were rounded up by the hundred, with the police using outdated files from the 1930s. A series of 'show trials' were arranged at which twenty death sentences were pronounced. Additional numerous sentences of five to twenty years' imprisonment were given and hundreds were officially deprived by the courts of their civil rights, a sentence that has no parallel in English or Scottish law.

Those who suffered were leading figures in Breton cultural and political life – few, if any, had actually had anything to do with Bezen Perrot.

A Welsh delegation of eight was allowed to visit Brittany from 22 April to 14 May 1947. Their conclusion was 'the mere fact of having taken part in any Breton activity was a sufficient motive for the French Government to indulge in persecution'.[6] Welsh journalists managed to alert world opinion, causing the UK and USA Governments to exert pressure on France to end the continuing trials. It was some years before the Breton movement recovered.

The two resolutions at the 1947 Congress were political but those delegates wanting greater political measures from Congress sought a declaration of support for the movement towards political independence in all the Celtic countries.

In July 1947, a new Pan Celtic publication was launched; *An Aimsir Cheilteach: The Celtic Time*, subtitled 'monthly paper of the Celtic peoples'. Published from Cork under the editorship of a Breton domiciled in Ireland since the early 1930s, Leo V. Millarden, it was to be one of the most influential journals for shaping the principles and aims of Pan Celticism before it folded in March 1954. It did not address itself solely to academic and cultural questions, but was firmly committed to political independence for the Celtic peoples and to a Pan Celtic federation of self-governing states.[7]

The appearance of the first issue of *An Aimsir* to coincide with the Celtic Congress in Dublin became a talking point of the politically-minded Pan Celticists, and these gathered in Trinity College to discuss how a more political body could be brought into existence. The chairman of this meeting was Gwynfor Evans (b. 1912), a law graduate of Aberystwyth and Oxford; a lawyer turned market gardener from Carmarthen, Wales. He had become president of Plaid Cymru in 1945 and was to win a seat on Carmarthen County Council in 1949, retaining it, and becoming an Alderman, until his election to the House of Commons in 1966. Gwynfor Evans was an enthusiastic Pan Celticist.[8]

The result of the meeting was the formation of the Celtic Union with Gwynfor Evans as president. The purpose was to encourage solidarity and action between the Celtic peoples in their struggle for independence. An international secretary was appointed with national secretaries in each Celtic country.

The international secretary was Donal Breen, whose father Dan Breen (1894–1969) represented Tipperary for Fianna Fáil in the Dáil (Irish Parliament) continuously from 1932–69. Donal was secretary from July 1947 through to 1949, but became a religieux. His father was very much a folk hero in Ireland for he had taken part in the famous ambush at Soloheadbeg, Co. Tipperary, which event precipitated the start of the War of Independence in January 1919. He became one of the most popular IRA leaders with a price of £10,000 on his head. He was first elected as Sinn Féin TD for Tipperary in 1923 but was defeated in the General Election of 1927. His book, *My fight for Irish freedom* (1924), became a classic of Irish literature about the independence struggle. Donal had much to live up to.

Other national secretaries included, for Wales, Walter Dowding of Brynmawr[9]; for the Isle of Man, Mona Douglas; and for Brittany, Youenn Olier, whose reminiscences about this period are recorded in *Dulenn* 1947, *deizlevr ur mix* ('Dublin, 1947, the diary of a month') published by Imbourc'h, Kistreberzh, in 1989. The only major event held by the Celtic Union that attracted media attention was a rally on Friday, 15 October 1948, when Gwynfor Evans extended 'a cordial invitation to all fighters for Celtic freedom in London' to attend at the Conway Hall, in London's Red Lion Square.[10]

It was clear from the start that while members of the Celtic Union subscribed to political independence, and a federation of self-governing Celtic states, with official status for the languages, there were as many different views of the type of self-government and Pan Celtic federation, with ways of securing them, as there were members.

In Wales, the most enthusiastic supporters of the new body came not from Gwynfor Evans' own Plaid Cymru but from Mudiad Gweriniaethol Cymru (Welsh Republican Movement), whose manifesto for a Welsh Socialist Republic included the concept of a Pan Celtic union in the same terms as in the manifesto of Breiz Atao over twenty years previously. A law graduate from Carmarthen, Clifford Ifan Bere, was to draft the manifesto for the movement.[11]

Bere had served in the British Army during the war, eager to fight Fascism, but had consequently refused a military recall during the Korean War, preferring to work on the coal face in the Welsh mines – the alternative offered to military service. A socialist and republican, he has worked at the National Museum of Wales, and is a novelist in Welsh, producing *Pennod yn hanes milawr* ('Chapter in the story of a soldier') in 1989, and in English, *I was a king*, in 1976. As well as producing this early work on the Welsh Republic, his most significant theoretical contribution to Pan Celticism has been *Towards the political confederation of Celtia* (Gwasg yr Ynys Newydd & Y Lolfa Cyf, 1988). Article 11 of the Welsh Republican Manifesto makes a special point about the relationship an independent Wales should have with the other Celtic countries:

Federalism in Britain under English patronage would certainly not give the vital substance of freedom to the Welsh nation, only its ineffectual shadow. It is only to a continental or Celtic federation of nations that Wales can rightly belong and perhaps owe the moral duty to surrender some part of her sovereignty.

According to Article II:

The Republic of Wales shall live in close association with all the other Celtic peoples and shall endeavour in every way to cooperate fully with all nations and in particular its near neighbours in the Republic of Ireland, Scotland and England.

But not one of the major national independence parties, such as Plaid Cymru or the Scottish National Party, subscribed to the aims of the Celtic Union, although they did allow individual members to join it.

During 1947 and 1948, Pan Celticism succeeded only in attracting support for its 'cultural message', with a series of Inter Celtic Festivals arranged in Cornwall, Brittany and Wales. The accent was on language, literature and music. A Celtic Society of Australia began to send delegates to these festivals.[12] One unlikely venue for preaching the message of Pan Celticism in 1949 was Mitcham Football Stadium. A hurling match between Tipperary and Kilkenny had just been played there. The Catholic Archbishop of Cardiff, Dr MacGrath, asked to speak, told those gathered that the Welsh, Irish, Scots, Bretons, Manx and Cornish belonged to one of Europe's oldest peoples, the Celts, and that they should be proud of their cultural heritage and work together to preserve it.

In Ireland, in February 1948, De Valéra had dissolved the Dáil and gone to the polls. While Fianna Fáil retained its position as the largest party, the five opposition parties formed a Coalition led by Fine Gael, and John A. Costello became the new prime minister. This Coalition decided to 'tidy' the Irish constitution of 1937 by declaring the twenty-six counties to be a republic. The British Government deemed the Irish Republic to have left the British Commonwealth.

There was an immediate reaction in the Partitioned North of the country with Unionists falling back on the creation of sectarian hysteria to secure their power base. An election for the Stormont Parliament was called for to reaffirm a majority for Partition. This was merely window-dressing as the statelet had been designed to ensure a permanent Unionist majority in its Stormont Government. Nevertheless, Colonel Hall Thompson, Minister for Education, rode around his constituency on a white horse in imitation of William of Orange brandishing a blackthorn stick. Sir Basil Brooke (later Lord Brookeborough) called on 'the Protestant people' to 'cross the Boyne... with me as your leader and to fight for the same cause as King William fought in days gone by'.[13]

Violence was so extreme that 200 Labour MPs at Westminster called for the election in Northern Ireland to be suspended until it could be held in 'democratic conditions'. The election produced 234,202 votes for the continuance of the Union and 133,290 for the reunification of Ireland. This meant that the Unionists could demand a guarantee in perpetuity from Westminster for the position of the Partitioned Six Counties.

De Valéra, out of office, but determined to fight Partition, now used the Pan Celts as a platform. Paying his first visit to Wales on 23 October 1948, he went out of his way to court the supporters for Welsh independence and rally them to the Anti-Partition League, which had originally been formed in 1945, by James MacSparran, a Nationalist MP for Mourne. Gwynfor Evans of Plaid Cymru welcomed De Valéra, and in a stirring article in the *Welsh Nationalist* that month, declared 'Ireland – One Nation, One State':

> It presents itself to us as a matter of simple justice. Ireland is one nation; it is a crying injustice that she should be carved into two states. Her Partition is a wrong which must be righted.

De Valéra's first official engagement was as the guest of honour at a Plaid Cymru luncheon. During his speech De Valéra expressed his hope that the Celtic peoples would learn more of each other's languages and cultures, and he added that the new world society must be built on the deep rooted fundamental basis of nationhood and not on the relationships between empires or multi-national states dominated by one nation.[14]

But in fact, De Valéra's speeches did not make Pan Celts very happy. According to *An Aimsir*, November, 1948:

> ... it is regrettable that he did not make clear reference to England, responsible for the Partition of Ireland, to Wales as a potential friend and to the Welsh nationalists as the only active friends outside Irishmen – *because they were Celts* and for no other reason; he chose instead to speak about 'Britain' which is an unhappy expression of Imperialist make-up.

Some Pan Celts attended an Anti-Partition, Easter Sunday 1951, demonstration in Dun Laoghaire. The Welsh republican, Dr Tom Williams, was the principal speaker who called openly for a closer union between the Celtic peoples, in a speech reported in the *Welsh Republican*, May-June, 1951:

> If the Celtic nations wish to survive we must work together politically and economically in order to ensure that England shall not continue to hold sway over nations outside her rightful borders.

The following year De Valéra was in Scotland making similar appeals.[15] In May 1951, after the Coalition Government fell and his own Fianna Fáil were returned to office, De Valéra appeared no longer to be interested in Pan Celticism as part of a practical policy.

However, before the defeat of the Coalition, Seán MacBride, the Coalition Government's Minister for External Affairs, had been taking a deep interest in Pan Celticism. Unlike De Valéra, his interest was sincere and long lasting. As Minister, and thereby an important international figure, MacBride could have been an important asset to the Pan Celts had he remained in office long enough.

MacBride was the son of the executed 1916 leader, John

MacBride, and the feminist and nationalist leader, Maud Gonne. Seán became Chief of Staff of the IRA, a brilliant barrister, and then member of the Irish Supreme Court before becoming leader of Clann na Poblachta, a radical and progressive minority party. Clann na Poblachta participated in its first general election in 1948 and won ten seats in the Irish parliament. Seán, as leader, was offered a ministerial post in the Coalition Government. In 1951 the party was down to only two seats and their representation steadily decreased until they held only one seat in 1965 and eventually disappeared. Seán MacBride would go on to become an influential figure on the world stage, being awarded the Nobel Prize for Peace (1974), and the International Lenin Prize for Peace (1977), as well as many other international awards. He was a founder member of Amnesty International, Secretary-General of the International Commission of Jurists, Assistant Secretary-General of the United Nations and recipient of numerous honorary degrees from universities in many parts of the world. MacBride remained interested in Pan Celticism until his death in 1989 and he encouraged Pan Celts to think in terms of a prospective political Celtic union.

In an interview given in *Le Peuple Breton* he announced: 'I should like to be able to contribute to the establishment of closer ties between the Celtic peoples.'[16] He felt that the Celtic peoples of Ireland, Wales, Brittany and Scotland had an important part to play 'in the present international evolution':

> What the world is lacking is an ideal based on a system where human freedom and dignity are recognized, when the freedom, independence, and integrity of the people are protected... the Celtic peoples can help much in fostering that ideal which is lacking today.

MacBride held a two-hour private discussion with leading political Pan Celticists, such as Ithel Davies of Wales and Robert Blair Wilkie of Scotland, during the Easter Weekend of 1951.

'My talk with him, and our discussions with Robert Wilkie of Scotland, all point to a solid desire for a union of Celtic nations... and further, to coordinate our economic resources for our mutual benefit,' recalled Davies in a report on 'Celtic Unity' in the Bulletin of Mudiad Gweriniaethol Cymru.[17]

But whether MacBride would have been able to convince his colleagues in the Irish Government to take up his attitudes as official policy is a matter of speculation, for within weeks Seán MacBride and the Coalition Government were no longer in office.

Ithel Davies expanded further on his discussions with the Irish Minister.

> It was made clear to us that the ultimate fulfilment of Irish liberation depended largely on the common efforts of the Scots and Welsh to free themselves from the crippling vice of English authority and power, and destroy that authority and power in these islands. We all felt that in the common enjoyment of republican freedom we could revive the Celtic fringe of Europe to be the most prosperous area in the world in material wealth and the most advanced in culture and social achievement. England's Teutonic greed for power, and her highway robbery politics, must be deterred if we, as Celtic nations, are to live. In the immortal words of Wolfe Tone, the Irish Rebel, 'We invade none of her [England's] rights but we secure our own.'
>
> The one thing that stands out from the conversations we had is the belief in Ireland that the approach of Plaid Cymru to the freedom of Wales, and the emphasis of its leaders on 'freedom not independence' is both inadequate and wrong, and that a free Wales under the English Crown and within the English Empire, either as a Self-Governing Dominion or as a replica of Northern Ireland, is bound to prejudice any attempt at full and effective inter-Celtic unity and cooperation.
>
> We, in Wales, have to choose between a Union of the Celtic nations and immersion in the English Imperial system. I am satisfied that our Celtic cousins in Ireland expect us to put the claims of the Celtic peoples first. That came out clearly in all my conversations with leading Irishmen and women.

In Wales, Mudiad Gweriniaethol launched its own newspaper, *The Welsh Republican/Y Gweriniaethwr*, in August 1950, with Harri Webb as editor. Its contents carried a definite

Pan Celtic flavour from the start. Harri Webb, a native of Abertawe (Swansea) was an Oxford graduate, and is now regarded as one of Wales' leading poets and literary figures. He achieved prominence as the presenter of a BBC TV poetry series, 'Poems and Pints', which ran for several seasons. It is generally accepted by critics that his journalistic talent flourished at its best in the columns of *The Welsh Republican*, which he edited for most of its life until 1957. An attempt was made to revive it again in the mid-1970s.[18]

Among those involved in the production of the paper was the philosopher Ifor Huws Wilkes, who is now living in the United States.

Prominent among the political Pan Celticists at this time was Irish Senator, Tom Mullin, a Fianna Fáil representative who was outspoken about possibilities of creating political Celtic links. In 1951 Eoin O'Mahony (1904–1970), a barrister, became very involved in political Pan Celticism. He was chairman of the Irish Anti-Partition Association, stood unsuccessfully as Fianna Fáil candidate for the National University seat in the Irish Senate and, in 1966, was unsuccessful in securing nomination for the Irish Presidency, opposing De Valéra. 'We Celts have so few friends that it is desirable that we should cooperate industrially, culturally and politically,' he wrote in an article entitled 'Free Wales: United Ireland!'[19]

At a meeting in St Andrew's Hall, Glasgow, on 22 April 1951, O'Mahony took the platform with Seán MacBride, still Minister for External Affairs, and F. Boland, the Irish ambassador to the United Kingdom. O'Mahony told his audience that the rest of the Celtic peoples '… looked to the Irish Government, as the only leaders of a free Celtic nation in the world, to take the lead in stressing the importance to the world and to the other Celtic nations that the Celts had a mission to the world, that the Celtic spirit stood for fair play and decency.' Like most political Pan Celticists, O'Mahony combined an appeal for practical politics with an almost metaphysical approach to Celtic spiritual values which, for him, was the basis of a Celtic destiny once they had re-emerged as independent nations. In his speech, on a more practical level, he urged the setting up of special Irish consular representation in all the Celtic countries, an idea immediately supported by the Irish Minister of External Affairs and the Irish Ambassador.[20] But a few days later there was a new Irish Government and O'Mahony's proposal was considered impractical.

By 1950 the Celtic Union had become moribund. The reason for the decline and disappearance of the Celtic Union was claimed to be the activities of the French *Deuxième Bureau*, or secret service, at the time. The French were seeking out Breton political and cultural activists abroad as they continued their effort to destroy the Breton Movement. The Scottish secretary of the Celtic Union, Hugh MacDonald of Busby, speaking to Séamas Filbin, said that the Union was becoming so infiltrated that it was impossible to continue in any meaningful way.[21]

Cliff Bere confirms this:

Hugh MacDonald was probably near the mark with his suggestion concerning the demise of the 1947 League. We waged an active campaign on behalf of Andre Geoffroy, Breton patriot under sentence of death at that time in Fresnes Prison, Paris. We managed to make things very uncomfortable for the French Consul in Cardiff (I think his name was Langlais). We bearded and disconcerted him in his office in the dockland area here to great effect and were duly hauled in to the police court for the show of Celtic solidarity when a bunch of French journalists visited the city. Geoffroy was later freed and released... perhaps our little manifest-ations played a small part in that happy denouement. During that time a 'Breton' calling himself Pinault appeared from nowhere and tried to attach himself to us. There was suspicion of him and we treated him with due circumspection. He later disappeared just as mysteriously. Now, with hindsight, there can be no doubt that he was one of the French Secret Service people.[22]

Jord Pinault, giving his occupation as 'student' and an address in Ruthin, North Wales, applied to join Mudiad Gweriniaethol Cymru in October 1950.

In spite of the potential membership now subscribing to *An Aimsir*, and the occasional appeal for a new political Pan Celtic organization, no serious moves were made to organize in this field until 1952 when Wendy Wood, an individualistic and indefatigable worker for Scottish independence, formed a Celtic Alliance. She decided to launch her movement with no half measures and organized a mass rally in London, the 'heart of the empire', on Sunday 5 October. The rally gathered at Hyde Park at 1.45pm and marched to Trafalgar Square behind Irish and Scottish pipe bands.

The attendance was reported as varying from 3,000 (News Chronicle) to 10,000 (*The Scotsman*). A figure of probably 5,000 seems reasonable. The meeting was chaired by Liam O'Callaghan of Sinn Féin, later a leading member of Cumann na Poblachta. Speakers ranged across the Celtic national political spectrum. Each had different political attitudes and ideas as to how Pan Celticism could operate. Among them were Wendy Wood herself (Scottish Patriots), the historian Oliver Brown (Scottish Congress), Meredith Edwards (Plaid Cymru), Harri Webb (Welsh Republican Movement), and the Irish writer Éamon Ó Faoláin. The speeches of the rally consisted of stirring cries for independence, a reunited Ireland and a call for the audience to express their support for the political independence of the Celtic countries.[23]

Among those attending that rally was a young London Irishman, Seán Mac Stíofáin (b. 1928), who was to become Chief of Staff of the 'Provisional' IRA and who conducted its campaign from 1970–72. He took a prominent rôle in the IRA-British Government talks in July of 1972. He became a supporter of the Pan Celtic idea at this rally, having also purchased a copy of *An Aimsir*.[24] His influence may have led to the IRA statement in 1972 that no aggressive actions would be carried out by the organization in the Celtic regions of Britain should Active Service Units carry out actions in Britain. Only England would be 'targeted'.[25]

In spite of the 'bang' with which the Celtic Alliance had been launched, it disappeared and no further meetings or rallies were held. Why, after an apparently good start, the Celtic Alliance vanished must be a matter of speculation at this time. One of the things that has bedevilled Pan Celtic groups over the years is that most activists are also committed to their own national organizations and have little time to spare on the work required to establish and administrate inter Celtic groups. There is, therefore, a lack of volunteers standing for office in such groups. This seems to be a reason for the abrupt demise of the Celtic Alliance.

Later, an abortive attempt was made to form a Pan Celtic movement among students with the impetus coming from Mudiad Gweriniaethol Cymru. One of its founder members, Gwilym Prys Davies, a graduate of Aberystwyth University Law School and an able writer in Welsh and English, attempted to form a Celtic Congress of Students, sometime between 1952–4.

Gwilym Prys Davies later decided to leave the Welsh Republicans and join the Labour Party. In 1966 he was chosen to stand for a 'safe Labour seat' in Carmarthen. There was an irony in that Prys Davies took 13,743 votes while Gwynfor Evans of Plaid Cymru obtained 16,179 votes, becoming Plaid Cymru's first Member of Parliament on 14 July. Gwilym Prys Davies, who had rejected the idea of Welsh independence and Pan Celticism, gloomily told newspapers: 'I think this has been a protest vote and not a positive vote.' Later, Prys Davies did succeed in securing a seat in Parliament on a Labour Party ticket. He was eventually made a Life Peer and became a Labour Party spokesman on Northern Ireland. In 1990, he drafted a new Welsh Language Bill, and he has tried to evolve a more positive policy on the vexed question of current English inmigration to Wales.[26]

In 1952 Prys Davies wrote enthusiastically to Harri Webb:

We are in touch with Rennes University (Brittany) and they are prepared to send over some delegates to a meeting to be held in Aber(ystwyth) at the end of this term to investigate the possibility of founding a Congress of Celtic Students. As I envisage things the Union would have to confine itself to 'cultural activities' for the first year or two, thenceforward it could be placed on a par with the NUS (National Union of Students). The success of the plan is dependent on two things: 1) cooperation of Scotland and Ireland. At the moment we are experiencing great trouble with Scotland. 2) the state of student opinion in Wales during the next few years.[27]

But the idea would not come to fruition for another fifteen years when the Celtic Youth Congress was eventually formed – and its life would be a very brief one.

Notes

1   *Y Ddraig Goch*, March, 1946.
2   'Recording Native Manx Speech', Shorys y Creayrie (Dr George Broderick), pp. 308–320, *For A Celtic Future*, edited by Cathal Ó Luain (The Celtic League, Dublin, 1983).
3   *An Aimsir Cheilteach*, September, 1947.
4   *Irish Press*, 25 July 1947.
5   Ibid. For information on the French authorities' repression of the Breton national movement during the late 1940s, see: *Breton Nationalism*, published by Plaid Cymru, 1948, 84pp, preface by Gwynfor Evans, and *Separatism in Brittany*, M.J.C. O'Callaghan (Dyllansow Truran, 1983).
6   O'Callaghan, above, p. 76.
7   Leo V. Millarden was still alive in 1990 and answered questions from the present writer through the good offices of Alan Heusaff: letter to the author of 20 April 1989. Millarden had played an active rôle in the Breton independence movement during the 1920s but had settled in Ireland during the early 1930s where he had set up an export business in Cork.
8   Gwynfor Evans to the author, 12 March 1989.
9   *Welsh Nation*, November, 1947.
10 *An Aimsir Cheilteach*, October, 1948.
11 *The Welsh Republic*, Clifford Ifan Bere, n.d. c. 1948.
12 *An Aimsir Cheilteach*, August, 1949.
13 Clause 1(1B), Ireland Act, 1949. A detailed account of this period is to be found in *Northern Ireland: the Orange State*, Michael Farrell (Pluto Press, London, 1976), pp. 177–201.
14 *Welsh Nationalist*, October, 1948, November, 1948, and *An Aimsir Cheilteach*, November, 1948.
15 Séamas Filbin in conversation to author, 1 September 1989.
16 *Le Peuple Breton*, April, 1948, quoted in *An Aimsir Cheilteach*, May, 1948.

17 See 'Celtic Unity: a report by Ithel Davies' (duplicated publication (1950), Mudiad Gweriniaethol Cymru).

18 Webb became widely known for 'Poems and Pints', the most popular BBC television poetry programme ever broadcast, which ran for five years. The *Western Mail* was to describe him as 'the uncrowned poet laureate of Wales'. All his life he remained committed to the idea of a Welsh socialist republic and to the Pan Celtic idea.

19 *Welsh Republican*, April–May 1950.

20 MacBride to author, 1 July 1987.

21 Séamas Filbin in conversation with author (1 September 1989).

22 Bere to author, 2 January 1990.

23 *Daily Graphic*, 6 October 1952; *Irish Independent*, 6 October 1952; *Scotsman*, 6 October 1952 and *News Chronicle*, 6 October 1952.

24 *Memoirs of a Revolutionary*, Seán Mac Stíofáin (Gordon Cremonesi Ltd., London, 1975), p. 53.

25 *Inniu*, Eanáir 21, 1972.

26 *Wales, A Nation Again*, Peter Berresford Ellis (Library 33 Ltd., London, 1968), p. 156.

27 Letter from Prys Davies to Harri Webb, n.d. but circa 1952–4; original with Cliff Bere sent to author with information on 19 August 1989. Letter from Lord Gwilym Prys Davies to author, 2 February 1990.

7: The influence of *An Aimsir Cheilteach*

DURING the period 1947–54, the central pivot or mainspring of the Pan Celtic movement was certainly the publication *An Aimsir Cheilteach: The Celtic Time – Monthly Paper of the Celtic Peoples*. Many of the basic ideas and objectives which still exist in today's Pan Celtic movement could be found in the publication's pages, which were printed mainly in English as a lingua franca. The concept of a Celtic political union based on the Scandinavian rôle model, the establishment of a League of Celtic Nations and the evolution of closer cultural ties were all discussed in detail. Even Charles de Gaulle's argument for the creation of a Celtic *lingua franca* was developed in its pages. More interestingly, an argument for an attempt to achieve Celtic independence within a European political federation was put forward, as early as 1949 – this was a concept which was returned to by the Scottish National Party in the mid-1980s and which was adopted by Le Mouvement Pour L'Organisation de la Bretagne (MOB), one of the Breton independence parties formed in 1957. The Celts were, perhaps ironically from our current viewpoint, early adherents to the Pan-European idea which was outlined in Richard N. Coudenhove-Kalergi's book *Pan Europe* (New York, 1926).

An Aimsir Cheilteach did not give birth to any lasting Pan Celtic organization within its lifetime but those who read it, or who contributed to its pages, were to be among the founders of the modern Celtic League which was established in 1961.

An Aimsir, according to its first issue, sought to create a mass Pan Celtic movement. Leo V. Millarden, its editor, writing 'Our

Purpose and Our Outlook', commented that:

> Far too long have Celtic matters been the privilege, almost monopoly, of an intellectual minority, partly living in the past and partly interested in the subject as a hobby. In these moving times we have reached the stage were the Celtic peoples will truly have to enter the struggle for life or death.

Having identified what many political Pan Celts saw as a problem, exemplified by the predominantly academic attendance at the Celtic Congress, of Pan Celticism being confined to an intellectual élite, Millarden stated that *An Aimsir* was founded:

> To inform each Celtic people of the news from the others and to consider the problems facing each one of the Celtic countries as well as those which concern them as a whole.
>
> To place the true position of the Celtic nations before the public opinion of other countries by bringing it to the notice of their Press, public, organizations and personalities.
>
> To rally the now scattered Celts, at heart and in spirit, promote an inter-Celtic outlook, develop and strengthen the inter-Celtic bonds, bring about collaboration and, where and when mutual, help in the various national grounds (sic) and achievements in the inter-Celtic field.[1]

Copies of the newspaper were regularly sent to the major daily and weekly newspapers in the Celtic countries and also to major newspapers in Europe, America, Australia, Africa and Asia. A year after its launch, Millarden was to tell his readers that the paper had succeeded in attracting a qualitatively important group of subscribers and that the publication had been successful in helping 'to promote an inter-Celtic outlook'.[2] However, he admitted: 'Our life has been too short yet to bring about collaboration and mutual help in the various national grounds (sic), and achievements in the inter-Celtic fields which have been set as our most distant aims, but we have reason to believe that the paper constitutes a potential factor of beneficial influence in that respect.'

Millarden also admitted that: 'The two great Celtic defects of individualism and passivity have been our main source of weakness.'

In spite of the fact that *An Aimsir* was regularly mailed to the major newspapers, there is no evidence to suggest that they took it seriously or even bothered to mention it until it was in its last year of life. The *Irish Independent* then commented in an editorial:

> ... there is even a monthly paper of the Celtic peoples. *An Aimsir Cheilteach* it is called, printed and published in this country (Ireland) but edited, I gather, in Scotland. There are articles in Irish, Welsh and Breton, on partition in Ireland, patriotism in Brittany and the political situation in Wales, the aspirations of the Scots and much more that shows how the Celtic wind is blowing.
>
> And looking it over I began to think one half of the Celtic world does not know how the other half lives and that it might not be a bad thing if we all become closer neighbours, instead of living too much to ourselves.[3]

Some political commentators had, however, noticed with apparent concern the growth of Pan Celticism. In Wales and Scotland, members of Plaid Cymru and the Scottish National Party were standing for local and central government elections as 'Anti-Irish Partition' candidates as well. Particularly worried were Welsh and Scottish adherents of the UK Labour Party, the Party which had not only declared Irish Partition inviolable, supporting the continuance of a regime in the Partitioned area which was in breach of basic Human Rights, but it was a Party which had promised self-government for Wales and Scotland, between 1918 and 1945, and then rejected that policy when Labour formed a Government in 1945.

For example, the UK Labour Party published *Labour and Wales* (1945) which promised: 'True freedom for Wales would be the result and product of a Socialist Britain, and under such conditions could self-government in Wales be an effective and secure guardian of the life of the nation.' A similar promise for Scotland was issued in *Let us Face the Future*. Labour achieved a landslide victory in Wales in 1945, winning twenty-seven out of the thirty-two seats. James Griffith, one of seven Welsh MPs who became ministers in the 1945–50 Government, justified his *volte face* position by saying: 'Circumstances have changed greatly. My advice now is that Wales should remain a unit with England.'[4] John Taylor, secretary of the Labour Party for Scotland, where a similar swing to Labour had been achieved, was perhaps a little more honest when he told the people of Dundee: 'I myself ceased to desire self-government as soon as we secured a Socialist Government for Britain.'[5]

The raising of expectations and the *volte face* caused many to seek alternatives. In these circumstances the growth of Pan Celticism worried those who had tried to justify this turnabout in policy. The Labour Party magazine, *Workers' Education*, launched a fierce attack on the Welsh Gorsedd for paying ceremonial honours to delegates from other Celtic countries.[6] This provoked a firm denunciation of the article from Harri Webb, who commented, '*Workers' Education* in these dangerous hands is "Workers' Indoctrination".'[7]

While the English media were content to pour scorn on the idea of Pan Celticism, the French authorities resorted to more practical means to prevent the distribution of *An Aimsir*. The French Censor told the French firm of distributors that the journal did not meet with their approval.[8] Rather than openly ban the publication, thus exposing the French Government to charges of human rights violations, the Censor put pressure on the distributors to stop vending the journal.

Millarden, with the help of his sub-editors in the various Celtic countries, continued to produce the publication until the issue of December 1952. With that issue he handed over to a Scotsman, Tomás MacNeacail. But during the succeeding eighteen months there were no less than four more editors. MacNeacail had to stand down immediately because of ill-health, and the paper became jointly edited by David Stevenson of Stirling and Michael Haslam of Leeds. A year later J.H. Glendinning of Edinburgh took over until the Edinburgh lawyer, Archibald MacPherson, became the final editor from July 1953 to March 1954. The publication's appearance had begun to be very irregular and the subtitle 'Monthly Paper of the Celtic Peoples' was altered simply to 'Paper of the Celtic Peoples'. As noted earlier, after the March 1954 issue, this most influential and important Pan Celtic journal was no more.

Its demise did not seem to lie in lack of subscriptions but in a failure to choose an editor able to devote the necessary time and care to producing a regular publication for, with no supporting advertising, the editor's position was a purely voluntary, unpaid one, and none of those who succeeded Millarden seemed to possess his single-minded enthusiasm and ability. According to MacPherson, its last editor, no serious attempt was made to attract advertising to support the costs of the journal.[9]

Its main influence consisted of its polemic articles on how Pan Celticism should develop; it created a heightened awareness of the Pan Celtic idea. Several issues relating to the development of the movement were argued in detail for the first time. The first cogent argument for practical steps to be taken towards inter Celtic activities was published by *An Aimsir* in its issue of December 1947.[10] The paper argued that:

> It is becoming increasingly obvious that, if our Celtic civilization, culture and way of life is to survive the forces and influences ranged against it, and continue to develop, as it must, closer integration and cooperation between the nations is vitally necessary. In other words a united front must be established with Congress as the international organization.

For the Celtic Congress to take this rôle, however, it was clear that it would have to be reorganized away from its merely 'academic' character. Proposals were put forward to change the constitution of Congress and it appears that the Indian National Congress (founded in 1885) was seen as a rôle model.

There were nine proposals:

1. That Congress be established as a permanent international organization with a constitution, elected officials, and executive, and a regular secretariat, and such committees as may be necessary.

2. That in each of the constituent nations there be established a Congress Secretariat to carry out the day to day work of Congress.

3. That Congress be a delegate assembly.

4. That Congress International Headquarters and permanent Secretariat be established in Dublin.

5. That the Annual Assemblies be convened in each of the constituent nations in rotation.

6. That provision be made for the participation and cooperation of the Celtic organizations in other countries particularly America and Canada.

7. That the main functions of the Congress be:-

a) to provide a focal point for the Celtic nations.

b) to coordinate the activities of the constituent national organizations, promoting the fullest cooperation between them and stimulate activity.

c) to evolve common policies and action to deal with influences endangering Celtic civilization and culture.

d) to coordinate and correlate all aspects of Celtic culture including higher studies and research.

e) to establish itself as the world spokesman for the Celtic policy.

f) to maintain [a] a world news and information service; and [b] an inter-nation news and information service.

g) to publish a Pan Celtic periodical and such other journals, pamphlets and books as may be necessary or desirable.

h) to sponsor a regular international radio feature.

i) to organize an annual Pan Celtic Festival, Oireachtas, Mòd or Eisteddfod.

k) such other activities as are calculated to assist the consolidation and advancement of Celtic civilization within the existing territories.

8. That a special representative commission be appointed to prepare a constitution and work out the details of organization and other cognate matters.

9. That reorganization to be effected in time for the 1948 Congress Assembly.

Discussions on this subject were held prior to the 1948 Congress but the proposals were dismissed as too radical.[11] It is many of these 'radical' proposals which are today matters of fact.

Later issues included articles by John Legonna (1918–78), benefactor of the Legonna Celtic Research Prize under the auspices of the National Library of Wales.[12] Legonna suggested: 'A federated Union of Celtic Peoples within the British and European Federation of Nations.'[13] In his argument, entitled 'Towards a Union of Celtic Peoples', Legonna admitted that he was well aware of the difficulties of the task, for 'not only have we been subjected wrongly to other races but, our greatest shame, we have also been too willing to be the instruments of our own subjection.' He said:

> Divided we fell and there, to all intents and purposes, we remain.
> It is my opinion that our continued division, if persisted in, is likely to ensure for us in the future, misfortunes as severe as those borne by us in the past. In other words, we simply must rediscover our common affinities. The intense difficulties now besetting the European social entity are perilously magnifying the threats to the continued existence of the Celtic languages, and thereby of the Celtic peoples. Those difficulties also contain possibilities, in cooperation it will be easier to seize opportunity when it offers.

Legonna proposed:

> ... the widest way to obtain from England a proper respect for the Celtic peoples, for our languages and national rights, is for us to federate in defence of those rights. A federated Union of Celtic Peoples within the British and European Federation of Nations should, I suggest, be our goal.
> Few realize the salutary effect which the evolution of a Union of Celtic Peoples is going to have in Western European politics; and few within the Celtic countries realize today the strength and status which such a Union is going to bring to each individual unit. As Hugh MacDiarmid has so long and wisely pointed out, such a Union will not only save the Celtic Peoples from eventual extinction but will also by its example and its leadership provide for Europe a way of recovery out of the morass into which European civilization is gradually sinking. We have in the Celtic countries all the elements necessary for so historic a task. We Celts still have a mighty contribution to make to human civilization. Beneath our suffering and struggle there are deep stirrings.

Representatives of Emsav Pobl Vreizh, a new Breton group, wanted to see a 'Pan Celtic Union of Federalists inside the European Union… our final aim ought to be asserted as follows: Free Celtic nations in a United Europe'.[14] Indeed, Celtic delegates began to attend the Federal Union of European Nationalities, formed in 1949 as a pressure group to safeguard the rights of European national minorities. The first business session of the Council of Europe, inaugurated on 8 August 1949, had just opened at Strasbourg under the chairmanship of Belgium's Paul Spaak. But it gave little comfort to the Celtic nations. Attempts by the Irish delegates to open up the problem of Irish Partition were blocked by the United Kingdom while an attempt to establish a European Court of Human Rights was blocked by France, still pursuing its aggressive policy of smashing the Breton movement. From the Celtic point of view, the 'European idea' was beginning to emerge as merely another development in 'power politics'; whereby the smaller nationalities of Europe would still have no means of asserting themselves, especially if they were incorporated into one of the larger states.

The Federal Union of European Nationalities claimed its origins in the League of Nations' 'National Congresses', which had been formed to work within the League for the rights of national minorities and stateless nations. This body disappeared in 1938. The FUEN emerged in 1949 with a Breton, Joseph Martray, as its first Secretary General, and claimed it was merely a reformation of the earlier institution. It based its aims on Article 13 of the Declaration of Human Rights, approved by the United Nations Organization, which pledges itself to the 'preservation and cultivation of the national characteristics and culture of the European minorities'. However, neither the Council of Europe, the United Nations, nor subsequently the European Parliament, have given any consultative status to the organization which has held its annual congress regularly since 1949. Its work and publications cover a wide range of European countries and the problems suffered by minorities, including the Celts, Basques, Frisians, Flemings, the Rheto-Romanche, Slovenes, Lapps, Kossovars and so forth. Delegates from the Celtic countries regularly attend these congresses.

The first working 'rôle model' was clearly spelt out for the Pan Celts by Dr Noëlle Davies, an Irish socialist and academic, wife of the Welsh economist Dr D.J. Davies. Noëlle Davies had previously published several works on the Pan Nordic situation, such as *Education for life: a Danish pioneer* (Williams & Norgate, London, 1931); *Grundtvig of Denmark: a guide to small nations* (1944); *Grundtvig: selskabit* (Grundtvig studier, Denmark, 1948). Dr Davies had also written *Connolly of Ireland: patriot and socialist* (Dublin, 1946), a study of the Irish Marxist leader James Connolly, executed for his part in the 1916 uprising in Ireland. With her husband, a well known economist, who had formed most of Plaid Cymru's early economic programmes, she had written *Cymoedd tan Gwmwl*, 1938; *Can Wales afford self-government?*, 1939; *Is Monmouth in Wales?*, 1944, and *Wales – land of our children*, 1944

Dr Davies contributed to *An Aimsir* an article on 'Education in Nationalism'. She had long been interested in the Nordic Union and the rise of the Scandinavian concept.

> Those who stand for a closer union between the Celtic nations and for a strengthening of the influence of the Celtic ideas in the life of Europe may sometimes envy the progress of the six Scandinavian nations (including Iceland and the Faroes) towards a similar goal for Scandinavia.[15]

In the mid-nineteenth century, 'Scandinavism' had been an academic and literary movement inspired by Romanticism. Following Denmark's defeat in the war against Prussia and Austria in 1864, the idea of an economic and political unity between the major Scandinavian countries of Denmark, Norway and Sweden began to emerge. In 1905, the Nordic Union had been formed with aims and aspirations for cooperation on economic, cultural and political levels between the Scandinavian countries.

The parallel between the aspirations of the political Pan Celts and the Nordic Union was exact. However, the Nordic Union had succeeded where the Celts had not. The Nordic Inter Parliamentary Union had come into existence in 1907. Then came the establishment in 1952 of a Nordic Council, a consultative body consisting of members of the various Scandinavian parliaments. It was on 1 July 1962 that a Treaty of Cooperation was entered into and Scandinavia became a reality with its nations 'desirous of furthering the close connection between the Nordic nations in culture and in juridical and social conceptions, and of developing cooperation between the Nordic countries; endeavouring to create uniform rules in the Nordic countries in as many respects as possible.'[16] According to Dr Davies: 'It is an ideal with which Celtic readers will find themselves in sympathy.'

Her idea was expanded by another contributor, John Wilding, who proposed the establishment of a Celtic League on the same basis as the Nordic Union for pursuing the Scandinavian experiment in Celtic terms.[17] He suggested a detailed set of proposals as to how such a Celtic League could be organized:

> The potential of the Celtic countries united in a League is boundless, even greater than any other European large country such as France or even England. But if the Celtic nations are not united in a League and each goes its own way, their potential is worth nil. Therefore in future we may hear more Celts demanding their respective national parties to include in their party programme support for the formation of a 'League of Celtic Nations' when independence is reached![18]

However, the major independence parties such as Plaid Cymru, the Scottish National Party, even Irish parties such as MacBride's Clann na Poblachta, which was the most sympathetic to Pan Celticism and had welcomed Welsh and Scottish delegates at its 1951 Ard-Fhéis or annual convention, steered well clear of any Celtic dimensions to their political programmes. Only some minority parties, such as the Welsh Republican Movement, maintained support for Pan Celticism in their official manifestos.

As noted previously, one of the ideas given prominence in *An Aimsir* was Charles de Gaulle's original idea of developing a Celtic *lingua franca* as a means of communication between all six Celtic peoples, based on one or all of the Celtic languages. The Celts of Ireland, Scotland, Isle of Man, Wales and Cornwall found, like it or not, that they shared English as a *lingua franca*. This, however, excluded Brittany. Celtic-minded Bretons found themselves having to learn English as a means of communication with their fellow Celts on a general basis, unless they were sufficiently linguistically-minded to learn the other five languages. Additionally, many did not speak their own Celtic language fluently. Nor could the five Celtic nationalities in the English orbit expect to gain a complete knowledge of what was happening in Brittany with a knowledge of Breton only. A knowledge of French was also needed.

The arguments for adopting a 'Celtic Esperanto' began when Aodh MacAinmire echoed de Gaulle's original proposal in 'A rallying language for the Celts'.[19] MacAinmire believed, however, that the Celts should adopt Irish as a general means of communication, and failed to see the 'cultural imperialism' of his proposal. A more considered article was contributed to *An Aimsir* by Eoghan Ó Faircheallaigh in 'Language and Inter Celtic Relations'.[20] His idea was that the two linguistic groups – Brythonic and Goidelic – be drawn together by the production of basic words, sentences and essential grammatical forms, and that speakers could learn one composite language from both groups.

The suggestion provoked a series of articles by Don S. Piatt, a translator working for the Dáil (Irish Parliament). The series was entitled 'The basic unity of the Celtic languages'.[21]

The articles were not an attempt to create a Basic Celtic but to make a comparative study of the vocabulary, grammar and idiom of the Celtic languages, which illustrated their common origin.

The idea was not taken up again within the Pan Celtic movement until 1978 when Seán Ó Duinn proposed, in an article in *Carn*, 'the desirability of a common Celtic language'.[22] The proposal created some discussion. Some linguists contributed to the debate, arguing that a 'Common Celtic' could be a practical proposition.[23]

The debate went quiet for another ten years when Clifford Ifan Bere, in *Towards the political federation of Celtia* (1988), argued that standardization of the Brythonic languages and of the Goidelic languages could be a practical way of creating 'Common Celtic'.[24]

Youenn Olier, the prominent Breton writer and editor of the Breton magazine *Imbourc'h*, proposed that all Celts should learn Breton.[25] His fellow Breton, Alan Heusaff, replied that Olier had underestimated emotional factors in this proposal.[26] Dr Robert L. Thomson, the foremost Manx scholar, sought to explain the problems of switching from traditional Manx spelling to a spelling more easily recognized by the Irish and Scots.[27] The debate has not ended.

Most Celts are prepared to accept the *fait accompli* of English as a *lingua franca*. But others point out English is the language which is threatening five out of the six Celtic languages, and that to use it as a *lingua franca* is merely to reinforce its position of dominance in Celtic life.

It is obvious that the idea of a 'Common Celtic' will continue to intrigue linguistically-minded persons in the Pan Celtic movement. However, the main argument which has prevented any serious movement towards the creation of such a language so far has been the fact that the most immediate problem facing the Celtic movement is the restoration of the Celtic languages themselves. Most members of the Pan Celtic movement would agree that at this stage of its development, the idea of a 'Common Celtic' is a little too esoteric to be seriously considered.

Notes

1   *An Aimsir Cheilteach*, July, 1947.
2   *An Aimsir Cheilteach*, September, 1948.
3   *Irish Independent*, 28 September 1953
4   *Y Ddraig Goch*, April, 1947.
5   *Dundee Weekly News*, 19 December, 1947.
6   Quoted in *An Aimsir Cheilteach*, January–February, 1951.
7   *Welsh Republic*, January-February, 1951.
8   *An Aimsir Cheilteach*, July–August, 1951.
9   In conversation to author, 2 October 1989.
10 *An Aimsir Cheilteach*, December, 1947
11 *An Aimsir Cheilteach*, June, 1948.
12 The first person to be awarded the John Legonna Celtic Research Prize
    was Dr Miranda Green, tutor in Classical Studies at the Open University of
    Wales, in March 1986. The result of her researches published as *Symbol &
    Image in Celtic Religious Art* (Routledge, London, 1989).
13 *An Aimsir Cheilteach*, May, 1948.
14 *An Aimsir Cheilteach*, February, 1949.
15 *An Aimsir Cheilteach*, July–August, 1949.
16 *Five Northern Countries Pull Together* by Vegard Slettin, & *The Nordic
    Council and Cooperation in Scandinavia* by Franz Wendt (Nordic Council
    publications, 1968 edns).
17 *An Aimsir Cheilteach*, November, 1953.
18 Ibid.
19 *An Aimsir Cheilteach*, December, 1947
20 *An Aimsir Cheilteach*, August, 1948.
21 *An Aimsir* Cheilteach, December, 1948–May, 1949.
22 *Carn*, No. 22 (Summer, 1978).
23 *Carn*, No. 23 (Autumn, 1978).
24 *Towards the Political Confederation of Celtia*, Gwasg yr Ynys Newydd, Y
    Lolfa Cyf. (Talybont, Wales, 1989), pp. 12/13.
25 *Carn*, No. 65 (Spring, 1989).
26 *Carn*, No. 66 (Summer, 1989).
27 *Carn*, No. 67 (Autumn, 1989).

8: The Celtic League, 1961

W ITH the foundation of a new Celtic League during the
Eisteddfod week at Rhos, near Llangollen, in North
Wales in 1961, the most influential of the Pan Celtic movements
came into being and through the next three decades Pan
Celticism became a more widespread and convincing political
influence. While the League's main emphasis lay on the 'cultural
question', which it saw as the move to reverse the 'cultural
conquest' of the Celtic peoples, it translated this into a political
programme, a programme which included the aim of achieving
self-government for the Celtic countries and, moreover, a formal
association between them.[1]

With the demise of *An Aimsir* in 1954, apart from the regular
meetings of the Celtic Congress, there had been no central
rallying point for Pan Celticism. In the late 1950s a quarterly
journal called *Celtic Voice* was launched by a Scot named Alistair
Graham, but the journal concentrated on the issue that nuclear
bases and power-stations were being sited in Celtic areas. The
journal was part of the Campaign for Nuclear Disarmament
rather than a vehicle for the Pan Celtic ideology.

The meeting in Wales on 9 August 1961 was organized by a
Breton exile living in Ireland, Alan Heusaff. Alan Heusaff was
born on 23 July 1921, in Sant Ivi, Cornouaille, Brittany. He
was a native Breton speaker who learnt French only when he
went to school, after which he trained as a primary school teacher.
A member of the Breton National Party from 1938, he gave up
his teaching post to become an instructor in the Breton Special
Service and then, at only twenty-two years of age, he joined

the Bezen Perrot, in 1943. While not a supporter of Fascism, Heusaff had been persuaded that Brittany would have to fight for her independence and Bezen Perrot seemed to offer the only opportunity to do this at the time. At the end of the war he was sentenced to death *in absentia*. Heusaff arrived in Ireland in 1950, and completed a course in physics at the National University before joining the Irish Meteorological Service in 1952. He became a fluent Irish speaker, marrying Bríd Ní Dhochartaigh, a native speaker from Conamara, herself a graduate and active in the Irish language movement. Heusaff edited *Argoad*, a Breton news bulletin, and was a contributor to Breton language magazines such as *Hor Yezh* and *Al Liamm*. During the 1960s he also edited *Breton News*. He became an active member of Conradh na Gaeilge and served on its executive committee. His work was recognized by Ireland with the presentation of the Pearse Award by the then President of the Irish Republic, Dr Patrick Hilary – and he was honoured by the Welsh Gorsedd through inauguration as a Bard (Gwyddnerth).

Curiously enough, Heusaff's basic reason for proposing a new Pan Celtic organization more political in tone than the Celtic Congress was the fear of a new French repression in Brittany. There was a need to have an organization able to alert international opinion:

> The basic reason why I proposed the setting up of the organization to a few correspondents… was that in 1960–61 things were stirring in Brittany (farmers in revolt), which led me to hope that the (Breton) national movement might gain a new momentum. But this could lead again to French repression – it was important that in such an event an organization existed ready to mobilize international opinion, particularly among Celts anywhere in the world.
>
> The idea of an inter Celtic structure should (I thought) appeal to all Celtic nationalists since the Celts – each nation – were numerically small in the modern world and we had enough common points to be able to gain from maximizing contacts and

cooperation. It would have to be nationally-minded, committed to the languages, neutral in religious matters (not to be a vehicle for a 'Celtic religion' either) – capable of rallying people with different views on social matters (Right and Left). It should involve its members, but at the same time aim at being a link between the national parties and organizations of the different countries.[2]

Many of those who attended the first inaugural meeting in 1961 were former readers, and often contributors, to *An Aimsir*. There is some confusion as to who actually attended this first meeting. Among the founders was J.E. Jones, former general secretary of Plaid Cymru. 'J.E.' (1906–1970) was a veteran Pan Celt. According to Yann Fouéré, Professor Per Denez, later head of the Celtic Department at Rennes, also attended with Gwynfor Evans.[3] Heusaff also remembers Elwyn Roberts, then treasurer of Plaid Cymru, attending with Séamas Filbin and Alan Niven of Scotland.[4]

The aims of the Celtic League were to be:

> 1. to foster cooperation between the national movements in the Celtic countries, particularly in efforts to obtain international recognition of our national rights.
> 2. to share the experience of our national struggles and exchange constructive ideas.

Alan Heusaff was elected General Secretary, a position he held until 1985, while Gwynfor Evans, president of Plaid Cymru, was elected president of the League. Dr Noëlle Davies was elected treasurer. *Celtic Voice* was offered as a means of propagating the League. By the second annual meeting, on 30 September 1962, branches of the League had been established in all six Celtic countries as well as among Celtic exiles in London. By this time it was decided that the League could launch its own journal – *Celtic News*, edited by Welsh historian, Dr Ceinwen Thomas, of University College, Cardiff. It was decided that the League would publish an annual volume, the first of which appeared in 1963, also edited by Dr Ceinwen Thomas.

The annual volumes constituted substantial books averaging

Alan Heusaff (left) receives a copy of For A Celtic future, *published in honour of his long service to the Celtic League, from its editor Cathal Ó Luain, chairman of the League. Alan's wife, Bríd, looks on.*

Gwynfor Evans, President of the Celtic League from 1961-1971, who became Plaid Cymru's first Member of Parliament in 1966.

up to 180 pages. Most of the League's early finances went into the production of these volumes and members of the League, such as J.E. Jones, argued that publication should be the main function of the League. Dr Thomas, meanwhile, resigned as editor of the annual volume with the 1965 volume and George Thomas, then secretary of the Scottish Branch, who was to become an SNP MP in 1974–79, took over the editorship. Irish historian and writer Nollaig Ó Gadhra edited the 1967 volume and then, with the 1968 volume, Scottish editor and author, Frank Thompson, became editor until 1972. By the end of 1963, editorship of *Celtic News* was taken over by Pádraig Ó Conchúir. He remained editor until its demise in 1972. When a more professionally produced journal, *Carn*, was launched in Spring 1973, Frank Thompson was the first editor.

The annual volumes of the Celtic League contain a fascinating treasury of articles and papers on Pan Celticism by many diverse personalities ranging from politicians such as Dr Garrett Fitzgerald, at the time a Fine Gael Senator (he became Prime Minister of the Irish Republic in 1981),[5] to Winifred Ewing, then an SNP MP at Westminster (now an SNP Euro-MP), to prominent academics, poets, writers, artists and other leading figures in Celtic life.

Vice-Presidents of the League were also elected from each of the Celtic nations, being leaders of some of the main political national parties. These were Dr Yann Fouéré, president of the Mouvement Pour ·l'Organisation de la Bretagne; Dr Robert MacIntyre, of the Scottish National Party, who had been SNP's first elected Member of Parliament for Motherwell in 1945, and Robert Dunstone, the president of Mebyon Kernow, the Cornish national movement, formed in 1951. Mebyon Kernow had won its first election in 1953 when Helena Charles took a seat on the local Redruth Council. By 1963 the League was viable enough to make its world political debut. In June it gave evidence to the European Commission of Human Rights concerning the persecution of the Breton language. Its international status meant there was international media interest in the situation.[6] The League was also able to send an official delegation to the Fourteenth Congress of the Federal Union of European Nationalities on 11–14 June at Regensburg, Bavaria. In November 1965, the League delivered a 62-page memorandum, arguing the case for self-government for the Celtic countries, to the United Nations Organization in New York. The basis of this UNO Memorandum was published in the 1964/5 Annual Volume of the League edited by Dr Ceinwen Thomas, Dublin, 1965.[7] In addition, an examination was made by the Irish author Risteárd Ó Glaisne of the Partition of Ireland. Ó Glaisne, a graduate of Trinity College, Dublin, was both a Protestant and a republican as well as a highly respected writer in the Irish language. In 1966 the League also distributed copies of its memorandum on self-government to all members of the Council of Europe.

That the League had grown swiftly was seen at the 1966 annual meeting in Dublin, when 150 delegates attended, representing a membership of nearly 5,000. That year, during the same week that the League was meeting, the first meeting of a Celtic Youth Congress was held, organized by some of the younger members of the League. The Youth Congress was to exist for six years and sought to affiliate with the League. The Youth Congress believed in its members taking 'direct action', giving support, for example, to the 'civil disobedience' campaigns of Cymdeithas yr Iaith Gymraeg (Welsh Language Society) and Misneach (Courage), the Irish language group. The League, under Gwynfor Evans' influence, had an official policy of peaceful and constitutional protest. Indeed, during this time, the League was very much an appendage of the constitutional, pacifist policies of Plaid Cymru, which was also greatly influenced by its president Gwynfor Evans. It was decided that the two organizations, the League and Youth Congress, would remain independent from each other.[8] The Celtic Youth Congress produced a *Bulletin* during its five or six years of existence, edited by Tecwyn Evans. However, no library seems to have kept a run of this publication.

With Gwynfor Evans' election to Westminster in July 1966, the ensuing publicity gave a boost to League membership. He told the League, shortly after his election:

> The whole of the Celtic fraternity of nations is thus involved in a process of creative development and we can look forward to playing a far more significant part on the human stage than we have in recent centuries. All in all, the signs of a Celtic Renaissance are multiplying.[9]

The election of the president of the Celtic League to Parliament was reinforced by the election of the lawyer Winifred Ewing as Scottish National Party MP for Hamilton on 2 November 1967. She, also, contributed to the League's publications.

A further boost was given on BBC Radio 3 when the Celtic scholar Dr Anne Ross presented a series of eight programmes on 'The Celts' which, primarily concerned with the ancient Celts, did point out the contemporary situation and problems facing them.[10] By the end of the 1960s, thanks to the publicity generated by the Celtic League, Pan Celticism was no longer the province of a small group of middle class intellectuals; it was much more in the public domain as an issue. Numerous studies, both for and against, were being published in various journals, newspapers and in book form.

In November 1968, Routledge and Kegan Paul published the volume of essays entitled *Celtic Nationalism* which, they maintained, presented 'an insight into the factors, both political and cultural, which have led to the present upsurge of Celtic nationalist feeling'.[11] This work, however, singularly failed to address the main issues of Pan Celticism and confined itself simply to studying the cultural and political problems within each individual Celtic country.

One examination by William Greenberg, an English political pundit, *The flags of the forgotten: nationalism on the Celtic fringe,* was fairly typical of the confused attitudes which English political observers had to Pan Celticism.[12] It did contain a foreword by the Tory MP, Sir Gerald Nabarro, who correctly observed: 'The Celtic nationalists are no temporary phenomenon. They are here to stay.'[13]

But the author of *The flags of the forgotten* obviously had little grasp of the realities of the Celtic world. His book was full of prejudiced naïveté as seen, for example, when he interviewed Wing Commander Roy MacDonald RAF (Retired), who was then a Member of the Manx House of Keys (Parliament) and spokesman on behalf of Mec Vannin. MacDonald was also a Pan Celt. Greenberg observed: 'Wing Commander MacDonald would never be taken for a Celtic nationalist visionary.' One wondered what Greenberg thought a Celtic nationalist looked like. It appears that he thought them 'Anglophobic wildmen', 'mystic visionaries', and 'scruffy beatniks'. He found MacDonald to be a practical Manx politician. Greenberg reported that MacDonald expected 'international pressure to be brought to bear on behalf of the Manx by their fellow members of the Celtic Congress (sic) that works from Dublin – the Irish, the Scots, the Cornish and the Bretons'. He forgot the Welsh and, obviously, the purely academic Celtic Congress was not the body Greenberg meant. He was referring to the Celtic League. 'The effectiveness of the help they can give each other is apparently not to be despised', Greenberg warned. He believed that the 'Celtic Congress' 'was able to deliver the Irish vote in the Hamilton constituency to Mrs Winifred Ewing in the sensational 1967 by-election'. This was obviously a piece of Celtophobic fantasy.

But William Greenberg was not alone in being ignorant of Celtic affairs. As noted earlier, *The Times* in 1970 assured its readers that the Celts were extinct and left no written records. The fact that there has been a thriving literature in the Celtic languages for nearly 11,500 years seemed unknown to *The Times* as did the fact that some Celtic literary remains date to the third century BC, and the fact that Irish is regarded by academics in the field as containing Europe's oldest vernacular literature.

By now the political Pan Celts were returning to the debates of *An Aimsir* in seeking a clear political set of aims. It was clear, at this stage, that most members of the League saw themselves as left-wing, progressive anti-imperialists. In 1969 *The creed of the Celtic revolution* (Medusa Press) argued, in a clearly socialist framework, that independent Celtic countries should adopt the Scandinavian rôle model.[14] Its publication created much discussion.[15]

The English socialist historian, F.A. Ridley, commented: 'I do not think that I exaggerate in saying that *The creed of the Celtic revolution* marks the commencement of a new era in the cultural and political evolution of these islands.'[16]

However, 1969 saw the League go into a crisis. Gwynfor Evans MP, speaking to an audience of 2,000 at the League's Dublin annual meeting that year, talked about a 'British Federation' as a solution for Celtic problems. He dismissed the Civil Rights struggle in the Partitioned Six Counties of Ireland as 'merely sectarian' and went on to accuse the Breton movement, then undergoing a new repression by the French authorities, of bringing it on themselves by their recourse to acts of violence.[17] It had become clear that Gwynfor Evans was using the League as another platform for his Plaid Cymru policies. But he was speaking as president of the League and not as a Plaid Cymru MP. The Irish and Breton reaction was predictable. Their branches seemed about to break away from the League in disgust.[18] Indeed, Bernadette Devlin, the newly elected fiery MP for Mid-Ulster, attending the League's annual meeting, asked: 'Does it (the League) have any relevance?' While the respected Irish poet and playwright Caitlín Maude (1941–1981) made a blistering denunciation of Gwynfor Evans' attitude. Jakez Derouet, the Breton secretary, announced that he and his membership felt that they should disband the Breton branch as it was clear from what Mr Evans said that the League was not understanding of, nor helpful to, them and their problems. Even the General Secretary, Alan Heusaff, seriously considered his position within the League.[19]

Gwynfor Evans could not have been unaware of his audience's likely reaction to his comments on Northern Ireland and Brittany.

The campaign for Civil Rights for Catholics in the Partitioned North of Ireland had been met, during 1968 and 1969, with a fierce backlash by Protestant mobs, urged on by the Unionist Government in Stormont. Only a few weeks before Gwynfor Evans' address at the Celtic League AGM in Dublin, Harold Wilson's Labour Government had been forced to send in British troops to 'protect' the Catholics, although within a year, following the election of Edward Heath's Conservative Government, the rôle of the troops was inevitably changed to supporting the Unionists and the harassment of the nationalist population. British troops were to be part of the problem, as they had always been, and not part of the solution.

The Celtic League had supported the struggle for Civil Rights. Its president was well aware of the problem of Partition and, indeed, had been active in the Anti-Partition League in the late 1940s. To dismiss the Civil Rights struggle then in progress as nothing more than a 'sectarian disturbance' was an unwise choice of words to a majority Irish audience in Dublin.

Similarly, to blame the Bretons for the French repression they were then suffering was also unwise. At the time he was speaking, some forty Bretons were still in jail. Many of them had been held for nearly a year without charge or trial, on suspicion of being involved with the Front for the Liberation of Brittany. At the beginning of the year there had been sixty such political prisoners in French jails. On their release it was revealed that many had been severely beaten and otherwise ill-treated while in prison.

Throughout 1967 there had been many riots and demonstrations against the French Government's poor administration in Brittany. As protests had little effect, the shadowy FLB emerged, placing bombs (neither primed nor fused) in prefectures and tax offices with warnings that such bombs could easily be detonated if the National Assembly refused to listen to Breton grievances. The trigger point was General de Gaulle's provocative speech supporting the Québecqois nationalists in their campaign to separate from Canada – it being made at the same time as his Government were stamping on the rights of the small nation of Brittany. The General, ironically the nephew of the great nineteenth-century Pan Celt, was to make his notorious 'Vive Québec libre' speech in Montréal.

FLB launched a series of attacks on the French National Grid system during the months of July and August 1968. A four page manifesto was published by the FLB National Council, stating the socialist and anti-imperialist nature of their struggle. By 1969 some thirty-three successful attacks had been carried out: fourteen against tax offices, eight against administrative buildings, five against electrical installations, three against gendarmeries, two against water supplies and one against a military establishment. But events in Brittany were over-shadowed by the students' uprising in Paris.

By June 1969, public opinion, to which the Celtic League contributed, had led to the release of a third of the sixty Bretons who had been arrested by the French police. The authorities realized that they were heading for a major confrontation with the Bretons among whom there was widespread support for the FLB. Those arrested came from a surprising diversity of backgrounds; there were factory workers, farmers, university lecturers, military officers, artists, writers, businessmen and even four priests.[20]

Gwynfor Evans could not have been unaware of the alienation his remarks would cause in condemning the Breton movement. But the central point of his speech, the proposal of a British federation of nations, suggesting even that the Irish republic might rejoin, with England in such a federation, which,

149

of course, had no place for the Bretons, caused the Celtic League to be shaken to its ideological roots.

Matters simmered for a while after reassurances to the membership were made by the executive officers of the League. Indeed, the 1969 annual meeting, in spite of the President's remarks, passed a resolution expressing full support for the Civil Rights campaign in Northern Ireland. Moreover, official delegates were sent to a defiantly open meeting of the Front for the Liberation of Brittany, attended by 3,000 delegates on 14 November in Paris. The Bretons had decided to lay down a challenge to the French authorities by making FLB an open, mass movement. Even members of the French Socialist and Communist Parties attended and expressed their support for the Bretons.[21] An official spokesman for the League also attended and spelt out the League's aims.

But a clear weakness had been revealed in the League. The League was an organization concerned with six different nations and many differing political opinions. The office of President was occupied by a man who was leader and Member of Parliament for one particular political party. Instead of speaking for the League, Gwynfor Evans had been speaking for his own party policies of the time. Alan Heusaff later reflected that the League at the time aimed:

> ... at being a link between the national parties, but we maintained the line that we should avoid attacking the parties, so as to maintain their good will towards us. Our Welsh friends took that too far, however, tending to make the League a mere adjunct of the Blaid, which would deprive it of its freedom to take a stand on such matters as Human Rights in northern Ireland. This led to us taking a more independent position in the early 1970s.[22]

At the 1971 annual meeting in Glasgow, the turning point to the problem was reached. The constitution was changed so that the vice-presidential offices were abolished, whereby the links with specific national parties were dropped. The presidential office was made subject to annual election by the membership when it was pointed out that the constitution did not allow for this. The then Welsh branch secretary took this change of constitution as a personal attack on Gwynfor Evans, resigned and, on returning to Wales, attempted to set up an alternative Inter Celtic Movement which was not successful. During 1971/72 the Welsh branch ceased to function but a new secretary reconstituted it, fully subscribing to the League's constitution, and it was active again by the end of 1972.

J.E. Jones, the founder of the Welsh Branch and, as mentioned previously, one of the founder members of the League, had died from a heart attack on 30 May 1970.[23] The loss of 'J.E.'s' stabilizing influence was the main factor causing the disintegration of the Welsh branch. Branch records were lost and the branch had to be rebuilt from nothing during 1972 by J.G. Jones, and Meic Pattison of University College, Bangor.

The office of president was officially abolished in 1972 and that of chairman was established. Pádraig Ó Conchúir was elected and held the chairmanship for the next nine years. Pádraig Ó Conchúir was a graduate of University College, Galway, an Irish language teacher, and a member of Conradh na Gaeilge, the Irish Text Society, Irish Literary Society and other groups. He had been a Pan Celticist since the days of *An Aimsir*. He had edited *Celtic News* from 1966–1972 and held numerous branch offices in London.

Gwynfor Evans later admitted:

My personal interest in the League stemmed from an interest in the Celtic countries and particularly what we had in common in our history and culture as nations which had shared the great Celtic civilization which was dominant in Europe in 5–300 BC.

I have no Pan Celtic philosophy, but I have always wanted the Celtic countries to mix up more, to come closer together in a Celtic community of nations. I have not thought that a political structure for this is possible, although there can be political cooperation as there is in the SNP-Plaid Cymru alliance.[24]

The League was now moving officially to a left-of-centre position in political outlook.

Two more important aims were added to the League's constitution. Jakez Derouet and Cathal Ó Luain were instrumental in achieving this expression of 'social commitment' to be found in the League's constitution:

> 3. encouraging acceptance of the need for a formal association of the Celtic nations once two or more of them have attained independence.
> 4. advocating the use of the natural resources of each Celtic country for the benefit of all its people.

After 1972, the annual volume was no longer published but *Celtic News* was relaunched into a bigger and more professional campaigning publication called *Carn*, with the first issue dated Spring 1973. *Carn* has now become the oldest regularly published Pan Celtic journal. Its editors have been the Scottish author Frank G. Thompson (issues 1–4, 1973/74); the Irish poet, critic and author Pádraig Ó Snodaigh (issues 5–18, 1974/77), Irish writer and academic, Cathal Ó Luain (issues 19–38, 1977/81); Cornish political activist, Pedyr Pryor (issues 39–45, 1981/84); and Patricia Bridson (issue 46, 1984 onwards). Patricia Bridson, a Manxwoman and teacher, living in Dublin, has been the longest serving editor of *Carn* to date.

Individual branches were also publishing their own publications. *Omma* and *Phoenix* were published by the Cornish Branch; *A' Bhratach Ur* (The New Banner) was a very successful Scottish Branch publication from 1971–74. The Manx produced Celtic League and AMA News during the late 1970s into the 1980s, while the American Branch launched a prestigious magazine called *Keltoi* in 1988. London, also, produces a *Newsletter*.

Released of ties to the main national political parties, such as Plaid Cymru, the League commenced its second decade of existence with a clearer sense of political purpose and what it had to achieve. Its constitutional aims were eventually altered to make a clear statement of intent outlined in Article 1:

1. The fundamental aim of the Celtic League is to support, through peaceful means, the struggle of the Celtic nations, Brittany, Cornwall, Ireland, Mann, Scotland and Wales, to win or secure the political, cultural, social and economic freedom they need for their survival and development as distinct communities. This includes:

a) working towards the restoration of the Celtic languages, which are essential characteristics of nationality for each Celtic country, as ordinary means of communication;

b) developing the consciousness of the special relationship existing between the Celtic peoples;

c) fostering cooperation and solidarity between them;

d) making our national struggles and achievements better known abroad;

e) furthering the establishment of organized relations between the Celtic nations, based on their recognition as distinct nations, and with the long-term aim of formal associations between them;

f) recognizing that the Celtic peoples will be free only in a society which will give all the means to participate actively in the national affairs and the exploitation of national resources for the benefit of all.

The Celtic League had now overtaken the older Celtic Congress as the more dynamic and influential Pan Celtic movement. It was invited to the World Peace Conference in Moscow in October 1973, to present its case.[25]

However, its members were also busy setting up 'organized relations' between Celtic groups and were attempting the creation of infrastructures which could be used for future 'formal relations' between independent Celtic countries. These were seen as necessary first steps not only in their own right but in order to further the political programme of the League. In May 1971, Celtic League members were instrumental in organizing the first Pan Celtic Festival in Killarney, which, as observed earlier, has now grown into one of the premier music festivals in the Celtic world.[26] So successful was this festival that it was followed by the establishment of another music festival at Lorient in Brittany, the Inter-Celtic Festival, which, as also observed

Front cover of the Pan Celtic journal.

The flags of the six Celtic nations are carried through the streets of Lorient in Brittany at the commencement of the annual Inter-Celtic Festival.

earlier, began to attract huge audiences. The organizations running these festivals produced their own publications such as *Pan Celtic News* and *News from the Celtic Nations*.

Musically, Pan Celticism had always attracted the romantic in composers. Among the earliest to be attracted by the idea of Pan Celticism was Arnold Bax (1883–1953). Although born in London, Bax went to live in Ireland in 1902. and became a friend of many Irish Pan Celts. He wrote poetry under the name 'Dermot O'Byrne' and his music is regarded as making him the premier composer of the 'Celtic Renaissance' of the day. He died in Cork in 1953.

During the 1970s the idea of Pan Celticism won over Alan Stivell, folk/rock musician, whose popularity throughout the world, with his new brand of 'Celtic music', had a tremendous influence on the younger generation from the USA to the then Soviet Union. Works such as 'Pop Plinn', 'Suite Armoricaine' and his 'Symphonie Celtique' have become highly regarded. Stivell told *Le Peuple Breton*:

> I am interested in Celtic music. In order to recognize what is Celtic music, to throw it into relief, one has to familiarize oneself with the music of the Irish, Scottish and Bretons, and distinguish what is Celtic in them... We can afford to lose certain elements but others are essential and must be preserved. Celtic music must continue to exist. This requires us to keep what is strong and common to the Celtic countries.
>
> Pan Celticism is a quite concrete proposition. Music is not its only aspect. A synthesis of all aspects will create a Celtic culture...[27]

Indeed, there was, throughout the 1970s, a new resurgence in Celtic music, which had been launched by the composer Seán Ó Riada (1931–71). He trained 'classically' in Paris, but had rediscovered the traditional music of Ireland and launched the Ceoltoirí Cualann at the 1961 Dublin Theatre Festival, which had a dramatic effect on young Celtic musicians. To the new 'Celtic form' were attracted individuals such as Dafydd Iwan, Glenmor, Brenda Wooton, and bands such as Ossian, The

Chieftains (renamed from Ó Riada's group the Ceoltoirí), Run Rig and Ar Log among others.

Currently there has been a popularization of Celtic art. The first major authoritative study of Celtic art had been made by Paul Jacobsthal in 1944. The Scottish artist George Bain produced *Celtic art: the methods of construction*, in 1951, which is still one of the bestselling books in the field. The work of Dublin artist Jim Fitzpatrick started to hold popular attention in the mid-1970s. He was the first artist to adopt the Celtic myths in comic strip form and ran, for a while, a series called 'Nuada of the Silver Arm'. Since the 1980s, the fascination with Celtic art has created a small industry in the publication of Celtic art books on both sides of the Atlantic. From the 1980s, one of the most exciting and original talents in the reinterpretation of ancient Celtic art works has been the Welsh artist, Courtney Davies.

Such interests also went hand in hand with a rebirth of interest in fiction based on Celtic themes, especially in works rooted in history and mythology. Nowhere was there more activity in producing such works than among fantasy writers, on both sides of the Atlantic, who began to delve into the vast corpus of Celtic myths and legends for inspiration.

This new Celtic fascination emerged in the wake of the emergence of the Celtic League and the start of its activities designed to draw attention to the Celtic world.

New branches of the League were also being formed; an American Branch, a branch in Cape Breton, Nova Scotia, and an International Branch covering those who wanted to join but who did not live in an existing branch area. A Celtic League of Australia was also formed and affiliated to the League, and then an Australian Celtic Council.

A former *An Aimsir* reader, Pádraig Ó Broin, had formed a Canadian Celtic Congress during the 1950s and issued a magazine entitled *Teangadoir* (The Linguist) which ran to thirty issues, ceasing publication in May 1960. It carried material in all six Celtic languages. With the rise of the League, the Canadian

Celtic Congress was resuscitated and affiliated. The London Branch became the first international branch, however, and was formed in 1961 under the guidance of Pádraig Ó Conchúir. The New York Branch was formed in 1969. The general International Branch was formed in the mid-1980s while the Cape Breton (Nova Scotia) Branch was formed in 1988. (Scottish Gaelic has been spoken on Cape Breton Island as a first language since the time of the Highland Clearances in the late eighteenth century.) Nova Scotia, during the nineteenth and early twentieth centuries, was the centre of publishing in Scots Gaelic at the time the language was suppressed in Scotland. Groups such as the Australian Celtic Council, and Real Associacioñ Céltica (Buenos Aires, Argentina) are among several bodies affiliated to the League. The Celtic Society of Japan celebrated its twelfth annual congress in 1992.

The Celtic Congress was given new impetus by the League's dynamism. On 13 August 1974, 1,700 delegates attended the Congress in Nantes and departed from the usual academic programme by adopting a 'Charter of Cultural Rights' asking for the recognition of the languages and cultures of the Celtic peoples by the UK and French Governments. At the same time the League were submitting proposals regarding the weak, indeed, almost non-existent, position of broadcasting in the Celtic languages to the Committee on the Future of Broadcasting under Lord Annan.

It was at this time that the English Press and media singled out the League as an object of attack. The 1975 annual meeting in Peel, Isle of Man, found itself being slurred by the London *Guardian*. A militant Manx movement named Fo Halloo (Underground) had been active at this time, daubing Manx slogans and putting up posters, and issuing a regular newsheet which made allegations of corruption in the Tynwald and Athol Street (the Manx financial centre in Douglas). An arson campaign was laid at its door by government spokesmen but it was never proved that the movement was responsible. Fo Halloo appeared as a popular movement with popular support, which allowed it to sustain a vigorous campaign of action until the 1976 General Election on the Island in which Mec Vannin won its first seat (in a Manx Labour Party stronghold) and took 13 p.c. of the poll. Concessions were made to some of Fo Halloo's demands and the movement disappeared. The *Guardian*'s comment, at the time of the Celtic League's annual general meeting, was:

> The youthful Manx underground will be seeking fresh impetus from the more experienced Celtic campaigners amid a debate centering on the question of a Pan Celtic federation, economically and politically independent from the United Kingdom and France.[28]

This was a clear inference that the League was involved in criminal activities, in the arson attacks being laid at the door of Fo Halloo. Pádraig Ó Conchuir, as chairman of the League, wrote to the *Guardian* officially refuting such an inference. The *Guardian* refused to publish his letter and only after a telephone call and a further letter, one with a threat of legal action, was the original letter published on 17 October, just over a month after the offensive article – too late for the correction to be effective.

The next year the BBC attacked the League, this time with a precise but entirely false allegation. An attempted arson attack had been made against the French consulate in Edinburgh. A man named McGuigan was arrested. According to BBC Radio Scotland, on 24 September 1976 McGuigan had stated in court that 'the person who had incited him to set fire to the French consulate in Edinburgh was Alan Heusaff, General Secretary of the Celtic League'. It was claimed that McGuigan had set fire to the consulate because the French had imprisoned some Bretons and 'he had been asked to help by the secretary of the Celtic League' in a campaign to seek their release. Indeed, the Celtic League were running a publicity campaign to bring attention to the plight of the Bretons.

The fact was that McGuigan had told the court that he had

responded to a Celtic League general public appeal to bring attention to the plight of the Breton prisoners and he, of his own volition, had felt that his attack on the consulate was a way of doing so. But the BBC report had distorted what McGuigan had said, implicating Alan Heusaff and the League in a spurious criminal plot. A denial from Heusaff and the League was immediately forthcoming on 30 September. This was not acknowledged by the BBC nor, after a subsequent letter and reference to what was on record as being said in court, did they either acknowledge their misreport or redress its effect by refuting it.[29]

A statement to the Press, giving the correction, was not published in any Scottish newspaper. The *Irish Press* was among those who carried it. Heusaff emphasized:

> I wish to state that the Celtic League, an open organization set up to promote inter Celtic solidarity and understanding, confines itself to legal activities.[30]

Due to the slurs, innuendos and misreporting, a section of the general public began to see Celtic League members as some sort of 'fringe fanatics' who supported political violence. But in spite of the misrepresentation in the Press and media, the Celtic League continued to grow in influence among the Celtic populations.

It was during the 1980s that a veritable industry of research and writing activity produced books on the Celts ranging across archaeology, history, art, music, language, literature and religion, and this activity began to spread the idea of 'Celticism' and 'Pan Celticism' to a wider audience, not only in the Celtic countries but wherever Celtic migrants gathered. Many of these works were optimistic about the future of the Celts, such as the League's own 332-page volume *For a Celtic future*, edited by Cathal Ó Luain (1984), and C.I. Bere's *Towards the political confederation of Celtia* (1988). But the majority of them were pessimistic and more like obituaries for the Celtic world, such as Dr Durkacz's *The decline of the Celtic languages* (1983).

One of the most impressive volumes produced was *Celtic*

The flags of the six Celtic nations at the 1990 annual dinner of the American Branch of the League

Ron Stewart, a Welshman who organized the early Celtic Film and Television Festivals, which started in 1979.

consciousness. It was a large illustrated book of over 700 pages. It was edited by Dr Robert O'Driscoll, then head of the Celtic Department at St Michael's College, University of Toronto. The book was published by McClelland and Stewart (Toronto, 1981). This volume went into other editions in the USA and Ireland. If there was a criticism levelled at it, it could be argued that O'Driscoll threw in everything except the kitchen sink, but failed to examine the rise of the various Pan Celtic movements as an ongoing historical process. It was more a reflection of individual views and ideas.

The authors of these works, in speaking of Pan Celticism, ranged from those who subscribed to the League's aims to those who simply accepted the linguistic relationship between the Celts but would not be drawn into any other conclusions about cultural identity and political purpose in the modern world.

There seemed no stopping the creation of various cultural Pan Celtic organizations inspired by the League's activities. The establishment in 1979 of the Celtic Film and Television Festival, organized by the Association for Film and Television in the Celtic Countries, whose chief organizer at the time was Welsh-born Ron Stewart, an early supporter of the Celtic League and contributor to *Carn*, was an important event which opened Pan Celticism to a large world audience. This continues as an important window on Celtic cultural life.

Pan Celticism was now being discussed in the English media in a more serious fashion. Previously media commentators would attempt to equate Pan Celts with esoteric religiousness, or people waiting for King Arthur to reawaken and lead the Celts to a glorious new 'Golden Age'.[31] The first serious media examination was a series of programmes broadcast in January 1981 called 'The Celtic Connection' (BBC1 'Nationwide'). Then came a series on Channel 4 TV called 'How to be Celtic', which comprised five programmes shown through September 1983.[32] These programmes endeavoured to present the Celt to the non-Celt. The response to such programmes undoubtedly led BBC2 to start work on a series of six fifty-five minute programmes called 'The Celts', presented by Frank Delaney and shown during prime-time viewing in 1986.

The programmes, in spite of the involvement of Celtic scholars, were full of many elementary mistakes and succeeded in presenting a highly colourful but utterly confusing picture of modern Celts as fey mystics, given to composing poetry and dreaming impossible dreams.

Yet in spite of such programmes, gradually, through the Press and media, the public, both within the Celtic countries and outside, were being shown a new image of the Celts and were accepting that there existed a serious political intent for self-government and cultural fulfilment.

Celtic Vision, established in 1982, was another Pan Celtic venture, this time aimed at promoting Celtic art exhibitions, of both ancient and modern artists. Scríf-Celt, held under the auspices of the Celtic League in April 1985, was the first Celtic languages book fair. Some seventy-two Celtic language publishers exhibited. It was a one day affair but so successful was it that in 1986 it was expanded to a two day fair.[33]

In November 1965, the League had presented its memorandum to the United Nations which, among other things, outlined the cultural problems facing the Celts. The League continued to lobby UNESCO and found support with the Irish National Commission who, in May 1980, proposed a resolution which sought the active support of UNESCO to back a campaign for the promotion of the Celtic languages and their cultures. After discussions, which lasted until 1982, UNESCO established a Project for the Study and Promotion of Celtic Cultures.[34] A UNESCO *Celtic Cultures Newsletter* was launched in June 1983. The *Newsletter* paid tribute to the League for bringing the UNESCO project into existence.[35]

It can be argued that the success of the League in these three decades lies mainly in 'developing the consciousness of the special relationship existing between the Celtic peoples' (Article 1b of its constitution). Through the establishment of musical events, film and television exposure, literary, arts and educational festivals and gatherings, an informed awareness of Pan Celticism has become general in the Celtic countries.

The literature produced on Pan Celticism by Pan Celtic organizations and groups has been considerable during these decades. In addition to the League's own journal *Carn*, and journals produced by its various branches, many other Pan Celtic journals have been launched in the Celtic countries and among the countries of the Celtic diaspora.[36]

Several academic studies discussing Celtic nationalism seem to miss the essence of the phenomenon entirely. Professor Michael Hechter of the University of Washington (Seattle), in a lengthy study on the subject summed up his perception in these words: 'The most recent crystallization of Celtic nationalism may ultimately be understood as a trenchant critique of the principle of bureaucratic centralism.'[37] More recently, Malcolm Chapman has dismissed the concept as a 'myth'. In a study published early in 1993, provocatively called *The Celts: the construction of a myth*, he argued that modern Celticism had 'been constructed to serve the interests of a discourse external to them' (the original Celts). Chapman is not only a believer in the 'Celtic Twilight' but would welcome the onset of a 'Celtic Night' because he argues that these 'peripheral cultures' are doomed. The implication is that the sooner they vanish, the better for everyone. He also seems to have the novel idea that modern Celtic cultures are not 'authentically Celtic'. He is irritated with Celtic political movements, especially organizations such as the Celtic League and implies such movements lead to the emergence of 'terrorism'. This is like arguing that the victim not the bully is responsible for violence. Even the London *Guardian* wryly observed: 'all this reads like Conor Cruise O'Brien at his less persuasive'.

Another more helpful study towards the identification of Pan Celticism has been Jake Gaucher's *Histoire chronologique des pays celtiques*, published in French in Brittany by the Association Keltica International (1990).

As noted earlier it remains a curious fact that there have been few independent surveys of Pan Celticism, for most of the publications have emanated from those involved in the movement and not outside it.

As regards the League's relationship with other Pan Celtic organizations, individual Pan Celtic groups and organizations based in Australia, New Zealand, Argentina, etc, are affiliated to it. The League also maintains close links with other Pan Celtic movements, including the Congress. This is a tangible result of the League's campaigning rather than the combination of nearly a full century of the activities of the Celtic Congress.

This is not to detract from the continuing work within the Celtic Congress, though many Congress members and supporters are also members of the League. The Congress has become simply an annual gathering, a Pan Celtic Eisteddfod, with lectures, poetry readings and musical events. Congress, it can be argued, has given birth to many other Congresses, such as the Canadian Celtic Congress, the North American Celtic Congress and so forth.

The League has had some successes with several of its political campaigns. The achievement of persuading UNESCO to establish a project which would *promote* the Celtic languages and their cultures has already been mentioned. However, the League was instrumental in persuading the English National Trust to hand over the island bird sanctuary known as the Calf of Man to the Manx National Trust in 1986. The English National Trust had owned the small island off the south coast of Man for fifty years, in spite of the constitutional position of the Isle of Man and the fact that a Manx National Trust had come into being in 1951. The League began demonstrating outside the London National Trust Offices and took part in talks with the Trust, which immediately persuaded them to hand over the ownership of the island to their Manx counterparts.

Rather than show gratitude to the Celtic League, the Manx National Trust was highly embarrassed by the fact that since 1951 they themselves had done nothing to urge the return of the Calf of Man from the English National Trust. They blamed the League for 'interference' and refused to invite representatives of the League to the 'handing over' ceremony. This only provoked more publicity for the League and showed the Manx National Trust in a bad light.[38]

Another success, in Manx terms, came when, after the League had spent several years of protesting against the British Army base on the island, where training of the Ulster Defence Regiment was taking place, the British Army announced (in December 1988), that it was closing the base at Jurby. Yet a third success was announced in January 1991, when, after a decade of protesting to the Governments of the UK, USA, USSR, France etc about the sinking of fishing boats and other vessels in the Irish and Celtic Seas in incidents involving submarines, the British Ministry of Defence, the chief culprit, announced new guidelines for submarine commanders operating in those waters. The League had logged eighty-five incidents over 1981–90, in which fifty-nine lives had been lost. The League, initially starting out as a lone voice of protest, had, as casualties mounted, successfully persuaded representatives of many political parties to raise questions at Westminster,[39] in Tynwald and in the Dáil. One of the first Governments to make a positive response to the League's campaign was the Dutch Government. They told the League that the Royal Netherlands Navy had adopted a code of conduct for use by its submarine commanders.

The widespread publicity for the League, from Japan to Scandinavia, and from Poland to the USA, as well as in the United Kingdom, enhanced the image of the League as a progressive, campaigning movement.[40]

It can be argued that the League's successes are not uniquely 'Celtic', that such successes could have been achieved by other groups not supporting the 'Pan Celtic' idea. On the other hand, the successes have relied on peoples from the different Celtic countries working together on a common project. Herein is one of the 'hidden' but important successes of the League. The League has been able to gather six disparate peoples and bring them together in an international organization working for a common goal. Celtic individualism has become a stereotypical joke among people both inside and outside the Celtic countries. Among the English, the idea of Celts agreeing on common interests has been translated to the anti-Irish racist joke: 'Put two Irishmen in Parliament and you'll have two political parties.'[41] The League has demonstrated the lie.

The League has now set up a Celtic Environmental Council to consolidate its long-term ecological involvement. The sudden death of the Cornish barrister, Paul Smales, who was the organizer of this council, on 11 September 1990, has caused the project some setback. Smales was forty-four years old, a chairman of the Cornish Bar Association, the Cornish Literary Guild and many other organizations.[42]

By 1991 the Celtic League, entering its fourth decade of existence, had moved from being regarded by the Celtic general public as a group of mainly intellectual idealists, towards being a major influence in the Celtic world. Still funded only by its membership, and staffed by volunteers, it can be seen that the League was exerting a widespread influence on Celtic opinion, creating almost single-handedly the modern attitudes towards Pan Celticism – that it has a practical and achievable set of aims. Without the dynamism of the Celtic League, acting as a catalyst in many areas of the Celtic world, the widespread acceptance, not to mention the creation of Pan Celtic infrastructures and organizations, would doubtless not exist.

The League's General Secretaries have been: Alan Heusaff (1961–1984); J. Bernard Moffatt (1984–1988), a Manxman, born in Peel on 9 April 1946, a full-time official of the Transport and General Workers' Union and a founder member and chairman

The first Celtic languages book fair, Scríf-Celt 1985, which attracted 72 Celtic language publishers to display their productions.

A 1991 seminar in Dublin discussed the League's monitoring of submarine accidents in the Irish Sea. J. Bernard Moffat is seen with Orla Ní Éilí of Greenpeace, Deirdre Cantwell of the Irish CND, and Cathal Ó Luain.

of Mec Vannin, the Manx Socialist Republican Party; Davyth Fear (1988–1990), a Cornishman, born 17 March 1960, a graduate from Sussex University who taught geography through the medium of Welsh in a bilingual school in Caernarfon; and Séamas Ó Coileáin (1990–1991), a graduate with a degree in Cornish phonetics, who was an Irish language teacher in London. From 1991 J. Bernard Moffatt resumed control of the secretariat, following a constitutional crisis within the League.

This crisis was one of the most serious faced by the League. It started with a complaint to the League's chairman from a Cornish member in 1989. The complainant claimed that the Cornish Branch had been infiltrated by members of the English National Front or related groups. The chairman referred the matter to the General Secretary and General Council. Under the League's constitution, the Cornish Branch had to meet and consider the member's complaints. They did so in June, their officers having been advised on constitutional and procedural matters by the League's General Council whose officers had, coincidentally, been invited to give a presentation on League aims and activities at the annual Cornish Perranporth Conference in May that year.

It became apparent that the complainant was well-known in Cornwall, for running a grossly amateur and scurrilous gossip sheet, which, in the past, had attacked everyone in the Cornish movement; he was considered a mischief-maker. But the complaint had to be taken seriously. The member made thirty-two accusations to the Cornish Branch, naming some ten prominent Cornish members who had, he claimed, among other things poisoned his cats and made malicious telephone calls consisting of drill noises. Among the ten people named was a founder member of the Cornish Branch, then current treasurer of the League and General Council officer, Royston Green. This veteran Socialist and author, whose Marxist views had been in print for many decades, was accused of being an English

National Front activist.[43]

A hearing was set up for the complainant to present his evidence for his allegations. The meeting ended with the branch dismissing the claims of the member, for no evidence was presented – only a series of unsubstantiated opinions. On 3 July the branch committee published a statement to all branch members and also reported to the General Council that they 'were unanimous in agreeing that all of [the member's] allegations were based on supposition and were totally unsubstantiated'. But so serious were the allegations and such were the irresponsible activities of the complainant, who had already begun to circulate anonymous printed attacks on the League, that an extraordinary Cornish Branch meeting was held on 15 July and a proposal was heard that the member be expelled from the Cornish Branch and refused membership of any other branch of the League because of gross misconduct. The member was invited along to defend himself. He attended but, curiously, offered no further defence. The expulsion was unanimously agreed. Procedurally, the member was informed that he could appeal to the General Council. No such appeal was forthcoming.

At the League's AGM in Abergwaun later that month, the AGM, after considering a full report, unanimously endorsed the expulsion. Almost immediately, newspapers began to telephone the General Secretary asking for comments on a joint statement put out by the expelled member and another person who was not even a member of the League. Both individuals claimed they were members of the League, and alleged widespread Fascist 'infiltration', not now confined to Cornwall but to every branch of the League and its General Council. Several League officials now suffered a series of telephone calls designed to pester and irritate them, as well as some abusive anonymous mail.

Of the few newspapers which decided to comment on the story, most of them put the matter in proper context and gave full credence to the General Secretary's rebuttal statement. Only one newspaper, the Cornish *Camborne Packet*, refused the League the right of reply to the allegations which they published.[44]

Legal advice was sought about the allegations being made against the League and against individuals who were League members. It was decided that no action should be taken, one, because of the legal fees involved and two, because the ex-member and his companion were known not to have any financial backing to ensure that costs and damages would be forthcoming from them.

At this point, with the decision at the 1989 AGM, the matter should have come to an end. The expelled member had duly moved residence, perhaps significantly, to Northern Ireland. However, two members of the General Council, presumably working on the principle that 'there is no smoke without fire', decided to take the ex-member's allegations seriously. Indeed, one of them opened up a correspondence with the expelled member that was in contravention of the unanimous agreement of the 1989 AGM that any dealings with the individual had to go through the General Secretary.

With a change of leadership of the League at the 1990 AGM, credibility appeared to be given to the allegations and rumours of an 'infiltration' within the membership of the League by members of the English Fascist Movement seemed to continue. It was resolved that membership of the Celtic League was not open to past or present members of 'proscribed organizations' whose aims were contrary to the League, and a list of several English Fascist groups and their offshoots was drawn up. Many members thought the production of a 'banned list' would create administrative problems for the future, as it would have to be constantly updated. Also, such a stipulation was thought to be superfluous, for if a person was prepared to join the League to work against the aims of the League then they would, undoubtedly, be willing to lie about their political affiliations.

The most unfortunate aspect of this matter was that the wording of the resolution, by referring to a former member by name, gave credence to the expelled member's allegations and this brought a great deal of discontent in the Cornish Branch whose actions were, in fact, being brought into question by the new regime.

Perhaps the most important item, emanating from those who now seemed to give credence to the expelled member's claims, was a change to the League's Constitution which – dangerously, according to many members – allowed decisions on matters of importance to be made at AGM or General Council by a simple majority vote instead, as previously, of allowing each of the six national secretaries the power of veto. Also, a matter of importance was defined as something that was considered important by two national secretaries instead of one, as formerly. This constitutional change introduced a weakness into the League as a democratic international organization. The strength of the League until 1991 was the fact that each of the six nations was fully consulted on central League policy with each national branch being allowed a power of veto. Extraordinarily, the amendment to the constitution of 1990 created a position in which a decision could be binding on any one of the six Celtic national branches, whether the branch approved or conditions in that Celtic country were amendable to it or not. This created the possibility of a situation in which a national branch might find itself breaking away from the League because it disagreed with League policy as pertaining to its area – conditions in Ireland, for example, being different from conditions in Wales or in Brittany. The newly elected General Secretary, Séamas Ó Coileáin, pointed out that this amendment was in fact unconstitutional, as it had not been presented at the AGM in accordance with Standing Orders. This brought him into disagreement with the newly elected convenor who had, in fact, been the proposer of the amendment. Ó Coileáin resigned in March 1991, after only a few months in office amidst some acrimony.

By 1992, under the firm guidance of J. Bernard Moffatt, the

crisis was eventually overcome. But the constitutional weakness remained. The League had a lesson to learn. A tendency had emerged for one national branch, or powerful individuals within that branch, to take the moral high ground over another national branch, without understanding local events or conditions; and a certain naïveté on the part of some officials then allowed a 'witch-hunt' to start based solely on slurs, innuendos and rumours. This could have resulted in the collapse of the League through internal frictions and, thereby, could have led to victory for the persons who started the allegations with, undoubtedly, the very intention of discrediting and destroying the League.

It can be argued that this is 'democracy' at work.

As the Celtic League moved into its fourth decade, with the slow but continuous growth of support for decentralization, if not independent states, in those Celtic countries incorporated into the United Kingdom, the prospects for the growth of political Pan Celticism were more favourable than at any other time. While only a few of the political independence parties in the Celtic countries had adopted Pan Celticism as part of their political manifesto, individual members were not precluded from belonging to the League or other Pan Celtic groups. Indeed, several members of the various parliaments covering the Celtic countries, including the United Kingdom Westminster Parliament, are members of the League. And, interestingly enough, as will be considered in the next chapter, some Members of Parliament representing the UK Labour Party and Liberal Democratic Party see no contradiction in being members of the League. There is the prospect that Scotland, at least, will secure some form of devolved government during the decade ahead. By 1990, all UK political parties, with the notable exception of the Conservatives, had pledged some form of devolved parliament for Scotland. The SNP and Plaid Cymru, together with the SDLP from Ireland, formed an alliance as a voting block in Westminster during the 1987–1992. Parliament. They continued this alliance following the 1992. General Election.[45]

It has been argued that this alliance could continue after the emergence of devolved parliaments. Whether this can be achieved remains to be seen.

Notes

1   *Carn*, No. 56 (Winter, 1986).
2   Letter to author, 6 July 1989.
3   Letter to author, 4 June 1989.
4   Letter to author, 21 March 1989.
5   *Maintaining a National Identity*, Celtic League Annual Volume, edited by Frank G. Thompson (Celtic League, Dublin, 1968), pp. 89–94.
6   The early years of the League were outlined in 'The Celtic League – Twenty Years A-Growing: a personal view' by Peter Berresford Ellis (*Carn*, Autumn, 1981, and Winter, 1981).
7   Ibid.
8   *Celtic News*, No. 13 (Summer, 1966).
9   Introduction, Annual Volume, Celtic League 1964/5.
10 *The Celts*, Dr Anne Ross (BBC Publications, 1967). Notes for the programme broadcast on Radio 3,
11 *Celtic Nationalism*, essays by Owen Dudley Edwards, Gwynfor Evans, Ioan Rhys and Hugh MacDiarmid (Routledge & Kegan Paul, London, 1968).
12 *Flags of the Forgotten*, William Greenberg (Clifton Books, Brighton and London, 1969). (Foreword by Sir Gerald Nabarro MP.)
13 Ibid. The preliminary pages are not numbered.
14 *Creed of the Celtic Revolution*, Peter Berresford Ellis (Medusa Press, London, 1969). Foreword by F.A. Ridley.
15 *Irish Weekly*, 18 October 1969. The reviewer said: 'There is little doubt that most of the ideas proposed in this coolly revolutionary little book will be considered Utopian, but so have so many ideas of a similar nature in the past.'
16 Foreword to *Creed of the Celtic revolution*, p. 9.
17 *Irish Independent*, 16 September and *Struth*, 2 October 1969.
18 *Sav Breizh*, November, 1969, 'Conference Annuelle de la Ligue Celtique'.
19 *Carn*, Winter, 1981.
20 *Separatism in Brittany*, M.J.C. O'Callaghan (Dyllansow Truran, Redruth, 1983), p. 89.
21 Coverage of the meeting was given in: *Le Monde*, 7 November 1969; *Nouvel Observateur*, 10 November 1969; *La Bretagne à Paris*, 13 November 1969; *L'Avenir de la Bretagne*, 13 November 1969; and *Sav Breizh*, December, 1969 and *Struth*, 13 November 1969. The author was the League's official delegate and the full text of his speech can be found in

Bretagne Revolutionnaire, January, 1970, and *Sav Breizh*, January, 1970. A detailed interview on his views at this time was carried in the Breton language monthly *Imbourc'h*, February, 1970.

22 Letter to author, 6 July 1989.

23 *The Times*, 3 June 1970.

24 Letter to author, 3 March 1989.

25 *Carn*, No. 4 (Winter, 1973/4) and No. 5 (Spring, 1974).

26 *News from the Celtic Nations*, Killarney, No. 1 (1978). Also *Carn*, No. 3 (Autumn, 1973).

27 *Carn*, Autumn, 1973.

28 *Guardian*, 12 September 1975.

29 *Carn*, Spring, 1977.

30 Full text of statement, *Carn*, Autumn, 1976.

31 *Daily Telegraph Magazine*, 18 August 1967.

32 *How to be Celtic*, Channel 4, London (48pp, September, 1983). Published to accompany the five programmes shown on Channel 4 made by Pelicula Films.

33 Reports of Scríf-Celt 1985 appeared in *Carn*, Nos 47/48 (double issue, Autumn/Winter, 1984), and No. 50 (Summer, 1985). It was covered by television and radio and in some fifty newspaper and magazine reports ranging from the *Times Literary Supplement* (5 April 1985), *The Guardian*, London (13 April 1985) to the *Irish Times* (30 March 1985), the *Scotsman* (16 March 1985) and *Western Mail* (15 March 1985) through to magazines ranging from *Book Marketing News* (March, 1985) to Marxism Today (April, 1985). Never before had the Celtic languages and publishing in those languages had such widespread publicity.
The 1986 Scríf-Celt was covered in *Carn*, No. 54 (Summer, 1986) and No. 55 (Winter, 1986). Media and newspaper coverage was not so widespread on this second book fair but was confined to items in newspapers in the Celtic countries between March–April, 1986. Both fairs published Programme Booklets (1985 – 76pp; 1986 – 64pp).

34 UNESCO *Celtic Cultures Newsletter*, No. 1 (June, 1983), pp. 1, 5–16.

35 UNESCO *Celtic Cultures Newsletter*, No. 4 (November, 1986), pp. 42–43.

36 Pan Celtic journals published abroad have ranged from a thick, glossy *Keltica*, launched in Boston, Massachusetts, in 1983, and less professionally produced *Celtic Fringe*, in 1987, to a highly professional *Australian Celtic journal*, launched in 1988, to a less professional *Tir na nÓg*, journal of the Australian Celtic Association. See the Bibliography for the full range.

37 *International Colonialism: the Celtic Fringe in British National Development 1536–1966* (Routledge & Kegan Paul, 1975), p. 310.

38 Details of the Celtic League's campaign for the return of the Calf of Man to the Manx people can be followed in *Carn*, No. 49 (Spring, 1985), *Guardian* (London), 5 November 1986 and *Isle of Man Examiner*, 5 November 1986, *Isle of Man Examiner*, 12 November 1986, and *Carn*, No. 60 (Winter 1987/88).

39 *Hansard*, 28 November 1989, contains one of the first parliamentary questions asked in the campaign by Archie Hamilton MP.

40 Coverage on the issue ranged from newspapers as diversely placed as the *California Press-Telegram* (Long Beach), 8 July 1989, to Scandinavian and German newspapers through to the *Mainichi Times* (Tokyo, Japan) on 14 December 1989. In mid-September, 1989, the League circulated a list of all incidents logged to that date with known details and casualties. Many national and local newspapers carried the figures.

41 *Nothing but the Same Old Story: The Roots of Anti-Irish Racism*, Liz Curtis (Information on Ireland, London, 1984), pp. 86–94.

42 *Carn*, No. 72 (Winter, 1990/91) and *Covath* (Autumn, 1990).

43 A detailed report of what had taken place was circulated by the chairman/convenor of the League during this period, dated 31 February 1991, to all members of the General Council.

44 Letter to author from Dafydd Williams, secretary of Plaid Cymru, 22 February 1990, and letter to author from Gordon Wilson, National Convenor of Scottish National Party, 6 March 1990.

9: Philosophy and future development

WHAT becomes clear from the preceding chapters is that there are many differing attitudes within the modern Pan Celtic movement, but they all spring from one basic concept: that the six Celtic national communities, by virtue of a common linguistic origin, have a special relationship with one another. The relation is that of a *cultural* commonality and awareness and no other criteria are used.

People adhering to the basic concept, although interpreting the cultural and political attitudes arising from it origin in many ways, form a social movement becoming a specific form of collective expression concerned with social transformation with evaluated overtones of progression for the Celtic communities. The variation in the aims and objectives of the groups and individuals within the movement is such that measurements of success are rendered difficult.

It has been seen that in the Pan Celtic movement, the spectrum of opinion ranges from those who believe simply in the idea of keeping cultural links between the Celtic communities, as expressed in the Celtic Congress and by supporters of various Pan Celtic Festivals and cultural bodies, through to the more radically political Celtic League, which works for the establishment of formal political links between the movements seeking to gain independence for the Celtic communities, as well as the continuances of those links after independence.

In order to assess current ideas and possible future development of Pan Celticism we have to restrict ourselves to the only area where we have a foundation for specific discussion – that is, the rationale of the League. It has been seen that the League is in fact, the organized mainspring of the Pan Celtic movement. One is cognizant of the argument that once a social movement is organized then it is no longer a social movement. But the League, as has been demonstrated, is the hub around which the unaffiliated groups and individuals revolve – and they feed their consciousness and perceptions from the discussions, directly or indirectly, emanating from within the League. For the last three decades, the Celtic League has set the pace for the Pan Celtic movement, and its publications constitute a corpus of material which we may comment on and assess.

It must be said that within the League, in the subscription to the aim of formal links, there are differences of opinion as to how far those formal links should go; there are those who espouse cooperative links on cultural matters right through to those who advocate a complete political and economic confederation as Celtia with the Scandinavian rôle model in mind.[1]

The League, by consistently refraining from setting out specific policies for its members, has allowed a broad spectrum of left-of-centre opinion within its ranks. As well as members of the individual national independence parties, Plaid Cymru, Scottish National Party, Mebyon Kernow, Mec Vannin, Union Démocratique Bretonne etc, members of the UK Liberal Democrats, the Labour Party and Ireland's Fianna Fáil are also members.

In 1990, among the Members of Parliament who supported the League's aims was Charles Kennedy, chairman of the Liberal Democratic Party, and MP for Ross and Cromarty. Kennedy is a Gaelic-speaker and member of the Celtic Congress. He has stated: 'Unlike some, I do not see this' (the League's aims) 'posing a long-term threat to overall European unity, as I think diversity can be a positive strength.'[2] In the UK Labour Party, Paul Flynn, a Member of Parliament for Newport East, has been a long-standing member of the Welsh Branch of the League. Plaid

Cymru, whose president and first MP (Gwynfor Evans) was, for ten years, president of the League, retains a close relationship with the League. Dafydd Wigley, for example, MP for Caernarfon, has represented League interests in Parliament, especially in their campaigns on pollution and the problems facing the fishing industry in the Celtic countries. According to Plaid Cymru's General Secretary, Dafydd Williams:

> Plaid Cymru has always strongly supported the development of links between peoples in the Celtic countries, who share a common aim of winning the freedom we need to secure our sense of national identity.
>
> Plaid Cymru has consistently supported the aims of organizations such as the Celtic League and Celtic Congress, and many members of ours continue to play a role within these organizations; over the years this has had many practical benefits. Firm friendships have been established between people in Wales and in other Celtic countries. The growth of our own movement in Wales has meant that Plaid Cymru members have been able to organize, for example, the twinning of towns and villages, particularly between Wales and Brittany.
>
> Plaid Cymru seeks the goal of self-government for Wales within the European Community... the links with other Celtic countries will be especially strong, particularly in the cultural field, and this in turn could also produce certain economic links (one small example is the attempt by Welsh and Breton members of the European Free Alliance, on an unofficial basis, to improve maritime links between the two countries).
>
> I would hope that self-governing Celtic countries would ensure special links between them which would have practical economic and cultural results, and would not in our view be in any conflict with the future European community which we would hope to span both west and east.[3]

SNP's former chairman and first MP, Dr Robert MacIntyre, was a vice-president of the League and several SNP MPs have been and are found in support of the League and its aims.[4] Mrs Winifred Ewing, now SNP's Euro-MP for the Western Isles, when an MP at Westminster, was a supporter of the League and contributor to its publications. Hazel Hannan, an Independent

Member of the Manx House of Keys, a former general secretary of Mec Vannin (the Manx Republican Party), has felt 'that any support of the aims of the Celtic League would be the aims [sic] of any Celtic person'.[5]

> I do not see Pan Celticism as being purely a cultural phenomenon and I think the sooner that cultural people see a place for politics the better.
> I would hope that eventually through a rather more developed Europe that the Celtic nations could play their part in such a federation and they in turn would have support from that organization for their minority interests.

The constitution of the League is so phrased as to encompass a broad church of opinion, even to the type of autonomy that the Celtic peoples should achieve before formal links are set in place. Article 1 stresses that the fundamental aim of the League 'is to support through peaceful means, the struggle of the Celtic nations... to win or secure the political, cultural, social and economic freedom they need for their survival and development as distinct communities...'[6] This allows a considerable spectrum of opinion as to exactly what type of 'freedoms' are needed by each nation. Therefore, there are to be found within the League varying kinds of devolutionists, from 'home rulers' through to those who believe in total separation from England and France.

The League's aim – to develop 'the consciousness of the special relationship existing between the Celtic peoples' and foster 'cooperation and solidarity between them' as well as furthering 'the establishment of organized relations between the Celtic nations, based on their recognition as distinct nations, and with the long-term aim of formal associations between them' are also worded to encourage a broad spectrum of opinions within the League.

One thing is clear by Article 1(a) – that the Celtic languages, according to the League, must be restored as 'ordinary means of communication' because they 'are essential characteristics of nationality for each Celtic country'. This underscores the cultural and linguistic fundamentalism of the League.

The League, however, welcomes everyone who subscribes to its aims and objectives irrespective of race or creed, by virtue of the 'linguistic criterion'. As seen earlier, as language is regarded as the only realistic means of identifying a Celt, the League, and indeed, the Congress, have no problems regarding people of various ethnic backgrounds who have emigrated to Celtic areas as Celts – provided they are willing to be identified as such by the support of that definition, and do not identify themselves with the imperial nationality. Therefore the native Scots Gaelic-speaking Maxwell brothers, of West Indian parentage, were considered leading Celtic activists in the 1930s; and the Breton-speaking West African born mayor of a rural community near Plougastel in 1990 is identified as being as Celtic as any other speaker of a Celtic language. Pádraic Pearse (1879–1916), the Irish poet who led the 1916 uprising and was thereafter executed, was the son of an Englishman. Similarly, Cathal Ó Sándair, the most prolific modern Irish writer (author of 160 novels published in Irish), was born of an English father in London. No one would challenge their rights to be considered Celtic. The Celtic League has made it clear that it therefore considers itself an anti-racist organization.

Anti-Imperialism and Socialism in the League

It has been demonstrated that those subscribing to the political aims of Pan Celticism, especially within the League, see themselves as part of an 'anti-imperialist' movement; a movement seeking autonomy from the dominant nations of two powerful multi-national states – the United Kingdom and France. The League, with its constitutional 'social commitment', places itself left-of-centre in its political outlook.

Some of its officers and activists would have no hesitation in describing themselves as socialists, or indeed, as republicans following the teachings of James Connolly (1868–1916) – the

Irish Marxist theoretician and activist executed for his part in the 1916 uprising in Ireland – or John MacLean (1879–1923), founder of the Scottish Workers' Republican Party.

But these political and social attitudes do not dominate the League's thinking, and the League officially retains its broad church approach. However, the attitude is summed up by the argument that the League does not see national and social freedoms as two separate and unrelated issues. The issues are viewed as two sides of one great democratic principle, each being incomplete without the other. As stated, nationalism, in this interpretation, is the advocacy of the freedom of national communities defined by a common language and culture, from the cultural, political and economic exploitation of other nations.

In answer to the popular misconception, often levelled in criticism at Celtic nationalists, that 'nationalism' has been the cause of much suffering and misery in the world, spokesmen and women for the League argue that this is not so. 'Imperialism' is the cause of aggression and suffering whereas 'nationalism' is a defence against imperial aggression. The point is underscored by George Bernard Shaw in his preface to *John Bull's other island* (1904).

A healthy nation is as unconscious of its nationality as a healthy man is of his bones. But if you break a nation's nationality it will think of nothing else but getting it set again. It will listen to no reformer, to no philosopher and no preacher, until the demand of the Nationalist is granted. It will attend to no business, however vital, except the business of unification and liberation.

The League believes that the way to a sound internationalism lies through the recognition, not the repudiation, of the fact of nationality. The solidarity of the peoples of the world should rest upon a pact between national units, associated in a common purpose and destiny. This echoes a teaching of V.I. Lenin that the principal condition for securing a lasting world peace and prosperity is that every nationality, without exception, worldwide, should obtain political autonomy and the opportunity to decide for itself its future as part of the human family.[7]

However, there are others within the League who would disagree with the socialist and republican concepts. The League, from 1961, has certainly proved a forum for many diverse political opinions. Yet the dynamism of the League has a distinctly radical socialist approach.

Feminism in the League

It has been acknowledged that the Celtic League has played an active part in the feminist movement within the Celtic countries. Indeed, from the start feminists have played a prominent rôle in the development of the League as leading officers and members of its General Council. In 1989/90, for example, four of the national branch secretaryships were held by women and the editor of the League journal was a woman. Most of these Pan Celtic activists, such as the poet Caitlín Maude (1941–1981), have also been active in the feminist movements of their respective countries. In 1978 the Celtic League's Manx branch instigated the foundation of EVE (Equality versus Exploitation) to investigate discrimination against women on the Island.[8] One of the leading members of EVE was Patricia Bridson, General Council officer and editor of the League's magazine *Carn*.

In a polemical article in *Carn*[9] entitled 'Descent into Civilization', the authors, Margaret O'Hara and Bernadette Bulfin, argued: 'In the area of women's rights much of the long struggle is only to regain what was once enjoyed by Celtic women 1,500 years ago.' While this might seem extreme from a non-Celtic view, it has been pointed out that in pre-conquest Celtic society, women enjoyed a unique rôle, their rights enshrined in the Brehon Law system of Ireland and the Welsh laws of Hywel Dda.[10]

The place of equality women had in Celtic society until the conquests by England and France has continued to fascinate historians and feminists. *The Welsh law of women*, edited by Dafydd Jenkins and Morfydd E. Owen on behalf of the Board of Celtic Studies (University of Wales Press, Cardiff, 1988), has opened up new conceptions in this field through examination of the laws of Hywel Dda respecting women and comparison of them to the Irish Brehon Laws.[11] In 1990 an Irish feminist historian, Mary Condren, published *The serpent and the goddess: women, religion and power in Celtic Ireland* (T. & T. Clarke, Edinburgh), which gives a philosophical account of the decline of the original matri-centred Irish society. It has been argued that this has left a tradition in Celtic society which is reflected in modern Celtic politics, where women have tended to play a more prominent rôle than their English or French sisters, pursuing equal rights.

In modern times, the Celts could be said to have actually led the way in the struggle for female emancipation, particularly the movement to obtain voting rights. In the Isle of Man a Women's Suffrage Act was passed in 1881, many years in advance of any other western society and thirty-seven years in advance of the United Kingdom. In Ireland, Constance Markiewicz (1868–1927) became the first woman to be elected to the Westminster Parliament in 1918. She stood on a Sinn Féin abstentionist ticket and therefore refused to take her seat, joining the revolutionary Dáil of 1919–21 in which she became Minister for Labour, the first woman to become a government minister in any modern democracy.

The paradox, however, demonstrated by this study, is that the authors of most literature dealing with the development of Pan Celtic ideology have been male. However, two notable exceptions were Dr Noëlle Davies, socialist and feminist, who was the first international treasurer of the League and developed the idea of the Scandinavian rôle model in the early 1950s for a future Celtic union (in the pages of *An Aimsir Cheilteach*) – and the Welsh historian, Dr Ceinwen Davies, editor of the League's publications in the early years. Yet while women seem to have been slow to commit themselves to paper they have certainly been prominent in the practical development of Pan Celticism.

Ecology: Pan Celticism as a 'Green' movement

Its long running campaign on pollution, its early commitment to a Nuclear Free Europe, enshrined in its controversial Military Monitoring Campaign, and other activities, have placed the Celtic League in the ecological or 'green' camp. The League pointed out to ecologists in the 1960s that the destruction of language and culture was as much an ecological issue as the destruction of plant or animal life or other environmental issues.[12]

The concept of 'cultural ecology' in a Celtic context was pursued by Seán de Fréine in 1965 in his book *An thost mhór*, reprinted in 1968, and translated into English as *The great silence* (Mercier Press, 1975). This was a study of the relationship between language and nationality in a Celtic context which raised the issue as an ecological matter. In 1971 *The Ecologist* published an article on 'Celtic Nationalism' in which the concept of 'cultural ecology' was also argued.

The arguments put forward were taken up by Professor Bruce Cox of Ottawa University, in considering the problems of the Canadian Indians and Eskimos, and were published in his 1973 study *Cultural ecology*.[13]

In 1990 the ideas were once again brought back into a Celtic context by Kevin Collins in his study *The cultural conquest of Ireland* (Mercier Press) which drew attention to the alienation of the Irish people from the spirit of their own culture. The author argued that this amounted to the destruction of an 'ecosystem', to use an ecologist buzz-word.

It is from a resolution passed at its 1988 annual meeting on the Isle of Man that the Celtic League established its Celtic Environmental Council, which, as noted previously, has suffered a setback.

A former General Secretary, Séamas Ó Coileáin, summed up the League's main ecological concern, however:

> Although we work on many levels, we have defined for ourselves a special rôle within Celtia and this includes giving unstinting support to those strongest characteristics of national identity, our languages. It is a strange world we live in, the Green Movement clamours to preserve endangered species of plant and creature, while hundreds of small linguistic communities, with their wisdom, experience, memories and unique insights into life on this planet, pass away unnoticed as they are absorbed into larger linguistic communities, which are often backed by a state which controls the media, education, and through propaganda, the language itself.
>
> We, too, are part of the Green Movement, we want to preserve the turns of phrase of our finest poets, the ways in which we express our interpretations of the world around us and our relationships with each other, the prayers and curses, sayings and songs, which have been handed down from generation to generation since time out of mind. We want our children to know who they are, where they are, how much their ancestors have contributed to the well-being of humankind, and how much they can contribute if they retain their cultural identity. In a world where four out of five children are bilingual before attending school, we reserve our deepest contempt for the blinkered monoglot who says: 'What use is a minority language?' It has something to do with freedom, independence of mind, or if you like, not wearing blinkers. Freedom, like truth, belongs by right to everyone.

Towards the League's formal association

It is particularly during the last thirty years that the concept of Pan Celticism has been established in the minds of most culturally informed Celtic people. There is now a general understanding of the cultural relationships between the Celtic peoples.

But can Pan Celticism be developed in terms of Article 1(e) of the League's constitution? That is, can the idea of formal links between autonomous Celtic nations became a reality? As discussed earlier, at this time only the Irish Republic, twenty-six out of the thirty-two counties of Ireland, has sovereignty over its affairs. It is a member of the European Community and United Nations. The Isle of Man has its own parliament, Tynwald, and is, under international law, a UK Crown dependency outside of the United Kingdom. But its Governor-General, representing the English monarchy and the interests of the UK Government, places constraints on the international politics of the island.

For the other Celtic areas, Wales, Scotland, Cornwall, the Partitioned Six Counties of Ireland, and Brittany, there is no autonomous status, and rule is from London or Paris. The UK remains a fairly centralized state which pays lip-service to the myth of a homogeneous 'British nation'. In France this concept of 'state equals nation' is even more doctrinaire and centralized.

For even the most minimal objectives of political Pan Celticism to be achieved, the other four Celtic nations must succeed in obtaining some degree of autonomy from England and France. Whether this can be done is a matter of ongoing debate and political activity. Much depends on the successes of the major national parties in the forthcoming years and their attitude towards the League or other political Pan Celtic groups.

'Formal association' can, of course, be interpreted in many ways. There can be formal association without fully independent states, and some have adhered to this concept. While waiting the advent of autonomous Celtic governments through which to secure a Celtic confederation, the Pan Celts continue to attempt the creation of infrastructures; the links between their nations which one day might well form the links of a Celtic confederation, in much the same way as the Nordic Association and Council worked during the early decades of this century.

The main dynamic of the League, in this respect, as seen earlier, has been to look to Scandinavia as a rôle model. This idea has continued to be debated with the most recent contribution from Clifford Ifan Bere in *Towards the political confederation of Celtia*. Not since Tomás Ó Ciara's 'Celtic cooperation' (*Carn*, Autumn, 1980) and *The Celtic revolution* (1985), had there been a detailed examination of the idea of a political union of self-governing Celtic states.

Bere stated:

> The aim of this short treatise is to present the concept of a coming together in political unity of the Celtic nations and communities around the Celtic Sea in a Confederation of Celtia as a means of taking back that vital power to ourselves.
>
> The dream of a uniting of the Celtic peoples for their mutual interests and protection may be as old as the time of the first tides of invasion against their civilization. It is reborn today as an idea of urgent consequence in a world under the threat of a vaster, more universal chaos.

He argued further:

> The idea of realigning our political thinking away from the direction east or south – as the case may be – of our borders is indeed one to which the Celtic peoples must be ready to adjust. It implies, no less importantly than the urgency of safeguarding Celtic identity against the invading, enslaving uniformity of the tritely vaunted 'freedom of the West', the vital importance also of being able to look in a new vision at the potential for self-reliance, and renewed self-confidence as a result, which would lie in the power of the sixteen millions or so of people of the Celtic lands collaborating in the unity of political confederation... In the power and confidence of such unity the present day heirs of the historic civilization of the Celtic peoples could assume again a rôle of influence in Europe and the world of tomorrow. That vision is of our emancipated vibrant Celtia of the future.

As Dr Davies and others before him, Bere turned to the Scandinavian rôle model. Already Ó Ciara had pointed out:

> It is not proposed that the Celtic countries should adopt the Scandinavian system in its entirety, but it does provide a useful and thought-provoking modern form which future Celtic development could be based on.

Bere agreed with this:

> There would be, in general terms, something of an analogy between the countries of Scandinavia and that which it is aimed to

achieve for the countries of Celtia, our Scandinavia of the Atlantic, the one like the other, faced to the east by powerful neighbours. Mass populations are broadly equal in number, land configuration and relief are not dissimilar; in both there are different native language groups within the same ethnic relationship. But the analogy between Norway and Denmark and the Riksmål language common to them both, which has helped to safeguard Denmark from Germanization, is related to Celtia in its southernmost part, Brittany.

One of the fascinating points of Bere's arguments is that he saw the problems raised by the Partition of Ireland being solved in a united Celtia or Celtic Union:

> The question of 'Ulster', or the northern counties of Ireland, within the context of Celtic confederation is, of course, one of paramount importance. It is a significance in the political and economic life of a confederation. Indeed, it is the concept of confederation which offers an answer to the hitherto unrelenting problem of the tragedy of Northern Ireland. It is in the interests of its people, Protestants and Catholics alike, to give their motivation towards the building of the confederation, for within the terms of that concept can come the best hope of being able to live in peace and prosperity with one another again. It is only within the political unity of Celtia that the people of Ulster will find their true home. It is hardly conceivable that, when faced with the choice, these Celtic people will not decide to place their future in the keeping of Celtia rather than that of England… And is it too much to hope that the close-knit, self-sustaining world of Celtia which we visualize might lead eventually to a relaxing of the extremes of religious conservatism in both the Catholic and Protestant faiths which might bring us to a better understanding of one another and make for the even closer unity of Celtia?

The future

In debating ideals, the Celtic League is thinking in terms of future decades, but more immediate considerations and problems have to be dealt with. Speaking of the 'rôle and impact' of the League in 1981, Alan Heusaff said: 'The Celtic League should be seen primarily as having an educative function, that of making people see the Celtic dimensions of the national struggles; also of making those inclined only towards 'cultural pursuits' see the political aspects.'[14] Heusaff referred, of course, not to academic education but to informing and educating the public on Celtic issues, and to the achievement of a general Celtic awareness.

While leading officers of the League, past and present, vary in what they see the League's rôle as being, the general consensus is that the League, as the main active body of the Pan Celtic movement, must continue in its educational rôle for the foreseeable future.

Alan Heusaff has stated:

The Celtic League has a rôle to play in stimulating Inter Celtic contacts, Inter Celtic solidarity, which could express itself in contributing to pressure on politicians and international/European institutions to steer developments in Europe towards full recognition of the rights of our nations including languages. Other Inter Celtic organizations exist (ie Celtic Congress), also Inter Celtic events (Film and Television Festival, Celtic Congress of Writers etc) – but we are the only association so far working on a continuous or permanent basis. We need to think about what contribution the Celtic peoples and their cultures can make to the development of European unity, to formulate proposals and suggestions, disseminating them, instead of adopting an aloof sort of attitude. We lack people to do this work.

Many European peoples have something like an attachment to Celtic matters. I believe we should appeal to them to help us to get recognition and the freedom we need to realize our national aims.

Our problem is to bring young people to join in the work. The cosmopolitanization of culture, which now rules supreme, the control of the media by the agents of uniformity, are great obstacles to our progress.[15]

The current General Secretary, J. Bernard Moffatt, argues:

The main practical development 'waiting to occur' is the fusion of the two mainstream Pan Celtic movements, ie the Celtic League and Celtic Congress.

The continuing pressures on Celtic integrity in the twenty-first century will not allow us to afford the luxury of two distinct groupings, loosely chasing the same ideal, and the reason for whose separate development is indeterminate.

The Celts may need to learn a difficult lesson, ie that after the thousands of years of distinct warring sub-cultures, the preservation of a Celtic identity will require more than lip service to that goal.

In short, the 'cultural Celt' must come of age, realizing the politics of culture, and having achieved that his place and identity will be secure, albeit on the fringes of an increasingly colourless European cultural conglomerate.[16]

Moffatt sees the League as facilitating that 'coming of age'. A former General Secretary, Davyth Fear (1988–90) believes that:

The rôle of Pan Celticism is now clear. It draws upon the common experience of all Celtic communities to further their interests. In particular, it can protect the smallest or weakest Celtic nation, rekindling their cultures, languages and economics. Pan Celticism draws upon a common root, and political parties have come to realize this. Pan Celticism is taken for granted as a truth, even if others do not necessarily go along with the political conclusions of its thought.

As for the future, the main challenge is that of the European Community and the vast changes being brought about within it... There is the chance of greater links with European minorities in other multi-national states. When we consider the power of the changes being wrought in Europe today and our chance as small nations of changing them and the potential benefits of concentrating our resources on establishing greater links with other minorities, I do not think there is much choice over the way we should turn.[17]

Davyth Fear's successor as General Secretary, Séamas Ó Coileáin (1990-91), has summed up the general perception of most Pan Celticists.

The Celtic League has been described as a federation of Celtic nationalists, and it would be difficult to better that description in as many words. In a way, there is no such thing as a 'Celt', there are only Scots, Manx, and Welsh, Cornish, Irish and Bretons. The League does not bring these different peoples down to a common denominator. It provides from what is held in common, a solid area of mutual support which assists each people to better build its own uniqueness. The Celtic heritage which we share has been romanticized, trivialized, Balmoralized and hijacked, and yet, when examined carefully, can be seen to go back to one of the foundation cultures of western Europe; our languages are closely related, our traditions often correspond even through the inevitable differences. On the negative side, we share in varying degrees the experience of being exploited; at worst persecuted, at best being undervalued or dismissed as irrelevant. What we share also is a determination to preserve and develop our cultural identities, and each Celtic nation has its own broad-based movement working on different levels to retain and develop the degree of independence of mind necessary to achieve sufficient effective control over its own affairs to guarantee the future flowering of that same independence of mind.

Reduced to its bare essentials, the fundamental aim of the Celtic League is: 'to support... the struggle of the Celtic nations... to win or secure the... freedom they need for their survival as distinct communities'. The emphasis on 'distinct communities' is significant, and shows that we are not a racist movement. Our concern is for the values and strengths passed on through the community rather than by blood and genes, and those values are best kept alive by being expressed in the people's native language and traditions.

Each national branch, while ideally reflecting all that is best and most relevant in its country's cultural and political life, including the independence movements, in practice tends to concentrate on what its active members do best, while the non-national branches, such as London, provide an opportunity for Celts in exile to cooperate and strengthen the links between the home nations.[18]

The current convenor/chairman of the Celtic League does not share the view of many of the Pan Celts that the European Community holds some of the answers which will help the Celtic people in attempting to reassert their independence. Cathal Ó Luain was chairman from 1983–85 and re-elected in 1990. He was editor of the League's journal *Carn* from 1977–81.

Pan Celticism has many facets, not the least important being the cultural one. To many people it is the most obvious one, Inter

Celtic festivals, bilateral exchanges etc. However, these are not sufficient in themselves. We are unfortunately only too well aware that the base of these cultures and their languages, which are the source of them, are being continually eroded. This is true even though progress is being made on many fronts in various countries.

The essential of Pan Celticism is the recognition that through Inter Celtic cooperation we base our strength on our nation and those of our fellow Celts. To achieve this in a realistic way must entail cooperation on a political level. It is only through the building of independence and new political structures that we can guarantee the survival of our nations and cultures. The one country which has independence (over most of its territory) is unfortunately acquiescing in the continuing relinquishment of such to a centalized EEC bureaucracy. It will be of no benefit to those Celtic nations under English or French control to be under an EEC master... which will certainly not allow them the political or fiscal control required to ensure their survival as nations. The 'Atlantic Periphery' is already well established unfortunately and the centralization continues. In this context, the need for political movements in the Celtic nations to recognize that their future lies not as regions in the EEC but as nations in a much greater Europe where other small nations also have their freedom, is paramount. The benefits of a Celtic federation supportive of their own cultures and with the advantages of a greater combined weight in economic and political terms should be obvious.

The rôle of the Celtic League must be to work for the promotion of that concept in a wider Europe and the encouragement of political cooperation at as many levels as possible and in as many issues as possible. The League has done much over the years since its founding to encourage the ideal of political federation and cooperation albeit with meagre and voluntary resources. Its successes have not been as significant as hoped, particularly with regard to the national parties in the UK. However, it has waged a long battle to publicize the Celtic movements, languages, cultures and problems.[19]

There has only been one voice which is less sanguine and a little dismissive of the achievements of the League, and it comes from within the leadership itself. Pádraig Ó Concháir, the League's chairman from 1972–1982 comments:

The Celtic League has accomplished very little. Any complacency ought to disappear at the sight of the frequent 'Brits Out' slogans found in the Six Counties. Although the sentiment is healthy in its way it nevertheless shows that the element most averse to English hegemony has succumbed to a long term tenet of English 'divide and rule' propaganda. Viewed within the context of a media essentially geared to the assimilation of non-English and non-French peripheral areas, perhaps the limited degree of Celtic solidarity that can be perceived is a matter for some surprise.[20]

This variation of views and priorities by individuals has led to an identification of a weakness in the Pan Celtic movement. Celtic individualism has become a stereotypical characterization. Nevertheless, there is some truth in it and the Pan Celtic movement's fortunes seem to have waxed and waned and waxed again with the attitudes and fortunes of its individual leaders. It can be argued that the individualism of leading figures and the individualism of the six Celtic communities has made, and will make, the creation of a homogeneous Pan Celtic movement difficult to say the least.

While this might well be an inherent weakness of the Pan Celtic movement, similar tendencies, of course, can be observed in the Pan Arab and Pan African movements. The difference being that the Pan Arab and Pan African movements have been more cohesive due to the fact that most Arab and African states accept the 'Pan' ideology as state policy. The fortunes of these movements tend to rise and fall according to how committed to those concepts the individual leaders and governments of independent Arab or African states are.

A second weakness has also become identifiable. This is that of the League, like all other Pan Celtic organizations, having to rely on volunteers to run it. There are no full-time or paid officials. Insomuch as officials are primarily committed to their own community's struggle, and are often officials of national movements (the current League General Secretary, J. Bernard Moffatt, for example, is chairman of Mec Vannin, a Manx political party) in addition to having full-time jobs, the time they can devote to Pan Celtic matters is restricted. This practical limitation has stopped development in many fields. Conversely, it places the achievements of the Pan Celtic movement in a rather more positive light.

This book has attempted to chart the growth and development of the Pan Celtic movement and has demonstrated how Pan Celticism has changed, especially during the last three decades, from an intellectual idealism, to a movement of practical political ideology. The transition from a general Celtic awareness, inspired by the Celtic League's activities, to mass support for the League's political aims has not, as yet, been achieved. Nevertheless, what has been achieved in terms of League membership and influence, taking into account the fact that it remains a purely voluntary organization with no salaried officials, is remarkable. It is not beyond the realms of possibility that, with the right stimuli at some future date, there will be a transition to a position of support for the League's long-term aims by a significant section of the Celtic populations.

In spite of the trend towards unions and federations throughout the world, and the approach of the new Europe, there is an equal dynamic in the world for the re-emergence of stateless nations. There is no contradiction between the two strands of political ideology. The emergence of small nation states, politically protecting their cultural boundaries, and then moving into a confederation where there is equality with other such states, would be a demonstration of a more fundamental internationalism than the union of centralist, multinational states, such as the UK and France. Spain was once an even more extreme example of a restrictive, centralized multi-national state, dominated by its mainly Castilian culture. Since 1980 home rule parliaments have been given to the Catalans, Galicians and Basques and their cultures are now protected. Thus Spain now serves as a progressive example of what may be achieved within a multinational state. The state's border integrity has been maintained, which demonstrates the fallaciousness of the argument that the establishment of parliaments in Wales and Scotland would herald the disintegration of the United Kingdom.

It is fascinating that the UK and France, for a long time exponents of imperialism, have been quick to alarm people about the dangers of 'nationalism'. Yugoslavia is now trotted out as an example of the dire consequences of 'nationalism'. Yet the war in the former Yugoslavia is not the result of 'nationalism', but of 'imperialism'. The Yugoslavian state was formed in 1921, with Serbia laying down the terms of union for the other five peoples who were incorporated into the state. In 1919 the Serbian King Alexander established a personal dictatorship, to impose a Serbian identity on all his subjects. He was assassinated in 1934. In 1939 the Prince Regent Paul gave Croatia a limited autonomy and he was overthrown by Serbian officers in March 1941.

The Germans seized the opportunity of dissent among the nations and invaded. It was, like the Breton war of 1793–1804, a highly confused struggle. The various Yugoslav national movements were not only fighting against Serbian royalists, they were resisting the German invasion and many were fighting the Yugoslav Communist guerrillas, who still sought to maintain the union. Indeed, some national groups did make the mistake of accepting German aid against the Serbians of whatever political complexion. Finally, in 1945 Josip Broz Tito (1892–1980), ironically a Croation-born Communist leader, emerged victorious as the head of a Yugoslav federal republic which replaced the Yugoslav kingdom. The new republic allowed some autonomy to the six constituent peoples: Slovenia, Croatia, Bosnia-Hercegovina, the dominant Serbia, Macedonia and Montenegro. Further decentralization was granted in the 1960s in which autonomous provinces emerged, protecting local culture and languages. After Tito's death, the economic and political crises intensified and once more the Serbians began attempting to reassert their domination over the other nationalities. The failure to assimilate them has led to the 'ethnic cleansing' policy, intended to eliminate all nationalities but Serbians from as much territory of the former Yugoslavia as Serbia could militarily annex. The problem, therefore, is not 'nationalism' but 'imperialism' – that of the Serbs over their neighbours. But it becomes obvious why the UK and France would be worried about the emergence of small nation states the closer these nations appeared to their state borders.

The contention that the rise of small national political units was inevitable in the modern world was put forward in 1957 by the Austrian political economist Professor Leopold Kohr. Kohr argued in his work, *The breakdown of nations* (a title he later realized was badly translated, for he meant 'The breakdown of states'), that this was a natural course of events. He attributed the universal cause of modern social diseases to the overgrowth of societies. Like Aristotle in *Politics* or Augustine in *City of God*, Kohr proposed that man's best social organization would be a world of small nation states. Kohr attributed the cause of historic changes to the size of the political society in which human beings lived:

> Oversimplified as this may seem, we shall find the idea more easily acceptable if we consider that bigness, or oversize, is really much more than just a social problem. It appears to be the one and only problem permeating all creation. Whenever something is wrong, something is too big. If the stars in the sky or the atoms of uranium disintegrate in spontaneous explosion, it is not because their substance has lost its balance. It is because matter has attempted to expand beyond the impassable barriers set to every accumulation. Their mass has become too big. If the human body becomes diseased it is, as in cancer, because a cell, or group of cells, has begun to outgrow its allotted narrow limits. And if the body of a people becomes diseased with the fever of aggression, brutality, collectivism, or massive idiocy, it is not because it has fallen victim to bad leadership or mental derangement. It is because human beings, so charming as individuals or in small aggregations, have been welded into over-concentrated social units such as mobs, unions, cartels, or great powers. That is why they begin to slide into uncontrollable catastrophe.[21]

Kohr, in this respect, was the originator of the 'Small Is Beautiful' philosophy which was later developed by Dr E.F. Schumacher.[22] Both Kohr and Schumacher had an effect on the thinking within the Celtic League, and both men spoke on the same platform with League officials in August 1968 at the London 'Fourth World Conference'. Indeed, between the publication of Kohr's book in 1957 and Schumacher's book in 1973, Dr Yann Fouéré, vice-president of the League 1961–71, produced his *L'Europe aux cent drapeaux; essai pour servir a la construction de l'Europe* (1968). Fouéré argued for a truly international European confederation in which all nationalities emerged within protective political borders and subscribed to a European structure.[23]

At first glance it might appear that we have a contradiction. The move to unions of varying sorts might seem at odds with the move for the emergence of more nation-states. Does the recent re-emergence, for example, of the constituent nations of the Union of Soviet Socialist Republics (USSR), as witnessed through 1989/90 and which is a continuing phenomenon, the splitting of Czechoslovakia into its two constituent nations, or the re-emergence of Slovenia, Croatia, Serbia and the other nationalities of the former Yugoslavian federation, indicate that unions, indeed 'Pan Movements', as Professor Peter Alter calls them, are no longer in the ascendant? In fact, the two movements are not incompatible at all. What is called for is a *new unionism* which is based on the fundamental rights of national communities to govern themselves and, of their *own choice*, enter into new agreements of confederation on equal terms with their partners. Certain republics of the former USSR now hope to achieve this through their new Commonwealth union. The USSR was a union created by *force majeure*, in spite of the rhetoric of its constitution and Lenin's teachings on the rights of nationalities. It was not created by a free coming together of equal nation states any more than the United Kingdom was created by a free union of equal nations. Even the union of England with Scotland in 1707, often cited as a union between equal nations, was not such a union. It was achieved by duplicity, and bribery, as an unequal union of the parliaments. A breaking of several of the Treaty of Union clauses within one year of its signing and subsequent military suppression of uprisings underscored what was actually taking place.[24]

Fundamental internationalism, says the League, recognizes the rights of all nationalities to self-government. Only when these rights are secured can confederations of equals be formed without the tensions which inevitably cause the collapse of the powerful multinational state, union or empire. The oft-cited argument is that the nationalism of the Celts is merely a step back to the time of small, primitive warring tribes. Yet Pan Celts argue that this is a demonstrable fallacy. They state that their idea is an attempt to reorganize the peoples of the world, in such a way that, with all groups' cultural and political rights protected, the period of the large warring empires and multi-national states and their dominance in world affairs would be finally ended, and mankind would be able to start along the real path to international unity.[25]

Can Pan Celticism, should all the Celtic nations gain their independence and come together in some sort of Celtic confederation, exist within the union of a greater Europe? Would not the European union make a Celtia, if it followed the Scandinavian model, superfluous? There are many Pan Celts who suggest that the European Community in its current guise, which treats the Celtic nations as a periphery of a periphery, is detrimental to Celtic interests.[26] There are others who see Europe as a means to by-pass the dead weight of London and Paris, who have treated them as provincials, and obtain aid from Brussels.[27] It can be argued that recent years have seen a spread of new unions and unions within unions – the continuation of 'Pan Movements'.

Professor Alter sees the growth of these 'Pan Movements' as easing and intensifying cooperation across national boundaries.[28]

He is optimistic about the rise of such movements in modern times. Alter looks to the Organization of American States (which succeeded the Pan American League in 1948), the rise of the European Community, the South-East Asian Nations, formed in 1967, the Andean Pact in 1969, and the Organization of Eastern Caribbean States in 1981, not to mention the 'elder statesman' of the 'Pan Movements' – Scandinavia.

Professor Alter, in examining the more successful movements, does not believe that the failure of some of the 'Pan Movements' is relevant. He quickly dismisses the imperial adventures of Pan Slavism and Pan Germanism and does not deal with the failure of Pan Arabism in this context. Neither is the partial failure of Pan Africanism – which movement manifested itself in the formation of the Organization of African Unity in 1963 to promote unity, development and defence of African states, eradicate colonialism and coordinate economic, health and other policies – considered. Though the OAU, it must be admitted, has shown an undeniable ability to mediate and conciliate when conflict arises between member states in spite of the general internal factionalization.

According to Alter: 'This political energy suggests that a rearrangement of the world order is possible.'[29]

He goes on to say:

> They [the Pan Movements] appear to be the foundation stones of a world order whose shape will become much clearer in future, an order in which nationalism and the nation-state principle will have forfeited their absolute validity. This will be true not only of relations between states, but also within those states, as federalism increasingly begins to take the place of centralism as a means of organizing large political entities.

Pan Celticism, therefore, existing for over a century as a political ideology, now seems to find itself part of a lauded new world internationalism. Whether the Celtic nations make themselves part of that 'rearrangement of the world order' brings us into the realm of political speculation.

What conclusions can be reached in relation to the question asked at the beginning of this study?

It is really a matter of debate and speculation as to whether the Celtic peoples are on the point of failing to survive or whether they are about to flourish. As discussed, once the Celtic languages have disappeared beyond the point of resuscitation, the Celts themselves will have finally been eradicated from the cultural fabric of Europe.[30] The Celtic languages are in a precarious state; some observers have speculated that the Celtic languages may not survive another century.[31] It has been seen that Pan Celticism is responsible for the upsurge of interest in all Celtic matter, and that restoring the Celtic languages is a fundamental aim of the Celtic League, the prime organization of Pan Celts. But whether Pan Celticism can continue in the future to create a renaissance in which its aims are achieved is a matter of debate. It is not possible to tell, for example, whether Pan Celticism will become a mass movement. It is not possible to say whether the links set in place in the Celtic communities by Pan Celticism (such as the Celtic Film and Television Festival, the UNESCO Project, Celtic literary, sporting, artistic and education groups) will survive; so much depends on voluntary workers. There is open hostility from the UK and French Governments for such activities and, perhaps sadly, only lip service from the Governments of the Irish Republic and Isle of Man for such movements. That Pan Celticism is an influential movement is a fact, and that it has and will continue to play a rôle within the Celtic communities, there is no doubt. In his warning about Pan Celticism to his fellow English Conservative politicians, Sir Gerald Nabarro MP stated, in 1968: 'Celtic nationalists... are here to stay'. Today, twenty-four years later, the Pan Celtic movement, specifically its political organization, has proved his observation to be accurate. But are we, as yet, witnessing the start of a new 'Celtic Dawn'? The answer lies, primarily, with the Celtic peoples in how they continue to press their claims for cultural and political independence and, importantly, in the reaction of their dominant neighbours to those demands.

1   Constitution of the Celtic League (amended, 1989).
2   Letter to author, 21 March 1990.
3   Letter to author, 23 February 1990.
4   Letter from Gordon Wilson, former National Convenor of the SNP, letter to author 6 March 1990.
5   Letter to author, 3 March 1990.
6   Constitution of the Celtic League (see above).
7   *The Celtic Revolution: a Study in Anti-Imperialism*, Peter Berresford Ellis (Y Lolfa Cyf, Talybont, 1985). Also 'The Socialist Revolution and the Rights of Nations to Self-determination', V.I. Lenin, see *Lenin on the National and Colonial Question* (Foreign Language Press, Peking, 1970).
8   *Celtic League Mannin and AMA News*, No. 11, n.d. (1978).
9   *Carn*, No. 26 (Summer, 1979).
10 An important work examining such attitudes was *La Femme Celte* (Editions Payots, Paris, 1972), by Jean Markle, a Breton professor of Celtic Studies at the Sorbonne. An English translation was published (Gordon Cremonesi, London, 1978), as *Women of the Celts*.
11 *The Brehon Laws: A Legal Handbook*, Laurence Ginnell, 1894.
12 See *Resurgence*, Autumn, 1968, also *Hampstead & Highgate Express*, 9 and 16 August 1968. *The Ecologist* also published an article on 'Celtic Nationalism' in which the concept of 'cultural ecology' was put forward (*The Ecologist*, October, 1971).
13 *Cultural Ecology*, Bruce Cox (McLelland & Stewart, Toronto, 1973).
14 *Carn*, No. 36 (Winter, 1981).
15 Letter to author, 21 March 1990.
16 Letter to author, 21 March 1990.
17 Letter to author, 25 June 1990.
18 Letter to author, 8 July 1990.
19 Letter to author, 6 June 1990.
20 Letter to author, 26 May 1990.
21 *The Breakdown of Nations*, Leopold Kohr (Routledge & Kegan Paul, London, 1957), p. ix.
22 *Small is Beautiful*, E.F. Schumacher (Blond & Briggs, London, 1973).
23 *Presse d'Europe*, Paris, 1968.
24 *The Anglo-Scottish Union of 1707*, Oliver Brown (Scots Independent Publication, Stirling n.d.) and *The Treaty of Union between Scotland and England, 1907* (Scottish Secretariat Ltd, Glasgow, 1955)
25 *Celtic Unity: Ten years on.* Introduction by Gwynfor Evans MP, President of the Celtic League (Celtic League Annual Volume, Dublin, 1971).
26 Cathal Ó Luain (League convenor), letter to the author, 21 March 1990.
27 *L'Europe aux Cent Drapeaux*, Yann Fouéré (Presse d'Europe, Paris, 1968), pp. 23 et seq.

28 *Nationalism*, Peter Alter, translated by Stuart MacKinnon-Evans (Edward Arnold, London, 1989), p. 152.
29 Ibid.
30 'The Linguistic Criteria', *Kernow*, No. 4 (August–September, 1989).
31 *The Death of the Irish Language*, Reg Hindley (Routledge, London, 1990).

10: Dawn Becomes Realilty

BERNARD Moffatt, General Secretary of the Celtic League, has stated: 'The ten year period since the first edition of *The Celtic Dawn* was published has been something of a roller-coaster for the national political and cultural movements in Britain, Ireland and the Isle of Man.'[1]

During the last decade some amazing changes have taken place within the Celtic world. Two more Celtic nations have achieved various forms of self-government. A parliament has been established in Scotland and a national assembly in Wales. In Northern Ireland a peace process was finally begun after thirty years of armed struggle. Four out of the six Celtic peoples now have varying forms of autonomy. To achieve this progress, first the dying clasp of the clutching imperial claws of the old English Tory had to be loosened. That loosening came in the May, 1997, UK General Election which resulted in a landslide victory for Tony Blair's New Labour Party after eighteen years of Tory rule.

Even Irish republicans, who each generation resorted to armed struggle to assert independence and the reunification of their country, had always argued that they could not succeed without a change of political attitude and will by England. Blair's Government immediately manifested that change in a way that left many people breathless.

The first matter to be dealt with was the situation in Northern Ireland. For some years the leaders of Sinn Féin had been exploring a way forward from the political stalemate caused when successive Conservative Governments refused to depart from their military policy. In 1994 after years of secret negotiations, Gerry Adams MP, Sinn Féin president, and John Hume MP, leader of the Social Democratic and Labour Party, announced a joint way forward for the nationalist community. This policy was wholeheartedly supported by the Irish Taoiseach (Prime Minister) Albert Reynolds, leading a Fianna Fáil majority coalition government.[2] A cease-fire by the IRA came into being on August 31, 1994, which eventually forced the Loyalist paramilitary groups to reluctantly declare a cease-fire six weeks later. The cease-fire was never entirely observed by them and sectarian murders of Catholics continued.[3]

The agreement was that talks on a political way forward would be held by all protagonists. The Unionists, having always said that there would be no talks before the IRA declared a cease-fire, were now presented with a problem. The IRA had declared a unilateral cease-fire. The Unionists had to find other ways of saying 'no!'. They now demanded the surrender of the IRA in the form of 'decommissioning', or handing over their weapons, before Sinn Féin, as a political party, could enter the talks. The UK Tory Prime Minister John Major, needing at this time the support of the Unionist vote in the House of Commons, supported this demand. He assured Unionists that there would be no 'joint authority' in any devolved assembly in Belfast, that the United Kingdom Government would not impose any agreement on the Unionists and everything would be subject to a referendum in Northern Ireland. These public assurances before any talks could be agreed on, demonstrated to the nationalist community that there would be no progress anyway even if talks were held.[4]

Former US Senator George Mitchell was called in to chair a three member international body, advising on arrangements to 'decommission' arms, as a ploy by which the UK Government hoped to reduce the impression that the IRA were being asked to surrender. However, Senator Mitchell went public in January, 1996, and argued that it was political naivety to demand a surrender of weapons by the IRA before Sinn Féin were allowed into talks. John Hume and other moderate nationalists as well as the Irish Government, a coalition now led by John Bruton of Fine Gael, tried to dissuade John Major and the Tories from pursuing this policy. Hume and Bruton feared that British delaying tactics had gone on too long. Instead of responding to their warnings, John Major set another hoop for the republicans to jump through – he insisted that before talks could take place, any delegates to the talks convention had to be elected and elections to the convention were called.

The reaction from the republicans was not long in coming. Having delayed and prevaricated for a full eighteen months since the beginning of the IRA cease-fire, John Major and the Tory Government could not have been surprised when the cease-fire was ended. On February 9, 1996, an IRA unit exploded a bomb that devastated the Docklands area of London, causing damage estimated at £85 million, killing two people and wounding more than one hundred. The Tories appeared content to return to the policy they knew best – the pursuit of a war of attrition.

On May 30, 1996, the elections to the Forum for Peace and Reconciliation were pushed ahead. John Major hoped that Sinn Féin would now lose any electoral mandate. Mistakenly, they thought that people would perceive that it was the republicans who had resumed the war. The public was fully aware that the Tory Government had created the situation by prevarication. The Ulster Unionist Party won 30 seats to the Forum, Democratic Unionists, 24 seats, SDLP, 21 seats, Sinn Féin, 17 seats, its best electoral showing yet, the Alliance Party, 7 seats and the UK Unionists, 3 seats. Talks opened on June 10 but since Sinn Féin were excluded in spite of its electoral mandate, such talks were a political farce.

In the year of frustration that followed, the right wing sectarian Orange Order continued to flex its muscles, especially against the Catholics of Portadown.[5] Sectarian killings continued with the vast majority of victims being Catholics. The UK

General Election was to change all that on May 1, 1997. Concurrently, Bruton's Fine Gael led coalition lost in the Irish General Election and was succeeded by Bertie Ahern's Fianna Fáil – Progressive Democrat coalition. UK Prime Minister Blair sent Dr 'Mo' Mowlam to the North as Secretary of State, declaring the peace process to be his highest priority. Now, without the colonial mandarin mentality to hold back progress, the discussions soon found a path to re-establishing the IRA cease-fire on July 20, 1997, and later six weeks Sinn Féin were formerly in talks.

Imaginative politics now came into being. The talks reached a conclusion at 5 p.m. on Good Friday, April 10, 1998. A referendum held on May 21, 1998, on both sides of the border endorsed the agreement. A Northern Ireland Assembly was to be established with a power-sharing executive with represent-atives of each community having a veto over the other. Legislation required parallel assent of a weighted majority of 60 per cent of voting members in order to be passed. A UK Secretary of State was to remain responsible for non-devolved matters, significantly law and order. There would be a ministerial council between the Northern Ireland and Irish Republic and north-south bodies to agree on transport, agriculture, education, health, environment research and tourism.[6]

There were commitments to enhance the status of the Irish language. As a sop to Loyalists the English dialect sometimes called 'Ulster-Scots' was hastily promoted to the status of a 'language' and Loyalists assured it would benefit in proportion to the Irish language. In the Irish Republic, in spite of Irish being the first official language since the state came into being, it was only in 2002 that an Official Language Equality Bill was proposed in the Dáil which would enact that all public bodies in Ireland would have to make documents available in Irish and English, promoting an equality for the first official language with English. Those involved in court proceedings could now have a legal right to choose to be heard in Irish or English, and the right of citizens to communicate with public bodies in either language was to be law.

Above all the lack of civil rights, from which Catholics had suffered in Northern Ireland over decades, was to vanish in a new society where there was 'parity of esteem'. There would be no turning back to the bad old days of the Special Powers Act, which was so admired by Adolf Hitler and Hendrik Verwoerd and Johannes Vorster.[7] More importantly the Royal Ulster Constabulary would be reformed as a genuine community police force.

On June 19, 1998, David Trimble was elected First Minister of the assembly with SDLP's Seamus Mallon as Deputy First Minister. But the negotiations continued to be blocked by Unionists, especially by Paisley's Democratic Unionist Party who used the excuse of lack of progress over 'decommissioning', and for over a year it seemed that the plan would collapse. Sinn Féin was to be excluded until IRA weapons were surrendered. Indeed, Seamus Mallon resigned his office in protest at the stonewall attitudes. Only when Senator George Mitchell came back into the peace process did he persuade the Ulster Unionist Council to agree that the assembly and its executive should be established before the decommissioning of weapons. As it was pointed out, no two parties agreeing a peace process in any armed conflict in history, could expect one or either side to surrender their weapons before engaging the process. In anyone's language, that was surrender. The Ulster Unionist Council accepted Mitchell's recommendations on November 27. Mallon was reinstated as Deputy First Minister. Ten ministers were now nominated.[8]

On November 30, 1999, the enabling laws for the assembly were rushed through the Westminster Parliament and on December 1, power passed from Westminster to Belfast at midnight. The following day the Irish Government reciprocated by removing its Constitution's territorial claim to Northern Ireland. The new Northern Ireland executive met for the first time and the IRA appointed a representative to the International Body on Decommissioning.

More problems arose and the new Northern Ireland Secretary Peter Mandelson tried to get tough by suspending the Assembly on February 7 because there was no overt progress on IRA decommissioning. The assembly's powers were restored on May 29, 2000 at midnight. Trimble also threw political spanners into the process when he tried to ban Sinn Féin ministers from participating in the north-south bodies in a bid to force IRA decommissioning in November, 2000. It was argued that such a move was beyond the powers granted to him and unconstitutional. Trimble threatened to resign on July 1, 2001, if decommissioning had not come about.

The most contentious matter was the future of Royal Ulster Constabulary. Fuel to nationalist resentment was added when the Queen awarded the George Cross medal to the RUC on April 12, 2000. Chris Pattern, former governor of Hong Kong, chaired a commission which recommended reforms, creating a new community Police Service to which Catholics and Protestants could join and be supportive. The sectarian, political police structure of the RUC was to be ended and the new Northern Ireland Police Service came into being at the beginning of 2002.[9]

The process in Northern Ireland is complex. It has been one imaginative attempt at a way forward in spite of the traditional obstructionism of the Unionists ('not an inch' and 'no surrender'); in spite of the emergence of splinter groups of IRA dissidents, and the large number of sectarian murders from Loyalist paramilitaries since the IRA cease-fire of 1997. The process still continues. But there are still troubled times ahead. In the UK General Election of June, 2001, Trimble's Ulster Unionist Party was badly mauled while Sinn Féin, for the first time, won a higher vote than the SDLP formed in 1970. The results were that the UUP won 26.8 p.c. of the vote, DUP won 22.5 p.c., SF won 21.7 p.c. and the SDLP 21.0 p.c. Sinn Féin had taken four Westminster seats. This was interpreted by pundits as a move towards a polarisation of attitudes to parties critical of the Good Friday Agreement. To reinforce the message that Sinn Féin was now accepted as a serious political contender, in the Irish Republic's General Election in 2002, the party increased their seats in the Dáil from one to five where Bertie Ahern's Fianna Fáil - Progressive Democrats coalition returned to Government. Overall, Sinn Féin had picked up 6.5% of the first preference votes.

It is a long, torturous path, but for many the reunification of the country by osmosis is seen as a more welcome reality than a continuance of the war. Whether that can be achieved depends on if and how devolution is allowed to work. The main movement against continuing the 'peace process' is, of course, Paisley's DUP. The more support they achieve, the more support the dissident breakaway republican groups will attract. Whatever lays ahead, the concept of a return to a sectarian administration, the denial of civil rights to the Catholics, with Unionists constantly supported in arms by the United Kingdom Government must surely be as dead as dreams of a return to the British Raj in India.

In July, 1997, two months after coming into office, the UK Labour Government published its White Papers on devolution. It proposed a parliament for Scotland and an assembly for Wales. Approved by a referendum in Scotland, the first elections for a Scottish Parliament, the first parliament in Edinburgh since 1707, were held on May 6. It had taken the UK Labour Party only one hundred and eleven years since Keir Hardie had first pledged the Labour Party to support home rule in an election address in 1888.

The Scottish Parliament consisted of 129 seats, 73 of these were elected by the 'first past the post' system while 56 more were elected by a form of proportional representation with seven additional members from each of the eight current European Parliamentary constituencies.[10]

As expected Labour took a total of 55 seats, the Scottish National Party 35 seats: Conservatives came in with a surprising 19 seats and the Liberal Democrats took 16 seats. The Scottish Socialist Party held one seat, Scottish Green Party one seat, and former Labour MP Dennis Canavan won a seat as an Independent for Falkirk West. Together with the Presiding Officer, who was the former Liberal leader Lord David Steele of Aikwood, holding the remaining seat.

The First Minister was Donald Dewar, who had been Secretary of State for Scotland, guiding Scotland into the new political phrase. The Queen performed the state opening of *Pàrlamaid na h-Alba*, the Scottish Parliament, on July 1, 1999. One wonders if there was any irony in her words welcoming the new body when many remembered how, in the Queen's Silver Jubilee address to members of both Houses of the London Parliament, in Westminster Hall in 1977, she reminded politicians that she had been crowned 'Queen of the United Kingdom of Great Britain and Northern Ireland' in an attempt to influence the then growing debate on devolution.

Donald Dewar died in office on October 11, 2000. His successor was Labour's Henry McLeish, of Fife Central, elected to office on October 26, 2001, but forced to resign on November 8, 2001, just over a year later. A third Labour First Minister appeared in the person of Jack McConnell, of Motherwell and Wishaw, on November 22, 2001.

At first it appeared that all might augur well for the cultural movement.[11] The Scottish Gaelic language, once the national language of all Scotland, was being used in the Parliament. Bilingual signs had been put up. However, to balance this, a 'Scots Language' Cross Party Group has been established in the Parliament to press for rights for the English dialect (Lallans) that had replaced the Celtic language in southern Scotland and had been made into a literary vehicle in the time of Robert Burns, born when the last native Gaelic speakers of his area were dying out. Hugh MacDiarmid, who thought he could use a revival of this 'Lallans' dialect as a halfway house on the road to the restoration of Scottish Gaelic had, to his dismay, realised in later years that many who followed him saw 'Lallans' as an end to itself (see Chapter Five).

After the centuries of repression and neglect, the dramatic revival of the Scottish Gaelic language was, at least, being acknowledged. With some 70,000 native speakers, enumerated in the 1991 Census, there were, nevertheless, 2,200 children being taught the language in 70 state schools, 8,000 more Scots had learnt it as a second language and a fifth of the Scottish population was now expressing the desire to learn it if facilities were made available. Some 500 Scots worked in Gaelic broadcasting and two million Scots were recorded as watching Gaelic television programmes.

The next step for Scottish Gaelic activists was to get Parliament to pass a Bill giving Secure Status for Gaelic as a living language. Proposals for such status envisaged obliging local authorities to make Gaelic medium education available where demand existed and to allow people to give evidence in Gaelic in courts and tribunals. Such recognition of the language would be an historic and vital development for those native speakers and those wanting to learn and use it. It would be an act that would engender hope and vigour in the Gaelic speaking communities in Scotland and world-wide. Comunn na Gàidhlig's Chief Executive, Allan Campbell, and a working group prepared the case for recognition. The signs were good: a Scottish Junior Minister, Alasdair Morrison, representing the Western Isles, had been given the portfolio of 'Enterprise, Lifelong Learning and Gaelic'. He soon became referred to as simply the 'Minister for Gaelic'.

The brief for a Gaelic Language Bill was presented in June, 1999. A Cross-Party Group on Gaelic was established from the MSPs. A Ministerial Advisory Group on Gaelic was established.[12]

On Monday, February 29, 2000, it was announced that the Scottish Parliament would be holding its first debate in the

Scottish Gaelic language on Thursday, March 2. It was the first known such occasion since it was recorded that King Robert the Bruce had held a parliament in Ardchatten in 1308 which had transacted all its business in Gaelic. Facilities for bilingual English and Scottish Gaelic simultaneous translations were available for all MSPs and press and media. Of course, many other parliaments in Europe had long had such simultaneous translation facilities as Celtic language enthusiasts have highlighted over the years.

Minister Alasdair Morrison introduced the motion: 'That the Parliament welcomes the Scottish Executive's programme of action in support of the Gaelic language, in particular its support for Gaelic medium education; recognises the cultural, economic and social contribution of Gaelic to Scotland; supports the Scottish Executive's participation in the Columba Initiative (Iomair Chaluim Chille) to strengthen the links between the Gaelic speaking communities of Scotland and Ireland, and commends the work of local authorities, schools, colleges, universities and voluntary bodies in making available Gaelic medium education at all levels from pre school to tertiary and continuing education and in promoting the Gaelic arts.'[13]

Hope that a Gaelic Language Bill would be among the first acts of the Scottish Parliament was soon dashed. The Scottish Gaelic language continues in a very uncertain position and even with a Scottish Parliament in control of education, the high level of ignorance and intolerance shown towards the language, the failure to teach some language awareness, challenging the falsehoods and stereotypes, makes the situation a bleak one with no prospect of the reversal of the language shift that has happened over the centuries in Scotland.

In spite of this, the UK General Election of 2001 saw SNP increasing its vote and returning five MPs to Westminster.

In July, 1997, two months after coming to office, the Labour Government also published its White Paper, 'A Voice for Wales' and outlined its proposals for devolution. The proposals were endorsed in a nail biting referendum on September 18, 1997. The Westminster Parliament approved the Government of Wales Act, 1998, and the National Assembly for Wales Order was approved in 1999. Ron Davies, Labour's MP for Caerphilly since 1983, had been appointed Secretary of State for Wales in 1997 to guide the creation of the Assembly.

The *Cynulliad Cenedlaethol Cymru* (National Assembly of Wales) had limited powers compared to the Scottish Parliament.[14] The Assembly decided on Welsh priorities to allocate funds from the UK Treasury, overseen by the Secretary of State for Wales, and Wales continued to return members to the Westminster Parliament as did the Scots and Northern Irish. The Assembly had sixty elected members, forty of them elected on a 'first past the post' vote and a second vote allowing twenty additional members elected from the five electoral regions. The first elections were held on May 6, 1999, and the first session of the Assembly took place at 11 a.m. on May 12, 1999.

For the first time since England had defeated Owain Glyndŵr whose last Welsh parliament had sat in Machynlleth, an elected democratic Welsh legislature was meeting on Welsh soil. The Welsh language was now a language of parliament, with the principal of bilingualism allowed, although apart from translators, it has been discovered that only 1% of staff working in the Assembly can speak Welsh. Even in Cardiff over 8% of the population is Welsh speaking.

It was predictable that Labour would take the majority of seats with 27 Constituency seats and 1 regional seat. Plaid Cymru came in as the second largest party with 9 Constituency seats and 8 Regional seats. The Liberal Democrats secured three constituency seats and three regional seats while the Conservatives had one Constituency seat but eight regional seats. *Yr Arglwydd*, The Presiding Officer, was Plaid Cymru's Lord Dafydd Elis Thomas. He had been elected as MP for Merionydd, serving until 1983 and continuing when the constituency included Nant Conwy from 1983-1992. He surprised many in the Celtic world by accepting a title from the Queen in 1992. He was chairman of the Welsh Language Board from 1994–1999.

On July 1 a new Office of the Secretary of State of Wales was established and on July 28, 1999, Paul Murphy, from Usk, in Gwent, who had previously been appointed as Minister of State in the Northern Ireland Office in 1997, now became Secretary of State.

Ron Davies became First Secretary but within months he was forced to resign from anomalies arising from his account of being mugged on Clapham Common in London. Indeed, within another few months he was also forced to resign from the Assembly's Economic Development Council. The new First Secretary was a London Government appointee, Alun Michael, MP for Cardiff South and Penarth since 1987. He managed to scrape into office on the votes of the electoral college and this caused resentment among his own party in Wales. In February, 2000, Alun Michael himself was forced to resign before a vote of no confidence called by Plaid Cymru could be held in the Welsh Assembly. The vote of confidence had been called by Plaid Cymru over lack of funding to the poorest regions of Wales. Ieuan Wyn Jones of Y Blaid felt that Alun Michael was not standing up to the UK Prime Minister and making the case for Wales.

The Rt. Hon. Rhodri Morgan of Cardiff West who had twice fought for the leadership in the Welsh Assembly became Michael's successor. The office was now First Minister. Morgan announced a coalition Cabinet of eight including the Acting Deputy First Minster, Liberal-Democrat Jenny Randerson of Cardiff Central who took up the brief of Minister for Culture and the Welsh language. With Labour taking all the portfolios except Culture and the Welsh Language, there was unease that Labour saw the language as unimportant and so were happy to give it to a Liberal-Democrat.

The 1993 Welsh Language Act, however, had finally established the principal of equal validity in public business and administration of justice throughout Wales. The Welsh Language Board had been established to promote the use and teaching of Welsh and there was a new positive attitude to the language and culture in spite of frequent attacks on Welsh and its speakers by many English incomers into Wales including claims of 'racism' sometimes backed up by the old anti-Welsh language political figures. All Assembly business and information was made available in Welsh.

Under the leadership of Rhodri Morgan the National Assembly has settled down and is heading towards its second term elections. Whether the creation of the Assembly has stopped the march of Plaid Cymru towards even greater independence, as hoped by the UK Government, remains to be seen. In the 2001 General Election Plaid Cymru's vote gained a little in English speaking areas and dropped a little in Welsh speaking areas. Its number of MPs at Westminster remained static at four, having lost one sea but gained another. It has to be remembered that fear of the break-up of the United Kingdom has been the single dominant reason why the UK Labour Party readopted its devolutionist policies, having previously abandoned them once they had won the 1945 General Election.

While Cornwall remains the only Celtic area within the United Kingdom which does not have any recognition from the central government in London, the events of 1997 were not lost on the Cornish electorate. Among the five Members of Parliament representing Cornwall who were elected in 1997 was a Cornish speaker. Andrew George won his seat at St Ives for the Liberal Democrats. A graduate of Sussex and Oxford Universities, George had specialised in Agricultural Economics.

In his maiden speech he became the first Member of Parliament to address the House of Commons in the Cornish language. On June 17, 1997, he tabled an early day motion on '*Keskerdh Kernow*: March of the Cornish People' and pointed out the demands of the Cornish for a) recognition of Cornwall's distinctive cultural, linguistic and historical identity; b) the need for a Cornish Assembly c) the establishment of a Cornish University and d) a fair deal for Cornish residents with regard to water bills, economic development aid, education and affordable housing. Thirty-three Members of Parliament, including Plaid Cymru and SNP MPs supported him.[15]

It was not the last time Andrew George was to raise the matter of Cornwall's Celtic identity. On July 30, 1997, he tabled an early day motion on the need to establish a University College in Cornwall. On February 23, 1999, he introduced an Adjournment Debate on official recognition for the Cornish language. In outlining some of the history of the language and its decline and revival, he told members there were now some 3,000 Cornish speakers and many more thousands learning the language.

There are three regular periodicals solely in Cornish, *An Gannas*, *An Gowser* and *A Garrick*, with two local radio stations having regular news broadcasts in Cornish and features for learners and enthusiasts. Local newspapers also carried features. George felt that Cornish should be specified within the European Charter for regional or minority languages. While central education had even withdrawn the GCSE in Cornish, in Aberystwyth, Wales, and Harvard, USA one could take a degree level course in the language. Yet there was no financial sponsorship from neither local nor central government sources. He also pointed out that the Cornish language was playing its part in tourism and souvenir manufacture, publishing and in other commercial life.

'Before Cornish can rightfully take its place as an officially recognised language, we need to sort out which Department is responsible for assessing Cornwall's case for being specified under part II of the European Charter for regional or minority languages. It has been considered by the Department of Education and Employment, the Home Office, the Department for Culture, Media and Sport, the Department of the Environment, Transport and the Regions and the Welsh Office. I have asked the Cabinet Office to determine responsibility, but it has put the question back to the Foreign Office.'[16]

A few months later, on July 8, 1999, George tabled an Early Day Motion on the 'Cornish Language and the Prayer Book Rebellion' against the imposition of the language in Cornwall in 1549: their declaration of insurrection read 'we the Cornish men (whereof certain of us understand no English) utterly refuse this new English'. George called for Government recognition of the Cornish language to be incorporated in the Council of Europe Charter for Regional or Minority Languages. These were not the only campaign matters of this active MP.

In spite of George's raising the matter in the House of Commons and the support by a respectable minority of Members, usually from the other Celtic areas, Cornish is now the only Celtic language in the UK that receives no support from Government. However, the London *Times* (August 10, 2002) reported that the Westminster Government is expected to announce that Cornish will be officially recognised as a minority language of the United Kingdom in the autumn. This would be in accordance with the European Charter for Regional or Minority Languages, which has now been ratified by the UK. Local Government Minister Nick Raynsford has given such assurances to Andrew George MP. Agan Tavas (Our Language) which exists to promote the language issued a statement *Agan Tavas ha'n stuth a Gernuak* (Agan Tavas and the Status of Cornish) in which they pointed out that the County Council has denied Cornish language tuition to children whose first language is Cornish and refused to survey Cornish parents to assess demand for such tuition. There have been continued delays and prevarication to recognise the language and failure to identify it as an area of culture to be promoted and protected in official documents on 'Southwest English government bodies'. The Cornwall Council has deleted Cornish language phrases in promotional material and the Department of Transport and Cornwall Council has suppressed Cornish language place-names on official signs in favour of obscure place names in English. Finally, there has been a continual failure to respond to letters and requests for meetings or to recognise Cornish language organisations when dealing with cultural proceedings.

On March 5, 2000 (St Piran's Day, the Cornish National Saint's Day), a campaign in support of a *Senedh Kernow* (Cornish Assembly) was duly launched by Mebyon Kernow but then, in November, taken over by *Omguntellyans rag Selreth Kernow* (the Cornish Constitutional Convention). Four of Cornwall's Members of Parliament sponsored a petition: these were Andrew George, Colin Breed, Paul Tyler and Matthew Taylor. All were Liberal Democrats while the Labour MP for Falmouth and Camborne, Candy Atherton supported her Party's anti-Cornish line, rejecting recognition of the language and the call for a Cornish Assembly. Some 50,000 signed the petition which was presented in Downing Street, coinciding with a House of Commons debate on 'English' Regional Devolution which would propose that Cornwall would become part of a South West Regional Assembly stretching up to Swindon and Gloucester.[17] In May, 2002, The Cornish Constitutional Convention publshed a brochure entitled *Devolution for One and All: Governance for Cornwall in the 21st Century* which explained the necessity for an assembly and how it would work and benefit the people of Cornwall. The Convention established its own website at www.senedhkernow.freeuk.com .

Curiously, there were objections from one part of the Cornish nationalist movement. These supported the Stannary Parliament, regarded as the ancient and still legal parliamentary institution of Cornwall, claiming that the campaign for a new assembly did not take into account the existing constitutional and legal principles of the Stannary Parliament. While Cornish representation showed no change in the General Election of 2001, Mebyon Kernow put up candidates in three seats, specifically against the Labour's centralist inclined Candy Atherton. Interestingly, Mebyon Kernow's number of votes was nearly quadrupled by Helen Wasley. In Cornwall South East, Dr Ken George more than doubled Mebyon Kernow's vote and so did Conan Jenkin, standing in Truro & St Austell. These increases, while the votes were minimal in comparison to the main parties, are interesting.

An intriguing development of this new political spirit was the establishment of a British-Irish Council, which came out of the Good Friday Agreement, on new political strategies for Northern Ireland. There is some irony that this Council was based on an idea put forward by Gwynfor Evans MP, when President of the Celtic League in 1969, and one which nearly caused the break-up of the League by a hostile reaction to it. The idea was that of a Britannic Federation. In fact, the move for the British-Irish Council was put forward by Unionists who saw that if there were to be North-South bodies in Ireland, assuming certain powers on an all Ireland basis, then both the Irish Government and Northern Ireland Assembly must be drawn into an overall British framework taking on board the United Kingdom plans for devolution.[18]

The British-Irish Council would consist, therefore, not only of representatives of the Dáil and the Northern Ireland Assembly but the UK central Government, the Scottish parliament, Manx Government, Welsh Assembly and States of Jersey and Guernsey. It was to be a forum for its members to exchange information, discuss and consult; an endeavour to reach agreement on co-operation on matters of mutual interest within their respective competencies.

The inaugural meeting of the Council was held on December 17, 1999. Taoiseach Bertie Ahern TD, Tánaiste Mary Harney TD, Minister for Foreign Affairs David Andrews TD and Minister for Justice John O'Donoghue TD represented the Irish Government. The UK Government was represented by Prime Minister Tony Blair; Secretary for State for Northern Ireland

Peter Mandelson and Minister, Northern Ireland Office George Howarth. The Northern Ireland Assembly was represented by First Minister David Trimble; Deputy First Minister Seamus Mallon; Minister for Enterprise Sir Reg Empey; Minister for Finance and Personnel Mark Durkan and Minister for Health, Social Services and Public Safety Bairbre de Brún. First Minister Donald Dewar, Deputy First Minister Jim Wallace and Permanent Secretary Muir Russell represented the Scottish Parliament. First Minister Alun Michael, Assembly Business Secretary Andrew Davies and Finance Secretary Edwina Hart represented the Welsh Assembly. Chief Minister Donald Gelling and Chief Secretary Fred Kissack represented the Manx Government. Senator Pierre Horsfall, President of the States of Jersey Policy and Resources Committee and its Chief Executive John Mills represented Jersey. Guernsey was represented by Counseiller Laurie Morgan, President of the States of Guernsey Advisory and Finance Committee and Chief Executive Mike Brown.

Whether this was an historic meeting or simply a quango remains to be seen. The meetings are few and far between.

The Celtic League has dismissed this Britannic federation. According the League's convenor, Cathal Ó Luain:

> There can be no real welcome from the Celtic League for a body so constituted. Indeed, to adopt any such stance would be in total contradiction to the League's constitution which aims for a Celtic Confederation inclusive of Breizh (Brittany) and Kernow (Cornwall) and without any controlling influence from England (or for that matter, France). Neither should Parliaments nor Assemblies for the Celtic countries be on any par with devolved regionalism in England.
>
> The only beneficial advantage of such a body is that representatives of the various Celtic bodies might make some use of it to make contacts and develop bilateral co-operation and work towards a Celtic Council. Let us hope that as the Scottish Parliament and the Welsh Assembly flex their muscles these bodies will move quickly to full independence and see the advantage of the Celtic League model. The active political co-operation

developed by the League in its campaigns (submarine threat, Sellafield, marine munitions dumps etc) involving public representatives from Scotland, Mann, Wales and Ireland must be built upon as indeed should the co-operation of the Irish and Manx Governments. The Irish Consulates in Scotland and Wales have great potential. In the meantime the Celtic League must aid Kernow and Breizh in their struggles even more, enlist the help of others in this and promote our aims and model with increased vigour.'[19]

With the Celtic world so rapidly on the move, it was going to be inevitable that there would be a backlash from English. However, the backlash was curious. Apart from the usual bout of sneering in the Press and Media and from certain English 'public opinion', there was a significant concentration on public debates as to what it meant to be 'British' and, indeed, what it meant to be English. English people tended to be content to be English but, interestingly, the communities representing recent immigrants to the United Kingdom appeared unnerved by seeing the disappearance of the 'British' catchall label. Immigrants were happy to be 'British' but not so happy to accept themselves as 'English'. There were some exceptions to the pattern who had no problem being part of the nationality of the country in which their families had settled - being Welsh or Scottish or Cornish.

By now serious consideration was being given to the real history of the peoples of these islands. Books such as *Kingdoms United: Integration and Diversity*, edited by S.J. Connolly, 1999, brought together current academic thought on the politics, culture, economics, law and administration in the islands. The most useful and fascinating of such studies came from Professor Norman Davies, from Bolton, Lancashire. His book *The Isles: A History,* 1999, weighing in at 1,222 pages, took a scalpel to many of the 'British myths'. Studies for and against Scots, Welsh, Irish independence rolled from the presses at an alarming rate.

One anti-Celtic attack emerged from a surprising source, however. *The Atlantic Celts: Ancient People or Modern Invention?*

by Dr Simon James, an archaeologist was published by the British Museum Press. This was, perhaps, the first time the British Museum had published something that could be described as overtly in the contemporary political field. Dr James had already published such studies as *Exploring the World of the Celts* (1993) and co-authored *Britain and the Celtic Iron Age* (1997) in which he had happily talked about the Celtic peoples. But he had an amazing 'Road to Damascus' conversion. He now argued that there was no evidence of the Celtic peoples in Britain or Ireland during the Iron Age and that the idea of an insular Celtic identity was really a product of the rise of nationalism in the 18th Century. 'Celticness', he argued, was a politically dangerous falsification of history which had implications for what he described as 'resurgent nationalism' in these islands.

Such dumbfounding claims had actually begun to emerge as soon as the Labour Party announced their plans for devolution as part of a political programme if they were elected. Dr James had initially made his arguments in an article in *British Museum Magazine*[20] and his comments were reprinted on the front page of the prestigious *Financial Times* Weekend Section[21] within weeks of Labour coming to power. Dr James arguments were written as a critique of the renowned Celtic art specialists, Ruth and Vincent Megaw, who had made clear their views in a paper 'Ancient Celts and modern ethnicity'.[22] John Collis of the University of Sheffield attacked these ideas in *Antiquity* in the summer of 1998 claiming that the definition of a Celtic identity was 'both false and dangerous'.[23] It became clear to many in the world of Celtic Studies, like Professor Barry Raftery of University College, Dublin, that these arguments were emanating from a small band of influential English archaeologists without reference to linguistic and historical disciplines. There was a view from Celtic scholars that if ignored these fallacious arguments would vanish back into the black hole from which they had arisen.

However, archaeological and historical programmes began to appear in the media talking about Iron Age People, then the

Romans, then the Saxons. The Celts were being purposefully 'eliminated' from history. *The Independent* asked me to write a brief rebuttal[24]. I was only allowed to deal with one point in the space allowed. But Dr James then published his book-length arguments.

When it was published, *The Scotsman*, invited me to exchange a series of letters debating points with Dr James, to be published in their entirety in one issue as a single feature.[25] BBC Radio 3 then invited Dr James and myself to 'slug it out' on the airwaves a few weeks later. Unfortunately, the programmers were not concerned by serious argument and changed the format at the last minute to bring in some strange esoteric contributors who had no concept of our original debating points and preferred to wax lyrical about pixies and poets.

The arguments have still not gone away in spite of the ease with which Dr James' ideas could be corrected.

The Megaws have argued that the new move to deny the existence of the Celts is motivated, subliminally if not consciously, by an underlying right wing English political view – in whatever political party those views emerge, As the Megaws are Australian, they have no particular axe to grind in terms of internal Celtic politics. But they did point out that the arguments come from a continued belief in the righteousness of England's 'civilising mission', in their imperial past, and an attempted justification of England's historic role towards their Celtic neighbours. In this, I believe that they are substantially correct and supported their thesis in the *Irish Democrat*.[26]

Dr James strenuously denies such motivations and denies them strenuously.[27] When the Megaws pointed to the evidence of the 'ethnic cleansing' of Celtic Britain during the 5th and 6th centuries, well documented by Gildas in *De excidio et conquestu Britanniae* (Concerning the Ruin and Conquest of Britain) and by other authorities, Dr James commented that it 'raises serious questions of their [the Megaws] judgement and sense of proportion'. Presumably we were asked to believe that Dr James denies the evidence of the massacres and enforced migrations of that time.

Dr James' main argument was, of course, that the term 'Celtic' should be abolished when referring to the pre Roman period. 'No one in Britain and Ireland called themselves a Celt before 1700'. *'Qui ipsorum lingua Celtae, nostra Galli appellantur'* – in their own language they are called Celts, in our tongue Gauls – writes Julius Caesar slightly before 1700! From the inception of Celtic scholarship, as we have seen in Chapter One, the definition of Celts is a people who speak, or were known to have spoken within modern historical times, one of the languages classified as the Celtic branch of Indo-European,

When these islands emerged into recorded history, one of the first known records was the *Massiliote Periplus*, now lost but quoted by other Classic writers, a work of the 6th Century BC, through which Albion and Ierne became known to the people of the Mediterranean. From this work and subsequent Greek and Latin commentaries, we see that the people living here spoke one or another form of a Celtic language. These were the insular Celtic forms of Goidelic and Brythonic. That much is made clear by the names recorded in the early references.

If Dr James could find no evidence of the Celts prior to the Roman invasion of Britain then he was surely dismissing such records and the Greek and Latin records of place names, tribal names, and personal names which are clearly Celtic. As an archaeologist, he is even ignoring the Celtic names recorded on British coins issued by British Celtic tribal kingdoms long before the Romans arrived. It is a fact that no place name survives anterior to the Celtic place names in these islands. In response to these facts, Dr James curiously suggests that while there were Celtic speaking peoples here in the Iron Age, *'they were not necessarily Celts'*. But Celtic is, and always has been, a linguistic term, not a biological one. To talk of biological attributes becomes very dangerous and to use it as some meaningful label to identify a people borders on racism.

The evidence, overwhelming to anyone who has studied the subject, of the commonality between language, a shared religious system, a shared mythology, legal system and social system, appears in the 'Iron Age' among the Celts and has continued ever since. We know that the language of the Celts of modern Belgium (the Treveri) and those of central modern Turkey (Galatia) were mutually intelligible and we have the evidence of St Jerome for that. We know that even prior to the 1st Century BC, Celtic princes ruled in Gaul as well as Southern Britain and we have Roman writers' evidence for that. We can compare the Brehon laws with the Laws of Hywel Dda; we can even compare the same systems with evidence of how Galatia was governed and fragments of Breton laws incorporated in the 1532 Treaty of Union in which Brittany became an autonomous state within the French kingdom.

In making his assertions, Dr James disarmingly admitted that he was not competent to compare Irish and Welsh mythologies, nor indeed other Celtic myths and legends, nor the law systems, nor was he competent to talk about comparative linguists.[28] How then was he capable of making his assertions? How then could he write authoritative books such as *Exploring the Celtic World* (1993)? When I pointed this out to him, he defensively said that his lack of knowledge 'should not disqualify' him from asking certain awkward questions. That is true. But he is doing more than ask questions; he is making assertions with the apparent weight of his academic authority behind him. And the questions are anything but 'awkward'. They could be dismissed by a first year Celtic Studies student.

When I outlined the rise of this school of Celtic Revisionism, 'Did the ancient Celts exist?' in the *Irish Democrat,* Dr James was swift to respond in the following issue. His response did not give one any further confidence in him as an academic as he could not refrain from indulging in personalities – comparing me to that of 'a blue rinse Tory lady in Tunbridge Wells'. When an academic presents such remarks in defence of his arguments, they obviously loose credibility. Perhaps he thought it would rattle me, knowing me to be a life long Socialist and Republican? Or perhaps it was meant to be subtle humour? His main argument, when the dross was cleared, was 'we must see whether the beliefs ... about ourselves, and our neighbours, still fit reality. If they have become an obstacle to understanding peace and prosperity, they can and must be modified'. It sounds superficially laudable. But I am not talking about a *belief system*, neither was Dr James. We are talking about facts that can be empirically validated and Dr James' evidence that the ancient Celts did not exist just doesn't stand up to scrutiny.

It was not long before academics in France decided to follow in Dr James' faltering footsteps. Christian Goudineau, a professor of history at the College de France, produced a book *Par Toutatis*. It seems that the Gauls never existed. Certainly one could agree that to label as propoganda the stance, adopted after the 1789 Revolution, that the French were all descended from Gauls, is resonable, but the Jamesian myth that the Gauls or Celts did not exist, is staggering for serious scholars. *The Times* were quick to devote a lengthy article to the notion as were the *London Review of Books* and *The Independent*. [29] But rather than these articles discussing the indisputable linguistic and archaeological evidence for a Celtic civilization in what is now France, the writers seem keen to attack René Goscinny and his famous fictional character of 'Asterix the Gaul'.

Perhaps we should not be surprised by all the semantics of this debate. Professor Norman Davies summed it up in his study when he wrote: 'For their part, the English cultivated a variety of attitudes to their Celtic neighbours stretching from lofty detachment to scathing disdain. Their notorious ignorance about Celtic matters was most usually attended by relaxed complacency and occasionally fierce pride. All these attitudes and feelings have found full expression in the perpetual debates about the period of history when the chasm first opened ... In the formative period of the British Union, the English were so jealous of their own history and of their own exclusive right to a history, that all non-English histories in the Isles were either ignored or ridiculed.' I would add that this was so not only in the 18th and 19th Century but has continued throughout the 20th Century. It may well be that the English will never accept the Celts as equal partners in these Isles.

For Brittany, the repressive situation has continued with little respite although, after the pioneer efforts of DIWAN, which set up the first Breton bilingual schools, Mitterand's Government allowed the French State Schools (DIVYEZH) to include Breton language classes. In the 1990s the private Catholic schools (DIHUN) allowed the language to be taught. There are now some 7,000 pupils who attend the three educational systems following a bilingual education. But demand exceeds availability of places and lack of financial support is always the major problem with some fifty more teachers needed to keep abreast of demands. However, in 2001 the Constitutional Court of the French State declared that French was the only language allowed in state schools, although Breton could be taught as a 'dead' language. There was hope that the French Socialists might provide the next President and adopt the UK Labour Party policies. But the results of the French Presidential elections in April, 2002 saw the French National Front extreme right candidate, Jean-Marie Le Pen, beating the Socialist, Lionel Jospin, into third place and eliminating him. The rightist Jacques Chirac and Le Pen went to the next round and, as expected Chirac was re-elected with 82% of the vote. This was an anti-Le Pen vote rather than being pro-Chirac. France had been saved from the extreme right but the vote still meant no change for Brittany. Bretons are still presented with a bleak future, both culturally and politically.

The year 2002 started with eight Breton political detainees still in French custody; some of these detainees are facing their third year in jail without trial. Skoazell Vreizh (Breton Aid) formed in 1969 following the repression of Bretons by the French state, and continues to aid imprisoned Bretons and their families.

Skoazell Vreizh liases with international and humanitarian organisations such as Amnesty International.

The Isle of Man Government continues to have problems dealing with its Celtic heritage. In 2001 a new Isle of Man Education Act was adopted in the House of Keys which for the first time stipulated that the Manx language, its culture and history must be part of the curriculum of schools on the island. Peter Karran MHK moved several amendments to try to strengthen the Act. He wanted an advisory committee drawn from the language groups to advise on Manx Gaelic education and sought to include provision for the training of more staff to resource the Manx Gaelic education programme as well as specific provision for the inclusion of Gaelic units in schools. These reasonable requests were turned down by Education Minister Steve Rodan MHK. When attacked by the *Manx Independent* newspaper Mr Karran said: 'This country shouldn't be ashamed of its past but proud of its heritage.' But, on a positive note, the preliminary figures from the Manx Census of 2001 show that 1,689 people now identify themselves as able to speak, read or write Manx, and that 46% of these are under the age of nineteen years. Pupils taking 'optional Manx classes' in schools have remained at 1,000, 90% being taught in primary schools. However, in 2001, the first ever Manx medium primary school was opened at Ballacottir. Since its introduction in 1997, an average of ten pupils pass the General Certificate in Manx and twenty adults have also passed this. A higher certification (equivalent to English A-Level) called the Advanced Certificate is soon to be introduced. During the last decade Laare-studeyrys Manninagh (Centre of Manx Studies) has become well established in Douglas, the Island's capital, and the MA degree course in Manx Studies has attracted a healthy interest.

The Celtic League realises that it still has a mountain to climb. In recent years it has lost several of its most influential founding fathers including its first General Secretary Alan Heusaff (1921-1999). Alan's major contribution to the development of the modern Celtic consciousness has assured him of a place in the history of the Celtic struggle. He died at his home in Co. Galway on November 3, 1999.[30]

The writer Cathal Ó Sándair (1922-1996) died in Dublin. A prolific novelist and journalist in the Irish language, he had been a dedicated Pan Celticist and had a knowledge of all six Celtic languages.[31] A great shock to the movement was the death in London of Pádraig Ó Conchúir (1928-1997). A graduate of Galway University College, he had been involved in Pan Celtic politics since the early 1950s and was chairman of the Celtic League for nine years.[32] Another great loss was the death of the writer Cliff Ifan Bere (1915-1997) who had written one of the most influential works on theoretical Pan-Celticism *Towards the Political Confederation of Celtia* in 1989. [33]

Phillipe Le Solliec (1950-2000) died on January 15 in Reunion where he was a teacher of literature. He had been one of the 1960s generation of radical young Bretons who was both active in the national movement of his own country and a dedicated Pan Celt and Celtic League activist.[34]

Another blow came from an unexpected quarter in London in 2000. The London Association for Celtic Education suddenly found itself homeless. Formed in 1989 it united, through the incentive of the Celtic League, those involved in all aspects of Celtic language, from nursery level to university level, in the UK capital. Since their foundation they had been given a home and meeting point in the Islington Irish Centre. An Islington Council by-election in December, 2000 saw the seat go to a Liberal Democrat, Paul Fox. By one seat, power on the Council changed from Labour, traditionally supported by Islington's large Irish population. Fox was elected in the ward where the Irish Centre was based. Supported by his wife, Councillor Bridget Fox, now deputy leader of the Liberal Democrat Council, Paul Fox proposed the immediate withdrawal of grant aid to the Centre, forcing its closure. Plans to sell the building were put in hand in order to lower the Council Tax for residents in spite of widespread protests and support. The London Association for Celtic Education wrote to Liberal Democrat leader Charles Kennedy MP who had expressed his support for Pan Celtic bodies. Embarrassed, he promised to raise the matter with the Council but the closure went ahead.[35]

LACE has been without a firm base ever since, making its work increasingly difficult. Its files and books have been dispersed into members' homes and its programme of lectures curtailed by the need to find inexpensive venues.

So what of the future of Pan Celticism? The Celtic League's long-serving General Secretary, Bernard Moffatt has observed that in spite of the 'roller-coaster' of the last ten years, 'paradoxically, the new found political strengths have not resulted in any move to consolidate an Inter-Celtic dimension by these bodies' (the devolved legislatures) 'and the attempt by London to bind the new structures into an artificial confederation through the British-Irish Council, has so far proved ineffectual.

'The Celtic League and the Celtic Congress are still the only bodies via which all the Celtic countries coalesce.'[36]

He points out that the Celtic League's dissemination of information via its main journal, *Carn*, and its websites continues to provide the only forum through which all the Celtic countries find a voice.

Anyone scanning the pages of *Carn* or surfing the website will still find that, if anything, in the past decade the League has stepped up its campaign work. More importantly despite the Parliament in Scotland, the Assembly in Wales and the devolved status Legislative Body established to the six counties (Northern Ireland), political and cultural tensions remain.

There is increased fiscal autonomy in a number of the Celtic countries and the Celtic languages in particular have benefited. Despite this the threat to languages and community is still real and some of the Celtic countries, notably Brittany and Cornwall, have not realised the advances of the others. France continues to frustrate any move towards autonomy for Brittany and the English Government of Tony Blair cynically disregarded Cornwall's claim to be regarded in the same way as Wales and Scotland. In other words the agenda of the old 'Nation States' is broadly unchanged.

Indeed, in some ways these are more dangerous times. The Nationalist Parties, Scottish National Party, Plaid Cymru and Sinn Féin seem almost seduced by the granting of varying degrees of limited autonomy.

Limited autonomy, however, can only at best be a stepping stone. For the Celtic people to retain their identity and realise a constructive role in the Europe of the new millennium the only option is independence.

Forty years ago a Celtic Dawn occurred. At the time groups organised or reorganised in Wales, Scotland, Isle of Man, Ireland, Cornwall and Brittany. The cry then was for freedom – some of us have not and will not deviate from that objective. The work of the Celtic League continues.

In practical terms, then, the next decade will see the Celtic League continuing to pursue its efforts to established the formal links between the legislatures of those four Celtic countries, as well as continuing to support the voluntary cultural links that have been growing among them, and moves to gain autonomy for Cornwall and Brittany. Today, there are few people, even among the fiercest critics of the Pan Celtic idea, who would not accept the fact of Pan Celticism – the special relationship that the six Celtic nationalities have with one another. Even such a critic as Dr James, denying the ancient Celts existed, is not ignoring that Pan Celticism is an entrenched modern concept. With four of those nationalities now enjoying varying degrees of political and cultural and fiscal autonomy, will the coming decade realise the next step in the Pan Celtic programme? Will it see the establishment of formal links between those countries? And will Cornwall and Brittany succeed in establishing political recognition and be allowed to join that fraternity? A Celtic Dawn has certainly come. How the Celtic morning now develops is going to be one of the most exciting historical periods for the sixteen millions who populate the Celtic countries.

Notes

1   J. Bernard Moffatt, official statement to author, April 29, 2002.
2   *The Road to National Democracy: the Story of the Irish Peace Process*, Owen Bennett, Connolly Association, London, 1998.
3   *The Longest War: Northern Ireland's Troubled History*, Marc Holland, Oxford University Press, Oxford, 2002.
4   *The Road to National Democracy* (op.cit).
5   *Drumcree: The Orange Order's Last Stand*, Chris Ryder and Vincent Kearney, Methuen, London, 2001. Also *Orange Parades: The Politics of Ritual, Tradition and Control*, Dominic Bryan, Pluto Press, London, 2000.
6   *Comhaontúr ar Thángthar air sna Caibidlí Ilpháirtí,* Dublin Stationery Office, 1998, and *Northern Ireland Peace Agreement*, HMSO, London, 1998.
7   *Irish Democrat*, April/May, 2002, and *South Africa and the Rule of Law*, South African Department of Foreign Affairs, April, 1968.
8   *Northern Ireland After the Good Friday Agreement: Victims, Grievance and Blame,* Mike Morrissey and Marie Smith, Pluto Press, London, 2002.
9   Ibid.
10 Apart from contemporary newspapers, such as *The Scotsman*, giving full details of the emergence of the Scottish Parliament, the Parliament has its own information website and publications that are accessible to everyone.
11 *Scottish Parliamentary News* (Gaelic Debate) February 29, 2000.
12 Comunn na Gaidhlig official website gives full details.
13 *Scottish Parliamentary News*, March 2, 2000.
14 *Western Mail* is the prime source covering the emergence of the Assembly. The Assembly has websites in Welsh and English covering all aspects of the history, activities and debates.
15 *Hansard* (Westminster) June 17, 1997.
16 *Hansard* (Westminster) February 23, 1999.
17 *Carn*, Winter, 2001.
18 British-Irish Council information is accessed via the Northern Ireland website *www.nics.gov.uk*
19 *Carn*, Spring, 2001.
20 *British Museum Magazine*, summer, 1997.
21 *Financial Times* (Weekend Section), June, 14/15, 1997.
22 *Antiquity*, March, 1997.
23 *Antiquity*, March, 1998.
24 *The Independent* (London), January 5, 1999.
25 *The Scotsman*, March 27, 1999.
26 *Irish Democrat*, June/July, 1999.
27 *Irish Democrat,* August/September, 1999.
28 *The Scotsman*, March 27, 1999.
29 *The Times* (London), April 1, 2002; *The Independent* (London), May 4, 2002, and *London Review of Books* (mentioned in The Independent).

30   *Cam*, Winter, 1999/2000 and Irish Democrat, December/January, 1999/2000.
31   *The Independent* (London, February 22, 1996.
32   *Irish Democrat*, October/November, 1997.
33   *An Phoblacht/Republican News*, October 30, 1997.
34   *Cam,* Summer, 2000.
35   *Irish Post*, April 15, 2002.
36   J. Bernard Moffatt, General Secretary of The Celtic League, in official statement to author, April 29, 2002.

Chronology

Significant dates in the history of modern Pan Celticism.

1820 Celtic Society of Edinburgh. Sir Walter Scott's 'drawing room Celts' group.

1838 Pan Celtic meeting at Abergavenny regarded as the first modern Celtic Congress.

1853 *Grammatica Celtica* by Johann Casper Zeuss published and becomes one of the cornerstones of modern Celtic Studies.

1854 *Polemic Essai sur la Poésie des Races Celtiques*; Ernest Renan (1823–1893) called for the study of the Celtic languages and cultures at academic level.

1864 De Gaulle's polemic *Les Celts au XIXe siècle* proposed basic philosophies and aims of political Pan Celticism.

1865 Welsh emigrants settle virgin land around the mouth of the Chubut in Patagonia and establish Y Wladfa, 'the new independent Wales'. Governed by a democratically elected senate, flying the red dragon flag, the first capital was Yr Hen Amddiffynta (which extended into Trerawson). In 1869, the colony was annexed by the Buenos Aires Government into Argentina. Some 80,000 people of Welsh descent still live in the area, but Welsh speakers are bilingual with Spanish.

1866 Tynwald, the Manx Paliament, is recognized by the United Kingdom Government as being the popularly elected government of the Island, exercising 'home rule'. The Island eventually becomes a Crown Dependency outside the United Kingdom. The Manx are therefore the first Celtic people to be recognized as achieving self-government in modern times since the suppression of the Breton Parliament by the French in 1790.

1867 Celtic Congress (regarded as second of modern times) at Saint Brieuc, Brittany.

Matthew Arnold makes an appeal for Celtic Studies in his 'On the Study of Celtic Literature' article (*Cornhill Magazine*), leading to the acceptance of the subject in universities and the appointment of the first chair of Celtic Studies at Oxford, followed by chairs at Trinity College, Dublin, and other universities.

1873 *Revue Celtique* launched in Paris.

1886 A Celtic League proposed at Bonar Bridge, Stirling, during a Land League meeting, but no evidence as to its formation.

1875–1888 *The Celtic Magazine* published.

1888 The Pan Celtic Society formed in Dublin and later merged into the Irish Literary Society in 1891.

1893 *The Celtic Monthly* launched.

1897 *Zeitschrift für Celtische Philologie* launched in Germany. Now one of the oldest Celtic Studies journals.

1899 The Celtic Association formed at Cardiff Eisteddfod, headquarters in Dublin.

1900 First major Celtic Congress held in Dublin, now the oldest Pan Celtic movement.

1901–1903 *Celtia* magazine launched.

1904 Celtic Review launched.

1922 The Irish Free State is recognized by Royal Proclamation by the United Kingdom on 5 December 1922. On 7 December 1922, Unionists at Stormont issue a petition to King George V requesting that the Six Counties of North-East Ireland opt out of the Free State and remain within the United Kingdom with their own provincial parliament. Partition becomes a fact.

1923 Breizh Atao, Brittany, first political party to adopt a Pan Celtic policy.

Pan Celtia magazine launched.

1929 Celtic League launched by Hon. Ruaraidh Erskine

with Hugh MacDiarmid in Scotland, branches formed in other Celtic countries.

1936 *Études Celtique* launched by Joseph Vendrèys in Paris. One of the most respected Celtic Studies journals.

1946–1966 *Celtica* published in Dublin.

1947 Celtic Congress in Dublin sponsored by the Irish Government of the day.

An Aimsir Cheilteach (Celtic Time) magazine launched (major Pan Celtic Newspaper which runs until 1954).

The Celtic Union formed at a meeting in Trinity College, Dublin, branches organized in each Celtic country. Gwynfor Evans elected President.

1948–1951 De Valéra and Fianna Fáil in Ireland (out of office) flirt with Pan Celticism.

1949 18 April: the former Irish Free State becomes the Republic of Ireland. The United Kingdom deem it to have left the British Commonwealth.

1948–1951 Seán MacBride, Irish Foreign Minister in Coalition Government, becomes a convert to Pan Celticism and remains so until his death.

Welsh Republican Movement adopts Pan Celticism in its Manifesto.

1952 Collapse of Celtic Union followed by a rally of 10,000 in Trafalgar Square, London, to launch a new Celtic Association, organized by Wendy Wood.

1953 First Celtic Congress of Canada and publication of the Toronto-based *An Teangadóir* (The Linguist) in all six Celtic languages. Continues being published until 1960.

1955 Irish Republic becomes first Celtic state to enter the United Nations Organisation.

1958–1962 *Celtic Voice* published.

1961 Celtic League formed at Rhos, north Wales. Headquarters in Dublin and branches in each Celtic country with several international branches. Now oldest of the political Pan Celtic movements. The Irish Republic applied to join the

European Economic Community.

1962 *Celtic News* launched as League journal.

1963 First annual volume of *Celtic League* published, produced until 1972.

League gives evidence to European Commission on Human Rights about the persecution of the Breton language.

1965 Celtic League Memorandum to United Nations on the situation in the Celtic countries.

1966 Celtic Youth Congress formed. Disappears by 1970. Publishes own *Bulletin*.

Celtic League sends Memorandum to all members of the Council of Europe.

1967 'The Celts' series of programmes broadcast on BBC Radio 3 from 14 February to 4 April and repeated from 8 August to 26 September. Though devoted to ancient Celts, it mentions modern plight of the Celtic peoples.

Gwynfor Evans, President of the Celtic League, elected as first Plaid Cymru MP at Westminster.

1968 Conference on Inter-Celtic Cooperation and National Freedom and Economic Progress at Bangor, Wales.

Welsh League of Youth starts annual Inter-Celtic Camps for the youth of all Celtic countries.

1969 Polemic *Creed of the Celtic revolution* published.

1971 Gorseddau of Wales (1791), Brittany (1901) and Cornwall (192–8) join together under Archdruid of Wales.

Pan Celtic Festival launched at Killarney, Ireland and Inter Celtic Festival launched at Lorient, Brittany. Two oldest Pan Celtic music festivals.

1972 After ten years, Gwynfor Evans steps down as President of Celtic League.

1973 First American Pan Celtic Congress. *Carn* launched as new League magazine, now oldest Pan Celtic journal.

1974 Celtic Congress in Nantes adopts a 'Charter of Cultural Rights'.

1976 Celtic Studies Association of North America formed.

1977 *Pan Celtic News* launched.

1978 *News from the Celtic Nations* launched. First Celtic Colloquium (annual conference) at the University of California, Los Angeles.

1979 First Celtic Film and Television Festival.

1980 Celtic Society of Japan inaugurated, holds first annual congress. Publication of the first Pan Celtic Calendar. Reál Associacioñ Céltica (Buenos Aires) formed.

1981 BBC 1 'Nationwide' television runs a series examining Pan Celticism through January and provides the media's first serious examination of its rise.

UNESCO conference on 'The History and Culture of the Celts' held in Bonn, Germany.

The Celtic Consciousness, a major work on all aspects of Celtic life from culture to politics, published.

1982 Celtic Council of Australia formed.

1983 UNESCO launch their permanent 'Project for the Study and Promotion of Celtic Cultures' and issue *Celtic Cultures Newsletter*. Major television series on Channel 4 'How to be Celtic' shown in September.

Society of Inter-Celtic Arts and Culture, Massachusetts, launched *Keltica* magazine.

First exhibition on 'Celtic Culture' held in Yugoslavia sponsored by the National Museum, Belgrade, tours Ljubljana, Zagreb and Belgrade and then moved to Munich in Germany.

1984 'The Future of the Celtic Nations within the EEC' conference sponsored by the Heriot-Watt University, Edinburgh, with l'Institut Français d'Ecosse and An Comunn Gàidhealach.

'London and the Future of the Celtic Languages' Conference at County Hall learns that there are some 100,000 speakers of a Celtic language living in the GLC area.

For a Celtic Future published.

1985 The first Scrìf Celtic, Celtic languages book fair.

League launches its Military Monitoring Programme in the

Celtic countries.

Commercial company The Celtic Idea Ltd launched from Scotland, selling and promoting items from all six Celtic countries.

'Celtic Peoples on the European Scene' organized by European Foundation for International Understanding in Copenhagen, Denmark.

1986 International Federation of Celtic Wrestling formed.

Major BBC 2 television series 'The Celts', six one hour programmes. First North American Congress of Celtic Studies.

1988 *Australian Celtic Journal* launched.

C.I. Bere's polemic *Towards the political confederation of Celtia*. Celtic Ecological Council formed.

Keltoi launched in the USA.

World-wide Register of Celticists (scholars) published by UNESCO.

1989 London Association for Celtic Education formed.

Societas Celtologica Nordica founded at Uppsala, Sweden.

1990 'Celtworld' opened in Waterford.

Histoire Chronologique des pays Celtiques by Jakez Gaucher published by Association Keltica International.

Major exhibition on 'Masterpieces of Celtic Metalwork – sixth to ninth centuries AD' entitled 'The Work of Angels' opens at British Museum prior to going to National Museums of Scotland and the National Museum of Ireland.

1991 Bwrdd Croeso Cymru (Wales Tourist Board) launch 'Celtica', a tourist promotion plan to interest tourists in the Celtic heritage of Wales and its relationship to other Celtic countries, providing an annual publication, 'Celtica'.

Major exhibition on 'The Celts' opens in Venice prior to European tour.

1993 Celtica Nederland, exhibition and series of lectures, Amsterdam. Welsh Language Bill, 1993, finally adopts the policy of equal validity for Welsh and English in Wales. First edition of *Celtic Dawn: A history of Pan Celticism* published. Celtic League activist Dr Brian Stowell elected International President of the Celtic Congress 1993-1996. *The Celtic Pen*, a quarterly magazine mainly in English dealing with Celtic languages and literature, launched in Belfast.

1994 February 28. Death of Professor Leopold Kohr, political economist who had a profound influence on the Pan Celtic movement. IRA cessation of armed struggle in August. Hume Adams Agreement *The Celtic History Review*, quarterly magazine launched in Belfast

1995 *Irish Democrat* examines the work of Leopold Kohr in its December 1994/January 1995, issue. Celtica, a £2 million Celtic Resource Centre opened in Machynlleth.

1996 World Conference on Linguistic Rights, June, Barcelona. Celtic League statement presented by chairman Cathal Ó Luain. IRA go back on offensive due to delays and prevarication by John Major's UK Tory Government. - 18 months have elapsed since IRA ceasefire and agreed talks have been blocked by UK Prime Minister John Major.

1997 May: UK Labour Party landslide victory, pledged to devolution and engagement in the Irish peace process. Celtic League demands UK and French Governments honour their pledges to recognise lesser-used languages. Manx Government is also asked to keep to their pledge. June 17 Andrew George MP for St Ives becomes first MP to address the House of Commons in the Cornish language demanding recognition for the language, an assembly for Cornwall and a Cornish University. Referendum on devolution in September, 1997. Death of Pádraig Ó Conchúir, chairman of the Celtic League 1972-1982 dies. Pan Celtic theoretician, Cliff Ifan Bere (1915-1997) dies in October. Astonishingly, the Celtic Film and Television Festival Association turns down a Manx entry on the grounds that the Isle of Manx is 'a Scottish Region'. Constitutionally, the Isle of Man is not even part of the United Kingdom. Protests from the island are led by Dr Brian Stowell and the Celtic League.

1998 Good Friday Agreement in Northern Ireland. May

21 first all Ireland poll since the 1918 General Election endorsed a 32 county republic. 71.2% of the North and 95% of the Republic are in favour of a new Northern Ireland Assembly on a power sharing basis with north-south bodies. David Trimble of the Ulster Unionist Party is elected First Minister with Seamus Mallon of SDLP as deputy first Minster. Sinn Féin given two ministerial portfolios for education and health. Parity of esteem for the Irish language with English.

1999 May 6: First elections for a Scottish Parliament and a Welsh Assembly. July 1, HM Queen state opening of Scottish Parliament, the first to meet in 300 years. May 12, first meeting of the Welsh Assembly. December 17, first meeting of the British-Irish Council comprising heads of all the governments in Britain and Ireland – Dublin and Belfast, London, Cardiff, Edinburgh, Douglas (Isle of Man), Jersey and Guernsey. November 3, Alan Heusaff, first General Secretary of the Celtic League dies. Simon James launched his attack on Pan Celticism with his book *The Atlantic Celts: Ancient People or Modern Invention?* But Norman Davies' *The Isles: A history* becomes a major study for dispelling the myths of a 'British' nation.

2000 March 2 the first full debate in the Scottish Gaelic language in the Scottish Parliament. March 5 (St Piran's Day) Petition for a Cornish Assembly launched. A bilingual memorial is unveiled to Pan Celtic activist and writer Seumas Mac a' Ghobhainn at Sighthill Cemtery, Glasgow, and a volume containing some of his essays is published – *Scotland Not Only Free But Gaelic.*

2001 Celtic League celebrates its 40th anniversary. Its annual general meeting is held in Rhosllanerchrugog in Wales where its inaugural meeting was held. Petition for a Cornish Assembly signed by 50,000 people and supported by four out of the five Cornish MPs taken to Downing Street. Peter Karran MHK moved several amendments to the Isle of Man Education Act, 2001, in order to consolidate the position of Gaelic Education. Alistair Moffat's *The Sea Kingdoms: The Story of Celtic Britain &*

Ireland becomes a corrective to *The Atlantic Celts*.

2002   Breton hopes of a French Socialist presidency which might follow the English Labour Party policy of devolution in the French state, giving back to Brittany some degree of autonomy, are dashed by the emergence of the extreme right wing which defeats the Socialist candidate. French courts decree that even allowing Breton language to be taught and used as in accordance with the European agreement on Lesser Used Language would be 'unconstitutional'. In the Irish Republic Fianna Fáil is returned in a new coalition with Progressive Democrats but Sinn Féin win five seats, two more than was expected making an electoral impact in the Republic. The Cornish Constitutional Convention – Omguntellyans rag Selreth Kernow, launched its publication *Devolution for One and All: Governance for Cornwall in the 21st Century*.

London *Times* (August 10) reports Government Minister Nick Raynsford's promise that Cornish will shortly be recognised by Westminster as an official minority language.

2003   Elections are due in Wales, Scotland and Northern Ireland.

Bibliography

Alter, Peter. *Nationalism* (trs. Stuart McKinnon-Evans), Edward Arnold, London, 1989.

Anon. *Our Changing Democracy: Devolution to Scotland and Wales*, HMSO, London, 1975.

Arnold, Matthew. *The Study of Celtic Literature*, Smith, Elder & Co, London, 1867.

Atkinson, William C. *A History of Spain & Portugal*, Penguin, London, 1960.

Aughey, Arthur. *Nationalism, Devolution and the Challenge to the United Kingdom State*, Pluto Press, London 2001.

Bennett, Owen. *The Road to National Democracy: The Story of the Irish Peace Process*, London, 1998.

Bere, Clifford Ifan. *The Welsh Republic*, WRM, Cardiff, 1948.

Bere, Clifford Ifan. *Towards the Political Confederation of Celtia*, Gwasg yr Ynys Newydd, Y Lolfa Cyf., Talybont, Wales, 1989.

Brand, J. *The National Movement in Scotland*, London, 1978.

Branderis, Louis D. *The Curse of Bigness*, Viking Press, New York, 1935.

Broderick, George. *Chronicles of the Kings of Man and the Isles*, Celtic League, Douglas, Isle of Man, 1988.

Brown, Oliver. *The Anglo-Scottish Union of 1707*, Scots Independent Publications, Stirling, n.d.

Bryan, Dominic. *Orange Parades: The Politics of Ritual, Tradition and Control*, London, 2000.

Buthlay, Kenneth. *Hugh MacDiarmid*, Oliver & Boyd, Edinburgh, 1964.

Caldecott, Moyra. *Women in Celtic Myth*, Arrow Books, London, 1988.

Celtic League – Annual Volumes, Dublin, 1963–1972.

    1963. *The Celtic Nations*, ed. Dr Ceinwen Thomas.

    1964/5. *Self-government for the Celtic Countries*, ed. Dr Ceinwen Thomas.

    1966. *Recent Developments in the Celtic Countries*, ed. George Thomson.

    1967. *Celtic Advance in the Atomic Age*, ed. Nollaig Ó Gadhra.

    1968. *Maintaining a National Identity*, ed. Frank G. Thompson.

    1969. *The Significance of Freedom*, ed. Frank G. Thompson.

    1970. *The Celts in the Seventies*, ed. Frank G. Thompson.

    1971. *Celtic Unity – Ten Years On*, ed. Frank G. Thompson.

    1972. *The Celtic Experience: Past & Present*, ed. Frank G. Thompson.

Celtic League, Douglas, 1990.

    Pollution in the Irish Sea (Foreword by J. Bernard Moffatt, 1990.

Learning the Celtic Languages: A Resource Guide & etc. by Alexei Kondratiev and Liam Ó Caiside, Celtic League, American Branch, New York, 1991.

Chadwick, Nora C. *The Celts*, Penguin, London, 1970.

Chadwick, Nora C. *The Colonisation of Brittany from Celtic Britain*, British Academy, London, 1965.

Chapman, Malcom. *The Celts: the Construction of a Myth*, St Martin's Press, London, 1993.

Clarke, Austin. *The Celtic Twilight of the Nineties*, Dublin, 1969.

Clewes, Roy, *To Dream of Freedom*, Y Lolfa Cyf., Talybont, Wales, 1980.

Cobban, Alfred. *The National State and National Self Determination*, Oxford University Press, Oxford, 1945.

Collins, Kevin. *The Cultural Conquest of Ireland*, Mercier Press, Cork & Dublin, 1990.

Condren, Mary. *The Serpent and the Goddess: Women, Religion and Power in Celtic Ireland*, T. & T. Clark Ltd. Edinburgh, 1990.

Connolly, S.J.(ed.) *Kingdoms United? Integration and Diversity*, Four Courts Press, Dublin, 1999.

Coudenhove-Kalegri, Richard. *Pan Europe*, NYUP, New York, 1926.

Coupland, Sir Reginald. *Welsh & Scottish Nationalism*, London, 1954.

Cronin, Seán. *Irish Nationalism: a History of its Roots and Ideology*, Academy Press, Dublin, 1988.

Cunliffe, Barry. *The Celtic World*, second edition, Constable & Co Ltd, London, 1992.

Davies, D. Hywel *The Welsh Nationalist Party 1925–1945: a Call to Nationhood*, Cardiff, 1983.

Davies, Dr D.J. *Towards Welsh Freedom*, Y Blaid, Denbigh, 1958.

Davies, John, Lord Gifford and Richards, Tony. *Political Policing in Wales*, Welsh Campaign for Civil and Political Liberty, Cardiff, 1984.

Davies, Norman. *The Isles: A History*, Macmillan, London, 1999.

De Gaulle, Charles. *Les Celtes au XIXe Siècle – Appel aux Représentants Actuels de la Race Celtique*, Paris, 1864.

De La Villemarqué, P. *La Bretagne et les Pays Celtiques*, Paris, 1920.

Deacon, Bernard; George, Anthony & Perry, Ronald. *Cornwall at the Crossroads: Living Communities or Leisure Zone?* The Cornish Economic Research Group, Redruth, 1988.

Delaney, Frank. *The Celts*, BBC Publications/Hodder & Stoughton, London, 1986.

Deniel, A. *Le Mouvement Breton*, Paris, 1976.

Durkacz, Victor Edward. *The Decline of the Celtic Languages*, John Donald, Edinburgh, 1983.

Edwards, Owen Dudley; Evans, Gwynfor; Rhys, Owen and MacDiarmid, Hugh. *Celtic Nationalism*, Routledge & Kegan Paul, London, 1968.
Education of Cornish Children, Mebyon Kernow Policy Document, Mebyon Kernow, Redruth, 1966.

Edwards, Ruth. *Patrick Pearse: the Triumph of Failure*, Victor Gollancz, London, 1977.

Ellis, Henry Havelock. *A Study of British Genius*, London, 1904.

Ellis, Peter Berresford Ellis. *The Celtic Revolution: a Study in Anti-imperialism*, Y Lolfa Cyf., Talybont, Wales, 1985.

Ellis, Peter Berresford. *Celt and Greek*, Constable, London 1997.

Ellis, Peter Berresford. *Celt and Roman*, Constable, London 1998.

Ellis, Peter Berresford. *Celt and Saxon: the Struggle for Britain 410–937*, Constable, London, 1993.

Ellis, Peter Berresford. *Celtic Women: Women in Celtic Society and Literature*, Constable, London 1995.

Ellis, Peter Berresford. *The Ancient World of the Celts*, Constable, London, 1998

Ellis, Peter Berresford. *The Celtic Empire: the First Millennium of Celtic History 1000 BC–51 AD*, Constable, London, 1990.

Ellis, Peter Berresford. *The Chronicles of the Celts*, Robinson, London, 1999.

Ellis, Peter Berresford. *The Creed of the Celtic Revolution*, Medusa Press, London, 1969.

Ellis, Peter Berresford. *Wales – a Nation Again* (Foreword by Gwynfor Evans MP), Library 33 Ltd., London, 1968.

Evans, Gwynfor. *Aros Mae*, Abertawe, Wales, 1971.

Farrell, Michael. *Northern Ireland: the Orange State*, Pluto, London, 1976.

Fernbach, David. ed. *The Revolution of 1848*. The Pelican Marx Library, Vol. 1, Penguin, London, 1973.

Finot, Jean. *Le Préjugé des Races*, Paris, third edition 1908.

Fouéré, Yann. *L'Europe aux Cent Drapeaux*, Presse d'Europe, Paris, 1968.

Fouéré, Yann. *La Patrie Interdite: Histoire d'un Breton*, Editions France-Empire, Paris, 1987.

Fraser, Kenneth C. *Bibliography of the Scottish National Movement 1928–1958*, Strathclyde University, Glasgow, 1968.

Galliou, Patrick, and Jones, Michael. *The Bretons*, Basil Blackwell, Oxford, 1991.

Gaucher, Jakez. *Histoire Chronologique des Pays Celtiques*, Association Keltica International, Guerande, Bretagne, 1990.

Gaucher, Jakez. *La Bretagne de A à Z*, Coop Breizh, Spézet, 1998.

Ginnell, Lawrence. *The Breton Laws: a Legal Handbook*, London, 1894.

Green, Miranda. *Symbol and Image in Celtic Religious Art*, Routledge, London, 1989.

Greenberg, William. *Flags of the Forgotten: Nationalism on the Celtic Fringe* (Foreword by Sir Gerald Nabarro MP), Clifton Books, London, 1969.

Gregor, D.B. *Celtic – A Comparative Study*, Oleander Press, Cambridge, 1980.

Halliday, F.E. *A History of Cornwall*, Duckworth, London, 1979.

Hanham, H.J. *Scottish Nationalism*, Faber & Faber, London, 1969.

Havinden, M.A., Quéniart. J., Stanyer, J. *Centre et Péripjérie: Centre and Periphery: Brittany and Cornwall & Devon Compared*, University of Exeter Press, 1991.

Hearne, Derrick. *The ABC of the Welsh Revolution*, Y Lolfa Cyf., Talybont, Wales, 1982.

Hearne, Derrick. *The Joy of Freedom: Towards an Ideology of Welsh Liberty*, Y

Lolfa Cyf., Talybont, Wales, 1977.

Hearne, Derrick. *The Rise of the Welsh Republic: Towards a Welsh Theory of Government*, Y Lolfa Cyf., Talybont, Wales, 1975.

Hechter, Michael. *Internal Colonialism: the Celtic Fringe in British National Development 1536–1966*, Routledge & Kegan Paul, London, 1975.

Hindley, Roy. *The Death of the Irish Language*, Routledge, London, 1990.

Holland, Marc. *The Longest War: Northern Ireland's Troubled History*, Oxford, 2002.

Hubert, Henri. *The Greatness & Decline of the Celts*, Routledge & Kegan Paul, London, 1934.

Hubert, Henri. *The Rise of the Celts*, Routledge & Kegan Paul, London, 1934

James, Simon. *The Atlantic Celts: Ancient People or Modern Invention?* British Museum Press, London, 1999.

Jenkins, John. *Prison Letters*, Y Lolfa Cyf., Talybont, Wales, 1981.

Kelly, Kevin. *The Longest War: Northern Ireland and the IRA*, Brandon Books, Kerry, 1982.

Kohn, Hans. *Pan Slavism: its History and Ideology*, Notre Dame (Indiana, USA), 1953.

Kohr, Leopold. *The Breakdown of Nations*, Routledge & Kegan Paul, London,1957.

Le Mat, Jean-Pierre. *The Sons of the Ermine: A History of Brittany*. An Clochán, Belfast, 1996.

Legum, C. *Pan-Africanism. A Short Political Guide*, London, 1962.

Lenin, V.I. *The National & Colonial Question*, Foreign Language Press, Peking, 1970.

Lichtheim, George. *Imperialism*. Praeger Publishers Inc., New York, USA, 1971.

Lloyd, J.E. *Owain Glendower*, Oxford University Press, Oxford, 1931.

Mac a' Ghobhainn, Seumas. *Scotland Not Only Free But Gaelic*, edited by Risnidh Mag Aoidh, Introduction by Professor Kenneth MacKinnon, biographical essay Seumas Mac a' Ghobhainn (1930-87) – Revolutionary Fundamentalist, Peter Berresford Ellis), Celtic Editions, Edinburgh, 2000.

Mac Stiofáin, Seán. *Memoirs of a Revolutionary*, Gordon Cremonesi, London,1974.

MacAllister, Ian. *The Northern Ireland Democratic and Labour Party: Political Opposition in a Divided Society*, Macmillan, London, 1977.

Macardle, Dorothy. *The Irish Republic*, Victor Gollancz Ltd., London, 1937.

MacCormick, N. (ed.). *The Scottish Debate. Essays on Scottish Nationalism*, Oxford University Press, 1970.

MacCulloch, J.A. *The Religion of the Ancient Celts*, T. & T. Clark, Edinburgh, 1911.

MacDiarmid, Hugh. *Lucky Poet*, Methuen, London, 1943.

MacDiarmid, Hugh. *Scotland in 1980*, Montrose, pp, 1935.

MacIntosh, J.P. *The Devolution of Power*, Penguin, London, 1968.

MacNeill, Eoin. *Phrases of Irish History*, Gill & Sons, Dublin, 1919.

Markle, Jean. *The Celts and their Civilization*, Gordon Cremonesi, London, 1974.

Markle, Jean. *Women of the Celts* (trs, A. Mygind, C. Hauch and P. Henry) Gordon Cremonesi, London, 1975.

Modrel, Oliver. *Breiz Atao: Histoire et a Chialté du Nationalisme Breton*, Paris, 1973.

Moffat, Alistair. *The Sea Kingdoms; The Story of Celtic Britain and Ireland*, HarperCollins, London, 2001.

Moody, T.W. & Martin, F.X. *The Course of Irish History*, Mercier Press, Cork, 1967.

Morgan, K.O. *Rebirth of a Nation*. Wales 1880–1980, Oxford University Press, 1981.

Morrissey, Mike and Smith, Marie. *Northern Ireland after the Good Friday Agreement: Victims Grievance and Blame*, London 2002.

Nairn, Tom. *The Break-up of Britain. Crisis and Neo-nationalism*, London, 1977.

O'Callaghan, M.J.C. *Separatism in Brittany*, Dyllansow Truran, Redruth, 1983.

O'Driscoll. Dr Robert (ed.). *The Celtic Consciousness*, McClelland & Stewart, Toronto, Canada, 1981.

O'Halloran, C. *Partition and the Limits of Irish Nationalism. An Ideology Under Stress*, Dublin, 1987.

Ó Glaisne, Risteárd. *Cad a Deir tú Leis na nAlbanaigh?* Cló Chois Fharraige, Gaillimhe, tire, 1978.

Ó Luain, Cathal, (ed.). *For a Celtic Future*, Celtic League, Dublin, 1983.

O'Rahilly, Cecile. *Ireland and Wales: their Historical and Literary Relations*,. Longmans, Green & Co., London, 1924.

Olier, Youenn. *Dulenn 1947. Deizlevr Ur Mix*, Imbourc'h, Kistrebezh (Brittany), 1989.

Orpen, G.H. *La Chanson Dermot et le Conte*, Oxford University Press, Oxford, 1892.

Osmond, John. *Police Conspiracy?* Y Lolfa, Talybont, Wales, 1984.

Pakulski, Jan. *Social Movements: the Politics of Moral Protest*, Longman Cheshire Pty, Tasmania, Australia, 1991.

Payton, Philip. *The Making of Modern Cornwall*, Dyllansow Truran, Redruth, Cornwall, 1992.

Perzon, Abbé Paul-Yves. *L'Antiquité de la Nation et la Langue des Celts*, Paris, 1703. (Translated by David Jones as *The Antiquities of Nations, More Particularly of the Celtae or Gauls, Taken to be Originally the Same People as our Ancient Britons*, London, 1706.

Petrovitch, M.B. *The Emergence of Russian Pan Slavism 1856–70*, New York, 1956.

Plaid Cymru (publisher). *Breton Nationalism*, n.d. (circa 1947). Preface by Gwynfor Evans, Y Blaid, Denbigh, Wales.

Plaid Cymru (publisher). *The Historical Basis of Welsh Nationalism* (series of lectures by A.W. Wade-Evans, T. Jones Pierce, Ceinwen Thomas, A.O.H. Jarman, D. Gwenallt Jones and Gwynfor Evans), Y Blaid, Cardiff, 1950.

Poisson, Henri & Le Mat, Jean-Pierre. *Histoire de Bretagne*, Coop Breizh, Spézet, 2000.

Raftery, Barry. *Philip's Atlas of the Celts*, George Philip, London, 2001.

Rowse, A.L. *Tudor Cornwall*, Jonathan Cape, London, 1941.

Ryan, W.P. *The Irish Literary Revival*, pp, London, 1894.

Ryder, Chris and Kearney, Vincent. *Drumcree: The Orange Order's Last Stand*, London, 2001.

Said, Edward W. *Culture and Imperialism*, Chatto and Windus, London, 1993.

Scott, A. *Ideology of the New Social Movements*, Unwin Hyman, London, 1990.

Scott, Robert McNair. *Robert the Bruce*, Hutchinson, London, 1982.

Seton-Watson, H. Nations and States. *An Enquiry into the Origins of Nations and the Politics of Nationalism*, London, 1977.

Sharpe, L.J. *Devolution and Celtic Nationalism in the United Kingdom*, Western European Politics No. 8 (1985).

Sletin, Vegard. *Five Northern Countries Pull Together*, Nordic Council (reprint, 1968).

Snyder, Edward D. *The Celtic Revival in English Literature*, Cambridge, Mass. 1923.

Snyder, L.L. *Macro-nationalism, a History of the Pan-Movements*, Westport (Conn.), 1984.

Snyder, L.L. *The Meaning of Nationalism*, New York, 1954.

Thomas, Ned. *The Welsh Extremist*. Victor Gollancz, London, 1969.

Webb, K. *The Growth of Nationalism in Scotland*, London, 1978.

Weber, M. *The Theory of Social and Economic Organization*, The Free Press, New York, 1947.

Wendt, Franz. *The Nordic Council and Cooperation in Scandinavia*, Nordic Council (reprint, 1968).

Wertheimer, M.S. *The Pan German League 1890–1914*, New York, 1971.

Williams, A.H. *An Introduction to the History of Wales*, University of Wales Press, Cardiff (2 vols), 1941–48.

Young, C.V.C. *A Brief History of the Isle of Man*, Mansk-Svenska Publishing Co, Peel, 1983.

Documents

Devolution for One and All: Governance for Cornwall in the 21st Century, Cornish Constitutional Convention, PO Box 7, Truro, Cornwall, TR1 1WW, May, 2002.

Northern Ireland Peace Agreement, London, 1998.

Periodicals

A' Bhratach Ur (Scottish Branch, Celtic League, Glasgow) 1970–1974.

Alba (Stirling) 1920–21.

An Aimsir Cheilteach (Cork and Edinburgh), July, 1947–March, 1954.

An Baner Kernewek (Cornwall) 1970–79.

An Claidheamh Soluis (Dublin) 1899–1909.

An Sgeulaiche (Scotland) 1909–1911.

Australian Celtic Journal (Celtic Council of Australia, University of Sydney) Vol. 1, No. 1. January, 1988-present.

Bulletin of the Canadian Celtic Arts Association, Vol. 1, No. 1, Spring, 1982–present.

Carn, Journal of the Celtic League (Dublin), No. 1, Spring, 1973–present.

Celtia, Journal of the Pan Celtic Association (Dublin), 1900–1903.

Celtic Cultures Newsletter (Journal of the UNESCO Project for the Study and Promotion of Celtic cultures), Dublin, No. 1, June, 1983–present.

Celtic Digest (Scotland) n.d.

Celtic Fringe (Journal of the Northern American Celtic Cultural Society), No. 1, September/October, 1987–present.

Celtic Magazine (Glasgow) 1930–?

Celtic Monthly (Glasgow) 1920–?

Celtic News (Journal of the Celtic League), No. 1, Autumn, 1962–No. 33, Summer, 1972.

Celtic Review (Dublin) 1904–19.

Celtic Voice (Gloucester) 1958–1962.

Celtic World (Journal of the Celtic Society of India, Chandigarh) 1991–present.

Cornish Nation (Liskeard) 1968–79.

Fáinne an Lae (Dublin) 1898–1900.

Gaelic Journal (Dublin) 1898–?

Guth na Bliadhna (Scotland) 1904–1925.

Imbourc'h (Brittany) 1970–present.

Keltica: The Inter-Celtic Journal (Inter-Celtic Society of America), Boston, Mass, No. 1, 1983–present.

Keltoi (Journal of the American Branch of the Celtic League, New York), No. 1, 1988–present.

Kernow (Liskeard), No. 1, 1989–present.

The London Celt (London) 1898–1904.

New Cornwall (Hayle) 1960–1975.

Omma (Cornish Branch, Celtic League, Journal), No. 1, 1970–present.

Pan Celtic News (Tralee), No. 1, 1977–1979.

Pan Celtica (Rennes) Supplement to Breizh Atao, 1930–35.

Phoenix (Cornish Branch, Celtic League, Journal), No. 1, May, 1989–present.

Revue Celtique (Paris) 1870–present.

Resurgence, Journal of the Fourth World (London) 1968.

Sav Breizh, Cahiers Combat Breton (Rennes), 1970–78.

Studia Celtic Japonica, Nagoya University, Japan, 1974–present.

Tir na nÓg: Newsletter of the Australian Celtic Association, 1970–present.

Welsh Nation (Paper of Plaid Cymru), Vol. 1, March, 1927–present.

The Welsh Republican/Y Gweriniaethwr (Journal of the Welsh Republican Movement), Vol. 1, No. 1. August–September, 1950 – Vol. 7 (1956); as *Y Gweriniaethwr: The Welsh Republican*, Vol. 8, No. 1, August–September, 1973–Vol 10, No. 1, Spring, 1976 (irregular).

Articles

'Are our Sister Celtic Nations on the Road to Freedom?' *Kerryman*, 18 March 1967.

'Minorities Unite to Become Independent'. *Herald of Wales*, 27 May 1967.

'Celtica Today'. A regular fortnightly column in *Sruth*, Scots Gaelic bilingual newspaper, Inverness, from 12 June 1969 to 9 July 1970.

'La Révolution Celtique'. *Sav Breizh*, March, 1970.

'The Celtic Cultural Problem'. *Freethinker*, 20 June 1970.

'The Celtic Revolution'. *Ein Wlas* (Wales), March, 1970.

'Celtic Nationalism'. *The Ecologist*, October, 1971.

'The Celtic Question'. *Hibernia*, 11 July 1975.

'The Promotion of Celtic Consciousness'. *Irish Post*, 17 January 1981.

'The Celtic Revolution'. *Llais Llyfrau* (Wales), Winter, 1984.

'Misty View of New Celtic Dawn'. *Hampstead & Highgate Express*, 24 October 1986.

'What is the Celtic League?' *Irish Democrat*, January, 1989.

'Pan Celiticism: Modern Myth or Historical Tradition'. *The Celtic History Review*, Autumn/Winter, 1994/5, Vol. 1. No 1.

'Did the Ancient Celts Really Exist?' *The Independent*, London, Janauary 5, 1999.

'Identity Crisis?' Debate between Peter Berresford Ellis and Simon James, *The Scotsman*, March 27, 1999.

'Did the ancient Celts exist?' Peter Berresford Ellis, *Irish Democrat*, 1999.

'The Challenge to the UK State'. *Irish Democrat*, August/September, 2001.

Miscellaneous publications

The Celtic Conference, 1917; report of the meetings held by the Celtic Congress at Birkenhead. Perth, 1918.

Celtic Film & Television Festival. Programme Books from 1980–present.

Scríf-Celt. Celtic Languages Book Fair Programme Books for 1985 and 1986, Celtic League.

How to be Celtic, Channel 4 booklet to accompany series of five programmes made by Pelicula Films, first shown in September, 1983.

The Celts, BBC Radio. Pamphlet to accompany radio series of the same name broadcast on Radio 3 from 14 February–4 April 1967. BBC Publications, London.

LACE Directory for 1989/1990; for 1990/1991 and for 1991/2, London Association for Celtic Education. LACE also produces a newsletter.

Information about the Celtic League may be obtained from its General Secretary, Bernard Moffatt, 11 Cleiy Rhennee, Kirk Michael, Mannin. Email: b.moffatt@advsys.co.im or Assistant General Secretary, Mark Kermode, at mkermode@mcb.net *Carn*, the journal of the Celtic League, can be ordered rom 33 Céide na Grianóige, Ráth Cúil, Átha Cliath, Éire. Email: patriciabridson@eircom.net . The Celtic League website is http://wwww.manxman.co.im/cleague and the American branch has a website at www.celticleague.org . The League has branches in all six Celtic countries, branches in the USA, in Cape Breton, Nova Scotia, Canada, and an International Branch for all other areas.

PETER BERRESFORD ELLIS, historian and novelist, was born in Coventry, Warwickshire. His father was a journalist from Cork City, Ireland. His mother was from Sussex but had a Breton mother. Her father's cousin was David Randell (1854-1912) of Llanelli, the Welsh Liberal/Cymru Fydd Member of Parliament for the Gower from 1888-1900, who, in the House of Commons campaigned for status for the Welsh language. Peter therefore grew up in a family of Irish, Welsh, Scots, Bretons and English.

He took his degrees in Celtic Studies (a first class honours and his master's) but followed his father into a career in journalism becoming deputy editor on an Irish weekly newspaper and then editor on a weekly magazine. He became a full-time writer in 1975. His books have won him many academic accolades and several Fellowships. He has guest-lectured at universities in the USA, Canada, Ireland, the British Isles and Spain.

In 1987 he was made a Bard of the Cornish Gorsedd (as Gwas-an-Geltyon, Servant of the Celts) for his book on the Cornish language; in 1985 and 1986 he was organising chairman of *Scríf-Celt*, the first and second Celtic Languages Book Fairs; in 1988-1990 he was chairman of the Celtic League, which he had joined in 1964; from 1989 he was organising chairman of the London Association for Celtic Education, then its vice president and is now an hon. life member. In 1989 he was given an *Irish Post* Award for his work on Celtic history. From 1989 he has been honorary life president of the Scottish 1820 Society. Having served as a committee member of the Irish Literary Society (founded in 1891 by Yeats and others), he has become only the second living member to become an honorary life member of the Society.

His work has been translated into nearly a score of languages and, as 'Peter Tremayne', a fiction writing pseudonym, he is the author of the international bestselling Sister Fidelma historical murder mysteries set in 7th Century Ireland, with his sleuth not only a member of the Celtic Church but a qualified *dálaigh*, or advocate, of the ancient Brehon laws of Ireland.

The Times Literary Supplement recently described him as 'the pre-eminent Celtic scholar now writing'.

More about the Celts...

The Celtic Revolution
Peter Berresford Ellis
0 86243 096 8
£7.95

**Tales from the
Celtic Countries**
Rhiannon Ifans
0 86243 501 3
£6.95

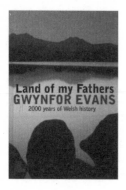

Land of My Fathers
Gwynfor Evans
0 86243 285 0
£12.95